ENSLAVED

RAHILA GUPTA is a campaigner and journalist.
She has written radio drama and is the editor of
*From Homebreakers to Jailbreakers: Southall Black
Sisters* and co-author of *Circle of Light*, now released
as a film *Provoked* which she also co-scripted.

FROM THE REVIEWS OF *ENSLAVED*:

'A well argued attempt to put a radical new policy on
immigration on the politicians' table. Fascinating.'
The Tablet

'Rahila Gupta is a wonderful interviewer, who enables
the reader to hear clearly the voices of these people who
are just emerging from enslavement. And behind the
interviews are intelligent analysis, a thorough going
commitment to justice and human rights and a vision of
how this could be achieved. Gupta explores the issues from
all angles and... controversially, but convincingly, makes
the case for dispensing with immigration controls
altogether.' *Red Pepper*

ENSLAVED

The New British Slavery

Rahila Gupta

Portobello
BOOKS

Published by Portobello Books Ltd 2007
This paperback edition published 2008

Portobello Books Ltd
Twelve Addison Avenue
London
W11 4QR, UK

A CIP catalogue record is available
from the British Library

9 8 7 6 5 4 3 2 1

ISBN 978 1 84627 066 6

www.portobellobooks.com

Designed and typeset in Minion
by Lindsay Nash

Printed in Great Britain by
CPI Bookmarque, Croydon, CR0 4TD

CONTENTS

INTRODUCTION

2007 marks the bicentenary of the abolition of the slave trade. The year has been bursting at the seams with commemorations, and debates have raged between those who credit William Wilberforce with bringing the trade to an end and those who talk up the lesser-known history of slave revolts and black resistance. Attempts have been made to pin down Prime Minister Tony Blair on the issue of an apology but, in his classic Third Way, he has talked of 'sorrow and regret', knowing that any deeper admission of guilt will open the door to the gilt-edged question of reparations. As always, the struggle to recast history sheds more light on the present than on the past. But amid feelings of regret for the past, are we adequately addressing the massive and continuing trade in human misery? Has slavery really ended?

Although it may sound like an oxymoron, slavery and Western civilization have co-existed from the earliest times, pre-dating slavery in classical Greece and Rome which, along with the infamous transatlantic trade of the seventeenth century, are the most familiar examples. It may suit us to think that slavery belongs to the past and, at best, only exists in under-developed countries, but in reality all our lives are touched by it and our demands sustain much of it. As consumers who put so much emphasis on low prices, we drive multinationals to search across the globe for cheap labour in order to protect their profit margins. Even where companies pay a 'living wage' to their workers, that living wage may be held down because, further down the chain, the food that workers eat may have been produced by slaves. As Kevin Bales, Director of Free the Slaves, points out, 'In Brazil slaves made the charcoal that tempered the steel that made the springs in your car and the blade on your lawnmower.'[1] Or the tea that we drink may have been grown by bonded labour in India.[2]

At a non-governmental level, only Kevin Bales has been brave enough to put his head above the parapet and come up with an estimate of 27m slaves in the world today, of which 15 to 20m are in bonded labour[3] – that is, working for nothing to pay off a debt. As is to be expected, there is no consensus on numbers. The International Labour Office (ILO), a UN agency, estimates a figure of 12.3m people engaged in forced labour but, as that is based on official government figures, it is generally accepted – even by governments – that it is likely to be an underestimate. Of this total, the ILO believes that 1.2m children have been trafficked internationally.[4] It is shocking to realize that the number of slaves today may far exceed the number, ranging from 15m to 28m, shipped during the 300 years of the transatlantic slave trade.

Worse still, we can find slavery closer to home. It is alive and well in the UK today. Conservative estimates for the number of people enslaved here range from 5,000 to 25,000.[5] Many are starved, imprisoned, beaten, sexually violated, physically abused and made to work eighteen hours a day, seven days per week. The scenarios are many and varied: a massage parlour on your local high street where a trafficked woman sells her body; a beach where cockle-pickers work in the middle of the night; the kitchen of a middle-class family where the 'servant' sleeps; or the bedroom in which a man imprisons his 'foreign' wife. This book looks into those corners of modern-day Britain that we know exist but are too uncomfortable to peer into.

These dark corners are illuminated by the personal stories of five slaves who have found some measure of freedom, even if it is to a life eroded by poverty: a Somali woman, Farhia Nur, a failed asylum seeker who cannot work or claim benefits but unofficially worked long hours for a roof over her head; Natasha Bulova, a seventeen-year-old Russian girl who was trafficked for sex; Naomi Conté, a street child from Sierra Leone who was brought here as a fifteen-year-old domestic slave; Liu Bao Ren, a Chinese man who fled persecution in China and was smuggled into the UK after a tortuous journey, to end up in dangerous construction work, sometimes only for board and lodging; and Amber Lobepreet, a woman in a forced marriage who was starved, imprisoned and assaulted. They came from different parts of the world – to escape poverty, war, sexual abuse, persecution, to name but a few of the factors that drove them to leave their homes. Four of the five are women and, of the five, two were children at the time they came to this country. This is roughly representative of those who are enslaved in the UK. It is always women and children who are the most powerless in these situations.

The defining feature of modern slavery is entrapment – physical, emotional, psychological and financial – often sustained through threats of violence or actual violence. While no human being legally owns another human being today, men, women and children continue to be bought and sold, finding themselves at the mercy of others, forced to work for long hours for little or no pay and unable to escape. Current immigration legislation plays a central role in keeping people trapped in slavery. An individual is powerless while her immigration status is in the hands of somebody else, whether it is an 'employer', a 'spouse', an 'agent', a 'trafficker' or indeed the government as in the case of failed asylum seekers. Until your passport is in your hands, until it has the right stamps on it, you are doomed to remain at the mercy of those who wave it in front of your eyes. You have few rights, no family life, no access to healthcare or housing; you are a non-person or an 'unperson'.[6] A new century demands a radical break with the past, highlighting a need to carve out a distinct response to the circumstances that face us now.

People are on the move all around the world for a variety of reasons. There were an estimated 191m migrants worldwide in 2005.[7]

Although it sounds like a lot, it constitutes only 2.5 per cent of the world's population as compared to migrants in the nineteenth century who constituted 10 per cent of world population. They may be refugees, students, immigrants looking for work or moving for purposes of marriage and family reunion, adventure and travel. And then there are those who are driven by desperation. I first became aware of the extent of this desperation when I read of two stowaways on a plane, two Sikh brothers from the Punjab, India. They hid in the wheel compartment of an aeroplane's undercarriage and flew eight hours to London at a temperature of −40° c. As the plane prepared to land at Heathrow, the wheels were lowered and the men fell frozen on to the runway. Amazingly, one of them survived. Since then there have been many similar stories: of pregnant women holding onto the undercarriage of Eurostar from Paris to London, of overcrowded boats decanting their load of desperate migrants into the sea to escape capture by immigration patrols, and of tourists pouring their last drops of Evian water down the throats of thirsty, shipwrecked Africans on the beaches of the Canary islands.

The complex subject of immigration and its connections to slavery is explored at some length in Chapter 6 – how can we prevent tragedies of this kind? – but I hope this book is also a response to the all too common view that migrants to the UK are either scroungers seeking a better life at our expense while building palaces back home with the money that they have acquired here, or are terrorists and suicide-bombers ready to blow up Britain on receiving a coded message from the likes of Osama Bin Laden. People who arrive here without the right papers do not get access to benefits or healthcare, nor are they allowed to work. The policing of 'illegals' does not stop at the borders – it continues at the GP's reception, the welfare office, with the employer and the marriage registrar. The social cohesion and inclusion debate does not even begin to touch their lives. They no more scratch at our consciousness than rats living below the floorboards, reminding us of their existence by their occasional scratching noises and their footprints in our flour. These are people who might be propping up marriages and families by doing the domestic chores that become major bones of contention between men and women, while having no right to family life themselves. By definition, they are mostly single people. Modern slavery destroys family life more effectively than the eighteenth-century slave trade.

Slavery is paradoxically both hidden and visible. If you take a walk on a Sunday in Hyde Park, you will spot many a family with a domestic worker in tow, someone of a Filipino or south Asian background, poorly dressed and lagging behind with a sense of deference. She may be a domestic worker on a work visa with satisfactory working conditions. But we know the majority of such workers are exploited and often paid less than the minimum wage, with the boundaries between slavery and employment becoming very blurred indeed. We find the same blurring in agriculture and cockle-picking. However, some slaves are truly invisible: African children imprisoned by families who depend on their domestic labour; Vietnamese children smuggled in to grow hashish; or women kept in flats to service men. We can live with this injustice not just because we cannot or will not see it but by denying the humanity of those whom we have enslaved. American historian Milton Meltzer points to 'the paradox that has existed at the heart of slavery throughout history. In theory, the slave is an object or tool; in reality, a human being.'[8] We deny her humanity by seeing her only as an object. This book is an attempt to restore the slave's humanity, the acknowledgement of which is the first step to healing the rupture at the heart of our civilization. Our debt to the past must be paid by a firm commitment to ending modern-day slavery.

FARHIA NUR: No Refuge

I have known Farhia Nur since 2004. We met while I was researching a documentary on the work of Southall Black Sisters (SBS). At that point she had been in this country for only two years, but her English was already good enough for her to volunteer as occasional interpreter for other Somali women who came to SBS. Her passion for languages contradicts the stereotype of the new immigrant who refuses to learn English and thereby refuses to 'integrate'. She uses phrases like 'lose consciousness' when she means 'faint'. Even when she was juggling her meagre benefits, she would not compromise on the costs of going to college, such is her thirst for education. She is a flower that will bloom with only a little watering.

Somalia is almost exclusively a Sunni Muslim country. Despite its religious and cultural homogeneity, Somali society has been riven by clan loyalties. President Siyad Barre, who had an unbroken rule of twenty-two years from 1969 to 1991, manipulated clan and sub-clan allegiances in order to remain in power and unleashed a vicious civil war which started in 1988. He claimed to have set up a socialist state with a policy of land distribution: in reality, he grabbed land from minority clans without paying compensation and gave it to members of his own clan, the Marehan, as a way of shoring up his power. This divide and rule tactic sowed the seeds of the inter-clan rivalry that is destabilizing Somalia today.[1] Since Siyad Barre was overthrown in 1991 by rival clans, anarchy has ruled. The north-west of Somalia seceded and declared itself to be the independent Republic of Somaliland. Without a central authority, the country has been carved into fiefdoms by war-lords from rival clans who lead armed factions.

Between January 1991 and August 2000, Somalia had no working government. A fragile parliamentary government was formed in 2000, but it collapsed in 2003 without establishing control of the country. Broadly speaking, the Somali people are divided into the Somali proper group (Samaale) made up of the Dir, Isaaq (Somaliland), Hawiye, and Daarood and the outcast Sab groups, consisting of the Digil and Rahanweyn, who are markedly different in their occupations and dialects from the rest of the population.[2] Minority clans who do not enjoy the protection of larger clans face the worst atrocities; the Eyle tribe, to which Farhia belongs, is one of these. The absence of a civil administration and a police force leaves minorities at the mercy of clan-based militias.

The anarchy fuelled by gun-toting militiamen, who set up check-points at will, has made the delivery of aid in Somalia a 'logistical nightmare' according to one United Nations (UN) official, and even when food is delivered it is often stolen by the militias. In March 2006 Pretoria News reported that levels of insecurity were seriously hampering efforts to feed 1 million hungry people. A UN report estimated that a checkpoint set up in a medium-sized town could raise more than £2m per annum for a war-lord. It is in their interests to ensure that chaos reigns.[3]

The election for the last government of Somalia took place in neighbouring Kenya in 2004 because Mogadishu, the capital, was judged too dangerous for it. Abdullahi Yusuf Ahmed was elected president and is still clinging onto power. The situation in Somalia changes by the day. Since May 2006, another key force has emerged: the Islamists, in the shape of the Islamic Court Union (ICU,) who draw their main support from the Hawiye clan. Despite their ruthless introduction of sharia law and highly unpopular actions, such as the shutting down of radio stations that played love songs and banning men and women from socializing in public, they were welcomed for bringing some semblance of law and order. They also appeared to be winning the military battle against the government, until Ethiopia, supported by the US, waded in on the side of the government. Instead of stabilizing the situation, foreign intervention appears to be accelerating the disintegration of Somalia. The US has justified its involvement on the basis that the ICU may be a new front for Al-Quaeda.

According to United Nations High Commissioner for Refugees (UNHCR) estimates, nearly 400,000 Somalis have fled the country since 1988. The 2001 census recorded the presence of 43,515 Somali people in Britain, most of whom arrived after the outbreak of the civil war. About half of Somali asylum seekers belong to a minority clan.[4] There is also a long-standing community of Somalis in the UK: Somali seamen from the then British colony of Somaliland first settled a century ago in places like Cardiff, Bristol, Liverpool and East London.

I will call myself Farhia Nur. I am thirty-two. Compared with London, Mogadishu is small. It has five or six hospitals, one big theatre, a few cinemas, villas and some large buildings. We don't have trains but you can use buses to go everywhere. If you go 30 km outside the city, you will find big farms and animals. Farmers bring milk from there to the city in these large, red, wooden pots. They burn incense in the pots the day before they put the milk in them so it has a strong scented flavour.

We lived in a 15 x 15 ft hut in an area called Medina where all the hospitals were situated. It was big enough for six children and my mother and father. Later, we had two huts and three more children. The amount of space you had depended upon how much you grabbed for yourself from the other families. We had one narrow, hard bed made from cow skin and wood, a *jimbar*. My father was a hunter and would sometimes be asked to kill and cook a cow for a funeral. If the family didn't want the skin, my father would bring it home. It would be stretched tight and hammered into the ground with a wooden peg at each of the four corners until it dried in the sun. We added salt so that it didn't smell, and dyed it. My father would sleep on the *jimbar* and all of us would sleep on the ground on thin mats made of palm fronds. I don't know how my mother ever got pregnant!

There was one toilet per family, which was a hole in the ground, surrounded by corrugated iron sheets for walls but with no roof. There were overhanging trees near by in which monkeys lived. People would say you should be careful of the monkeys, they will rape you – they had a habit of snatching your clothes away or jumping on you, but I think they were only being playful. There was no running water so we had to carry water and bathe ourselves in the same place as the toilet – it was quite smelly. We had a bucket and mug in the corner on a slab of concrete which tilted towards the hole in the ground so that the water could run away. This made it very slippery and I used to be scared that I would fall into the toilet.

My mother was really young when I was born. I think she had me when she was as young as fourteen. She said that she was married shortly after her first period and she got her periods at the age of thirteen. My brother was born after a gap of seven years. She left it a long time partly because she was afraid of another birth, but also because she couldn't go hunting with young children. She was about thirty-something when she had the last two. I don't know how to tell people's ages. My mother never knew dates or anything, she would count by the moon and things like that. She was illiterate, although my father knew how to read and write.

My mother told me that I was nearly born in the house. She was doing housework when her waters broke. A woman who had experience but no qualifications in delivering babies said 'the child isn't coming out, we must go to the hospital'. While they were walking to the hospital, my mother could feel me coming. She put her hand down there to stop me falling out. It must have looked very strange, but she was past caring. I was born within ten minutes of her getting to the hospital. She was actually giving birth as she was walking.

My father was away, hunting. He would go to the countryside every day at around 4 a.m. before the animals and the birds woke up.

He used a bow and arrow; the arrow head was really sharp and made of iron. He used to make the arrows himself. He'd buy the wood from a village, but the iron tips were expensive so he'd retrieve them from the dead animals and use them again. He would finish hunting by 11 a.m. and bring the animals back in a big bag. We didn't have a fridge, and we couldn't afford to buy ice from the local market, so we had to make sure that we sold all the meat on the same day. I would cut the heads off the chickens we'd reared at home and skin them.

On a good day, my father would bring back three or four rabbits or *sagaaros* – they are a bit like a fox. Sometimes he would bring back big birds. We were not the only hunters and butchers in the area, so selling your meat depended on who you knew. I would go and sell to the families of the young girls I went to school with. It was fun. When we got some money, we would buy enough sugar and flour for the day's meals. We didn't always get to eat meat just because my father was a hunter. Sometimes we had to sell all the meat so that we could buy other things.

It might seem odd that, as hunters, we were living in town but we needed to sell the meat somewhere. Rabbit was not available in the market. Nor was *sagaaro*, which was popular because the meat is very tender and sweet. Although we were Muslims, we were not really bothered about halal. Some people criticized us for slaughtering animals without saying bismillah. We used to say that it's just as good to say bismillah after cooking it! People weren't such strict Muslims when I was growing up. We never used to cover our heads with the *hijab*, we just used to wear this cloth, the *fasaleeti*, and when we went out we would drape a large shawl, the *garbasaar*, around our head and necks. It might seem like there is not much difference because both restrict women's freedom, but the *hijab* is religious and the *garbasaar* is cultural. But true religious women should wear the *jilbaab*, the whole-body cover.

The Eyle tribe, which is Farhia's tribe, believed themselves to be of Falasha (or Jewish) origin before they were Islamized. The main Somali

*clans despise them and consider them to be religious outcasts. It is esti-
mated that before the war broke out there were 1,000 Eyle families in
southern Somalia. They fled to Kenya, Ethiopia and Yemen and their
numbers have now dwindled to two to three hundred families.*

We would eat bread called *muufo* or *anjero* or *roti* made from maize.
You put butter or oil on it and eat it with milk. We would make the
cornmeal ourselves by pounding the maize in a large pestle and
mortar and sell the husks to people who fed their animals on it. We
might buy tomatoes and a bitter, green, cabbage-like salad called
bagel, which we had with lemon. We would eat grapefruit and water-
melon, which we could afford sometimes. I remember my brother,
when he was young, crying, 'No, I don't want water-melon for dinner,
I'll get hungry again.'

I was seven when I started school. We used to go to school from 7
a.m. to noon. It was a free government school. It wasn't really fun
because I had no friends. People looked down on me because my
father was a butcher and because I was from the Eyle tribe. I had the
same uniform for the three years that I was there. It was too big at first.
I used to beg my mum to make it smaller and she would say, 'don't
worry, you will grow into it'. When it got worn, my mother would sew
it up. I would wear it all week. If I came back dirty, my mother would
pick up a stick and say she'd beat me because she would have to wash
it at night and iron it with the coal iron in the morning. My mother
never beat me though. Nor did my father except once when he
slapped me because I couldn't get the maths questions right.

When I was eight years old, I was taken to this house near where we
lived. I had been woken when it was still dark, and was given a bath
and covered with a big cloth like a shawl. There was a long queue of
people outside the house, they had been waiting from early morning
with their children. I joined the queue, clutching my cloth to hide my
naked body. When my turn came, they took me into a room and put
me on this big table. My mother and a neighbour held me tight and
kept my legs apart. You are supposed not to cry because it is shameful.

I remember crying and the children were all saying 'you cried, you cried, you are not a brave girl'. They give you a cloth to chew on if you feel pain. The doctor brings all his tools, some to cut and some to sew, in his box – sometimes it's not a doctor, just someone who practises this thing. Sometimes they use anaesthetic, and sometimes the anaesthetic is not good and you can feel everything. It's really very painful and it takes them fifteen to twenty minutes to do it. I'm talking about female genital mutilation (FGM), or *gudniin*, the word for circumcision in Somalia. When the operation is done, they run their hand over the area. It has to be very flat for them to think it's a good job. Then they tied my legs together with a rope to make sure that I didn't open them. You can't move or walk or do anything that could open the wound. You feel like a roll of salami. In ten days or so they remove the stitches.

There are four types of FGM. The one I have had done is called pharaonic and there is another one called Sunna. My one is the worst type of FGM. They see it as the best one – where the woman is closed completely. That is the most common kind of FGM, so that the woman remains a virgin until marriage. It involves cutting all the parts and sewing everything. They just leave you a small place through which you can pass urine.

I couldn't wee because the pain was so bad. You have to wee in front of the doctor. If the wee comes out of the wrong place or it comes out in a rush, it will force it open and they will do it again. Painful! In my case they didn't have to. The terror of having it done again made me cry all night and all day. My mum started shouting at me. It took me nearly two days to do it. That's why I feel sometimes that my kidneys were damaged. The urine accumulates and doesn't come out properly and it hurts down there even now. Not as badly as it used to. It burns a lot because wee is acid and it's all open and cut. They give you very little water to drink, even though the weather is hot, so that you won't feel the need to wee. Your mother holds you horizontally over a place where you can wee and, when you wee, it drips through the back of your thighs and then someone pours water through the gap at the top of your legs. Somali girls are quite thin so there is a gap. My mother said that in the countryside they would hold girls over a hole in the ground in which they would burn incense, and that had healing powers too. I think they used nylon thread on me but my mother had hers done in the village and they used thorns to hold her skin together.

I remember my first period was so painful because it couldn't come out. Year after year blood clots build up inside you and the pain is indescribable. I ended up with an abscess. Every time I went to the doctor, he would say 'this is because of your operation'. They cleaned it under anaesthetic in hospital. During my periods I couldn't go to school and couldn't do very much. That was the only health problem I had with FGM until I was raped at eighteen. Then I bled and got an infection. There wasn't any medicine that I could use to clean myself. I could only use hot water. Horrible! I'm surprised that I didn't get AIDs.

The idea is that your husband should open you up with sex. They feel proud of doing it. If your husband can't do it and you have to get it done in hospital, your family honour is stained. It is expected that a 'real' man will open up a woman with his penis. The wedding night feels like rape. Even though it feels better afterwards, it is really painful getting there. If it is not done in the right way, you can tear. It can take up to six months and you suffer every single time. Sometimes men use a knife. By that time, the skin has joined together so they are not cutting the stitches but the skin. That's why you bleed. He has to have sex with you every night after that, even if he doesn't want to, to stop the skin sealing up again. A lot of women ask their husbands to take them to hospital secretly. Some men feel insulted and become violent. They won't even take their wives to hospital when they're bleeding or infected. A new bride doesn't go back to her maternal home until the seventh day after her wedding; her family could take her to hospital, but by then it might be too late.

It took four years for me to feel better. My periods started coming through once it was open. There's no sexual pleasure because it's all been taken away. There is also fear. You stop enjoying sex when you think it's going to hurt. You tense up. It's not something that should be done to a human being. It's no better for those who are single. They continue to have urine and period problems because the place is still closed, and you get a lot of infections.

Girls are not 'halal' and until it is done they are considered 'haram'. It is strange to call it halal or haram because it has nothing to do with religion. It's tradition. Men think that a woman without FGM is not good because she can sleep with every man, she's open. It isn't true that if you have FGM, you are good and if you don't have FGM, you are not good. Parents believe that: 'I want to be proud of my girl. I want her to be a virgin when she gets married.' I have not had children, but women tell me that FGM makes it more painful to give birth. Some women are stitched up again after childbirth. My mother told me that she was never stitched up again. That becomes a talking point among the older women and a source of shame. They say FGM came to Somalia from Arab countries like Egypt. That's why I think it is called *pharaonic*, because the pharaoh used to put a belt on his wife when he left her and he carried out FGM so that she couldn't have an affair with other men. In some parts of Africa they do a worse cut where they take it all out.

According to Amnesty International, the most severe form of FGM is infibulation, also known as pharaonic circumcision. An estimated 15 per cent of all mutilations in Africa are infibulations but the comparable figure for Somalia is 80 per cent. It is estimated that 98 per cent of all women undergo some kind of FGM. The procedure consists of clitoridectomy (where all, or part of, the clitoris is removed), excision (removal of all, or part of, the labia minora), and cutting of the labia majora to create raw surfaces, which are then stitched or held together in order to form a cover over the vagina when they heal. A small hole is left to allow urine and menstrual blood to escape. The less severe type of genital mutilation is clitoridectomy. The least radical procedure consists of the removal of the clitoral hood. An estimated one hundred and thirty-five million girls and women have undergone genital mutilation world-wide and approximately six thousand girls are at risk of mutilation per day. It is practised extensively in Africa and is common in some Middle Eastern countries.[5]

According to FORWARD, a leading African women's group in the UK, there are 74,000 women in the UK who have undergone FGM and 7,000 girls under the age of sixteen at risk of FGM. Although the government criminalized FGM here and the taking of girls overseas for that purpose in 2003, not a single case has been prosecuted because of the hidden nature and widespread acceptance of this practice in some African communities.

Apart from the FGM, I had a good childhood. We were poor but happy. Of course, as the oldest child who took care of all her brothers and sisters, I developed a sense of responsibility early. My worst fear as a child was not knowing whether we would have food for our next meal. If my brothers and sisters were crying from hunger, sometimes I could only give them bread with water. I used to worry about my mother dying in childbirth. In Somalia the number of women who die in childbirth is very high. My childhood ended at ten when I stopped school to help my mother look after my sisters and brothers. When I was sixteen, my father worked really hard to send me to evening school, where I learned English and mathematics for nearly two years. I remember he didn't have money for photos so I never got my leaving certificate. I cried a lot about that. My mother was not very keen. She used to say, 'what's the point, she's only going to get married and have children?' I was the boy that my father would have liked as his first-born. My father saw education as very important. I should have been married by fifteen, so for my father to send me to school at sixteen was quite radical. He used to say that we couldn't live off hunting any longer. Hunting was forbidden in Somalia. But these were the traditions of our Eyle tribe. He wanted me to understand how to deal with money. I remember that I had to study all night by the light of the *feynuus* – a kind of hurricane lamp which uses naphtha for fuel.

When my parents first came to Medina, the area around our home was just empty land, but then smart villas started to spring up near by. My mother used to do cooking and cleaning for our new, rich neighbours in the surrounding villas. I asked for work too – they would pay 5 or 7 Somali shillings depending on how many hours I worked. My mother would also make incense at home, *uunsi*, to sell to them. When I went to the market to buy tomatoes, flour, cooking oil for that day, my mother would give me 2 shillings. We would buy blackened bananas and rotting tomatoes. We would eat the gut of the animal which others, the 'noble' Somalis, wouldn't touch. We would clean all the shit out of it, boil it, cut it and have it with lemon.

This is widespread in the developing world. In India, shopkeepers are prepared to sell two teaspoons of chilli powder, salt and a cup of oil for a meal. Meat was an important part of the diet of Muslims, but poor ones who could not afford it would make curries from congealed blood to provide a source of protein for their children.

One or two years before the war, I fell in love with this boy who was from a different tribe. I was sixteen and he was about twenty. I'll call him Ahmed. I met him in a shop. I didn't tell him where I lived because I was embarrassed. He would hang around in the area where he first met me. That was how we met again. We weren't allowed to go out with boys. Once you get older, you have to stay at home and wear a *fasaleeti* and do housework. We didn't hold hands. He tried to put his arm around my shoulders once, and I started to shake in case anyone saw us. Although the seaside was about five minutes from where we lived, we didn't go to the beach because people could see you and all the romantic couples used to go there. We used to meet at the hospital. There was a big garden at the back where visitors would sit with patients. We would sit in the garden and talk and that's it. We didn't even kiss. But I can say that I fell in love.

We were found out because of my brother, who used to go everywhere with me. One day I said, 'I am going to the hospital and you're not coming with me'. Stupid me, I mentioned the hospital. My brother followed me and told my mum. I came back quite late that day. My mother threw her sandal at me. She wouldn't say why. After some days, I said I was going to the hospital again and she asked me who I was going to meet. She said, 'I know you are going to meet this boy'. I was so embarrassed. She wanted me to bring him home. I was embarrassed by what he might think of my mother. Whatever happens, I thought, this is your mum, you can't change that.

My mother liked him. She offered us drinks. Later he met my father. My parents would have allowed me to marry him, but he came from a very religious tribe, the Reer Hamars, and would have had problems. In any case, when the war broke out we lost each other. But, unbelievably, I met him again in London. I was walking down the street in Southall with Meena from SBS and I heard someone call my name. I thought, who can that be, nobody knows me here. It was Ahmed. I was jumping with excitement. He told me all about his life and I told him about mine. He is married with five children. I want to write a book about it some day. We are in contact as friends.

The war broke out on a Sunday in early December 1990. I used to work occasionally for the Yusuf family when their full-time servant was on holiday. They lived in a villa with gates and two cars, it was a ten- or fifteen-minute walk from my house. The old couple had grown-up children, two daughters and a son. The daughters were married and the son, Daahir, lived with them. The older daughter, Farida, had three children and a very quiet husband. The younger one, Hamida, was a widow with two children. Daahir's wife had died of an illness so his two children were being brought up by his mother. The old woman was very quiet. She would come and ask how much money she owed and give it to me. I used to give the money to my mum and sometimes she would give me a little back so I could buy things like shampoo. Normally we used the dishwashing soap for our hair. That Sunday afternoon, heavy gun-fighting started. Boom, boom, boom. I had no idea what it was all about because I didn't read the newspapers and just wasn't interested in politics – although my father used to listen to the BBC Somali news. That's why he had bought a radio.

Siyad Barre, the President, who fled in January 1991, belonged to a sub-clan of Daarood, while Aidid, who replaced him, belonged to the Hawiye clan, as did the Yusuf family that Farhia worked for. Most of the fighting took place between the Daarood and the Hawiye clans.

Trouble started originally, in 1988, in north Somalia, where the Isaak tribe lives. They had educated young men who stood up to President Siyad Barre because all the jobs were going to his tribesmen. They were fed up with the corruption that had flourished under his twenty-year dictatorship. Barre bombarded the north and started killing his opponents. The other tribes in the south knew that when he had finished with the north he would come after them. Aidid, who was in Ethiopia at that time, mobilized the Hawiye clan against the President. So the President turned his attention to the Hawiyes. Our neighbours started locking their doors at night. The fathers wouldn't stay at home because the President was rounding up all the men in the families. We knew something was going to happen but nobody knew that it was going to be so fast and so terrible.

That Sunday, I did all the washing and cleaning as usual. There was nothing about the fighting on the radio, apparently, but as I was working I couldn't listen to it anyway and TV didn't start till 6 p.m. When I'd finished my work, the old woman paid me, but said that it was too dangerous for me to go home. I didn't know what to do. At the back they had two rooms for servants to sleep in. I went there, but I couldn't sleep. It was my first time away from my family. I just assumed that the fighting was going to be a one-day thing, but the morning after, the boom, boom, boom continued. It was worse, though, because people had started to gather their stuff and run. The old man was a powerful man in the military, as was his son, but he didn't go to work that day because even he would have been in danger. People said that there was heavy gun-fighting, missiles were blowing holes into buildings, houses were exploding. Again I said, 'I have to go', and again she said, 'stay here till things become calmer'. All day the heavy fighting continued so I just got on with the cooking and cleaning while everyone was praying. Fear makes you religious.

Gun-fighting continued on the second night. The family said that they were going to go to Afgoe where they had their farm and second home. I asked them to take me home. They said, 'your family is not going to be there because everyone's leaving'. I didn't know what to do. They said, 'it's only temporary; when it's finished, we'll come back'. Nobody realized at that time that this would be a civil war which would go on for fifteen years and is still continuing.

We needed a van to take us to the country. We had to walk to the army barracks where all the vans were parked. It's normally a fifteen-minute walk but it took us much longer because I was lugging a big sack of clothes and they were carrying the money. Not only that, but we had to stop and take cover whenever the gunfire sounded really close. By now, it was dark. It was 9 p.m. and it gets dark by 6 p.m. I remember tripping over something and coming face to face with a dead body. It was horrifying. His eyes were still open. He was cold and petrified. I still dream of that face and wake up in the night seeing those staring eyes. We had to walk around the back of the President's house to get to the barracks. All the fighting was happening around his house. There were many dead people, but they weren't wearing uniforms so I think they were the people who were attacking the government. The later it got, the heavier the fighting became because they thought that ordinary people were at home and those who were out and about were up to no good. There was fallen masonry everywhere from the houses that were being destroyed. It was a mess, and we had to be careful not to fall. The children were crying. There were other families with children like us who were also fleeing. We tried to keep the children quiet, even though at that time they were not attacking refugees.

When we got to the station, a lot of people were there, shouting 'me first, me first'. I was really worried about my family. They did not have a car to drive them away or another house to go to. And it was too far to walk to Buur Eyle, our village. I was tempted to run to my family's hut, but I thought I might die on the way so changed my mind. The vans belonged to the army and they were only letting military families use them. It was a big open van and we put everything in it. We jumped in, all the women and children and two young men with guns. They were members of the extended family riding with us for protection. We were seven children, four women including me, five men, sixteen in all. Apart from Daahir and his father who were sitting with the driver in his cab, we were all sitting in the back. We could feel the wind in our hair. Of course we were too anxious to notice the weather. Our journey took about forty minutes. The roads were crowded with people fleeing. There was crying and confusion.

We unloaded the van when we arrived and settled in. It was a large house with eight rooms on one floor and was situated in the middle of farms which were also owned by the family. The farmers who worked the land brought vegetables like carrots, sweet potatoes, fruit like papaya, mangoes, and maize for the family. They sold what they did not need. I cooked and cleaned as I felt it was expected of me. After a couple of days, I went to the old woman and said I wanted to go back and find my family. She said, 'I will send my son to find out what is happening in Mogadishu'. Other members of their clan were visiting to discuss what was going on. On the radio they said that people from all the tribes were meeting for a conference. But many people died during that conference. After twenty days or so, it was reported that the President, Siyad Barre, had fled to Kenya and that a new government would have to be formed. Daahir reported that people were coming back to Mogadishu and there was going to be peace. I had hope. I would say thanks to God that I was going back.

However, different sub-clans of the Hawiye, led by men like Aidid and Ali Mahdi, were fighting for power and their followers were killing each other on the streets of Mogadishu. My employers belonged to the Aidid faction. These were the people whose fighting had led to the collapse of Siyad Barre's government. There was no single successor to Barre, but Aidid was the most powerful of all the war-lords. He was responsible for some of Somalia's worst outbreaks of civil war. The Americans tried unsuccessfully to remove Aidid in 1992 because he was the cause of all the problems. If you see the film *Black Hawk Down*, you will understand everything. There was no government for four years until Aidid ended up becoming president briefly in 1995. He was killed in 1996. Everybody believes it was the Americans who did it. The current president, Abdullahi Yusuf, belongs to a sub-clan of the Daarood. People recognize different clans by accent and dress. People know where the clans live and they'll go there and kill them.

During the fifteen days of heavy war, there was no radio or TV. The only news we got was BBC news, but because the reporters were not based in Mogadishu there was not enough detail. People who could afford it started leaving the country. At around the time of the American 'invasion', the family started treating me badly. They stopped paying me. They said, 'we'll keep your money because you're not going anywhere'. The idea was that they would give me the money when I left. We didn't even discuss how much they would pay me. They behaved as if they were doing me a favour because they were letting me stay with them. They gave me a small room at the back. I was cooking and cleaning for fourteen people, sometimes more. Militiamen who were cousins, friends and members of the same tribe guarded the family. They would come to my room when they wanted to eat, and ask for dinner, sometimes late at night. The sisters would say 'where's that skivvy?' If I took a little longer than usual to make tea, they would start taunting me. They would beat me and shout at me.

A normal day would start at 6 a.m., when the children woke up, and finish at 10 or 11 p.m. One of my jobs was to bathe the children. To start with, they were quite helpful, but once they knew that I couldn't leave they started acting up. The children were very young. The oldest, the twelve-year-old, was always with his mother, Farida, who was horrible to me. She would slap me if I had not cooked something correctly or if I had overheated the child's milk. She would say that all the protein was lost and would throw the hot milk at me. One day she slapped me because I put lemon on the salad. She went to the kitchen and made it again herself. I couldn't fight back. That's when I began to see myself as weak, because I didn't stand up for myself. They would taunt me by saying that my Eyle people were going to be killed. The old woman would say that bullets were too good for us. It would be better to slaughter us with knives. If women could talk like that, can you imagine how the men would behave?

I would usually eat the leftovers. I would cook rice, chicken, lamb, *anjero* and pasta for the family. When I first started cooking, I didn't know how to cook things like rice and lamb because we hadn't been able to afford them. Hamida, the second daughter, would serve the food for everybody and leave nothing for me. When the plates came back, I would eat what was left on them. You know how it is in our part of the world. The best food goes to the men, then the children, and then the women. Sometimes I would eat with the children. I am ashamed to tell you that, as I fed them, I would eat their food because I was so hungry and because I used to work all day. Now when I am hungry I deal with it mentally. I can manage my hunger. I learned to wait for whatever God will give me. The other way I dealt with my hunger was by fasting. Of course, I didn't even have food to break the fast. I was very weak.

I used to be brave but when I thought of running away I would think, I am only a woman, I could be raped or killed. I may be powerful as a human being, but as a member of the Eyle tribe I was nothing. I was not armed. I didn't have my father by my side to defend me. I started to become religious. Things were getting worse every day. Daahir used to go to Mogadishu frequently, sometimes for two to three days at a stretch, sometimes for just half a day. He was hoping to be part of the next government. He was a militiaman. All these big families were armed. The UN food that used to come into port was commandeered by militiamen and sold off to wholesalers, so the poor never got to see the food. As there was no government, these men would guard the airport and the docks. Daahir worked for one of the war-lords, all of whom had their own private armies. Towards the end of 1991, when infighting began among the Hawiyes, Daahir and his men would come back from Mogadishu, excited and noisy, like soldiers are when they come back from war. They would bang doors shut, shout loudly 'where's my food?', and throw their guns about. Daahir would sit with his father, who was disabled by now, in the courtyard and tell him what had happened. Although I was never told the full details, I think his father's legs had been injured in a gun battle when his car was ambushed by rival militiamen. Daahir would have arguments with his mother, who would beg them to stop the fighting. He was her little boy. I had been in Afgoe for nearly a year by then.

Around this time, Daahir started being nice to me. He would smile. He would look at me. I didn't understand – stupid me! Once he asked me to make tea for his militiamen, who slept in the two rooms at the back. They were eating *qat* – a bitter-tasting leaf that the men chew; it's a stimulant and is supposed to stop them feeling hungry or tired. He came into the kitchen and said he would take the teapot out. He then came and knocked on my door and said 'there's no milk'. The milk was in the kitchen and he could've taken it himself. Instead, I had to go back to the kitchen to get the milk. When I returned to my room, he was there. He started to touch me. He put his hand on my mouth and I tried to bite him. He pulled my hair, slapped me, threw me on the bed and said, 'don't say anything, it will be worse for you if you do'. Then he raped me.

That's when I gave up. I wished I was dead. I used to pray to God that Daahir would die and never return, but it continued to happen. He would come two or three times a week. He stole the best years of my life. In the beginning it was horrible. I wanted to shout out loudly. Don't ask me to give you a more precise image of what I suffered, then I won't have to dwell in that memory. It felt like an animal chewing your body all the time. You knew it was going to come and chew on the same place again. It's very difficult to cope with pain that does not end. I wished I was a man, that I didn't have a vagina. I was bleeding and had no one to talk to. The only good thing was that he would take his pleasure quickly at the beginning – maybe because it was tight. They like it when it hurts. Maybe that's why in the West men want anal sex. Thank God he didn't want that. There's always somebody worse off to give you a little comfort! As soon as he was finished, he would go to his own bedroom. Later he started taking his time. Then it was worse because he went on and on.

I never got pregnant. Maybe I can't get pregnant. They asked me that at the immigration tribunal. 'You were with this man for so long and you never got pregnant?' Maybe he didn't want a child with me. I certainly didn't want a child with him. He always removed himself before ejaculation. And it never happened accidentally. I used to jump up and down after he came, and wear tight things around my stomach, just in case. I have never told anyone about that. If I had got pregnant, they would have killed me. If I couldn't do the job I would be useless.

After I had been raped, I felt that I had crossed a bridge, and now I needed to worry only about being killed. I used to think that the best that could happen to me was that I might marry a farmer and carry on working for this family until I die. Even the farmers won't marry me because I'm from a different tribe. Although they used to say to me, 'you're beautiful, you have beautiful eyes'. That kept me going.

Then in 1995, everything changed. Aidid died. People hoped that things would improve. The family, however, continued to live in Afgoe. One day, the old man saw me crying. He didn't know how I was being treated. I wasn't allowed to clean his room when he was in there, only when he had gone to the hospital. His wife would take his food to his room. He gave me some money and said, 'go to the shops and buy something nice, a dress, for yourself'. He said I could take the next day off. I knew this was my chance. I also had some money – I had been saving any money I had been given and I'd collected nearly 30,000 shillings – though I have to admit that I used to steal money from them too. Not as much as they owed me. If I saw money lying around, I would take it. I used to carry it around in my bra. I still have the marks on my skin because the paper had sharp edges and kept digging into my skin as I worked. I couldn't leave it in my room in case somebody found it. All the time that I was planning to leave, I was worried about the money losing its value. Two thousand shillings would just buy a bag of sugar now. Thirty thousand shillings would be enough to get me to Mogadishu. I told the old woman that I was going to the market in Afgoe to buy something for myself. She didn't seem to mind, and told me to be careful.

That was the day I left. I just walked down the sandy road. My heart was pumping. I was twenty-two years old. I hadn't seen my mother for five years. I had gone with only the clothes I was wearing, a pair of worn-out sandals and the money. My head was covered with a *fasaleeti* and *garbasaar*. I was wearing the *dirac*.[6] In the war it was not safe to wear fine clothes in case people thought you had money and robbed you. I didn't know that. Everything had changed. I came to the big road and saw a woman who was a friend of the family who had, in fact, given me the *dirac* that I was wearing. I had nothing to fear from her because she knew that I was badly treated by them. She was the first person who had been nice to me. She used to smoke and offer me cigarettes and give me her old clothes to wear.

At first, I told her that the family had given me some money to go and look for my mum. She felt sorry for me and offered to help me to get to Mogadishu – she said we could hire a small car and driver. I told her I only had 7,000 shillings because I didn't want to give all my money away. She went off to negotiate a price with a driver she knew – she used to sell him *qat*. That's how she made a living. She was divorced and had no children, so she was very independent. On the journey I started to cry, and then I told her that I was running away from the family. She suggested that I look for my family in the refugee camp which was just behind our hut. The camp was in a big university which was closed to students now. When people ran away from the fighting, their houses were looted. When they came back, they would find other people, often militiamen, living there. They lived there by force and said 'this is mine now'.

The United Somali Congress (USC), the political party of the Hawiyes, were in charge in Mogadishu. When we reached a checkpoint (an *isbaaro*) the militiamen demanded money to let us into Mogadishu. Once we got through, we went our separate ways. The driver dropped me off in an area called KM4 and I started walking towards Medina, towards my home. Everything looked different. The buildings were empty, looted. No doors, no windows. Every building had been sprayed with gunfire. Women were wearing the clothes they would normally wear at home, cotton dresses called *baati*. I had to ask for directions to the place where I used to live. I was confused. When I got there, I knew no one. There was only one man from the old days. They said he had gone shopping and he might be back in the evening. The place where my hut had stood was just open ground, there was nothing left of it.

I felt terrible. I didn't know whether my family was dead or alive. I kept thinking about the missiles and how entire families would dive down on the ground to escape them. If one landed on a hut, the whole family would be found like that in the morning, dead. When I saw that even the hut wasn't standing, I couldn't find the calm (*sic*) to sit down. I thought that if I didn't have any luck at the camp, I would come back and talk to the old man. I also had to find somewhere to stay that night.

The refugee camp was spread over a number of large university buildings of two to three storeys each, so there was enough room for a family to have a small room to themselves. At the beginning, the militiamen stayed in nice big villas and weren't interested in the refugee camps, but when the war had been going on for some time they started charging money for the rooms.

I started my search here. I stopped people and asked them how long they had been there, before asking about my mother. Normally you ask by tribe, but, as the place was run by the Hawiye clan, I thought it best not to use the name of my clan because it might work against me. There were three buildings: one building had three floors, the other two had two floors only. The big building had approximately twenty rooms on each floor and the other buildings had maybe fifteen rooms on each floor. I hadn't been there before the war, but my mum had told me that they had lovely gardens. There were no flowers when I saw it. There was shit everywhere. Even in the empty rooms you would find shit. There were no toilets. At night-time people went out to shit. Sometimes you would go into a room and find a dead person. They were burying people everywhere. You'd come across them in the garden. They would put up a stone to mark the burial place.

I was walking around, crying, thinking I'll never find my mum. There were people selling food – *bur*, a kind of fried bread and tea. I came across this woman who was selling tea. A little boy was attached to her leg, crying mum, mum, mum. She was carrying a baby girl. She wore a *hijab*, and had a wrinkled face. Then she smiled. If it hadn't been for the smile, I wouldn't have recognized her. It was my mother. It was unbelievable. She must have been in her thirties, and yet she had aged so much. She looked very tired. We hugged each other and started to cry. She asked her friend if she would sell her kettle of tea for her so we could go to her room at the back and talk. For some time, we just sat and looked at each other. We started to tell each other what had happened. She hoped that I hadn't asked for her by her clan because she had changed her name and had claimed to be from the Rahanweyn clan, which was the truth in one way because they had accepted the Eyle people into their clan. The children who I didn't recognize were my little brother and sister, who were born after the war started.

I asked about the others. She had to tell me everything in a whisper because she didn't want people to hear. They first took shelter at the hospital for a month because there was very heavy gun-fighting. Then they returned home. The militiamen left them alone. They were not interested in hut-dwellers, because there was not much to loot. Despite that, they had taken everything from the hut. The hut was still standing back then although there were holes in it. That was in 1992.

It was no longer possible to hunt. My mother said the animals had run deeper into the forest because of all the shooting. My father started working for some militiamen, who didn't pay him because they thought he got enough money from killing and cooking animals. He told them that he couldn't work for them any longer because he needed to feed his children. One night, two men came in search of him. They pointed guns at my mother and all my brothers and sisters and told them to lie flat on the floor. My father was arguing with the men. He was shouting 'don't do this' as he wrestled with one man's gun with both his hands and tried to stop it from pointing at him. The other man thought my father was attacking his 'friend' and he shot my father. He fell to the ground and all the children started to cry. My mother didn't know what to do. None of the neighbours came out to help. Everybody would stay in their own huts at times like these. He had been shot in the stomach and he was bleeding. The next morning the neighbours looked after the younger children while my mother and the two oldest children (thirteen and fourteen) took my father to hospital on a stretcher. He was still alive although he had lost a lot of blood. There was a doctor who knew him and tried to help him. He cleaned his wound. But in the end he died the night after he was shot, from tetanus. That was 1994.

My sister was married at that time. It might seem odd that she was married when I wasn't. During the war young girls were married off for their own protection after their first periods, which could come as early as nine. This was because families couldn't look after them. If there was a young boy around, you talked to his parents and arranged the marriage. If she gets raped after she's married, it's not so bad because she belongs to that family anyway. It is a way of making sure that girls get married rather than remain single from the stigma of rape. They think they're saving the girl. Her husband went along with my mother to the hospital. He was about fourteen or fifteen, a neighbour's child, from the same tribe. They used to play together. At fourteen you are already grown-up, already responsible. They were married some months before my father died.

My sister, her husband and my brother decided to take the younger children to Buur Eyle. They hoped to find family there if they said they were the children of so and so. They're very welcoming in the village. There are a lot of farms there so they hoped they might get work. My brothers and sisters were also worried that those men might come back and finish off the rest of the family. They must have walked all the way to the village – all 50 or 70 km. My mother told them to go ahead of her because she had to bury my father. The doctor and the neighbours helped with the costs of the burial. Buying a grave costs a lot of money, especially during wartime because so many people are dying. You have to pay men to dig the ground and you have to buy white cotton to wrap the body. This cloth was also very expensive because of the war. Normally you buy a cow and cook it for everyone who comes to the funeral. We had no money. Even though neighbours contributed to the cost of the meat, we could only afford a small goat. My mother and the two youngest stayed behind. She got news about the others once when some woman came back from the village. The older boys were working and trying to make a living to feed the younger ones. They were living in a *mudul*, a house which was bigger than our hut.

My mother found it difficult to cope with the younger children after my father died. She used to sell tomatoes, lemons and oranges in the market. She would buy big sackfuls at the same checkpoint in KM4 that I came through. The stuff came from Afgoe. Could it have been from my employer's farm? Had we been connected all this time? She couldn't carry the big sack so she would divide it into two bags. Leaving the little children with a neighbour, she would then have to make two journeys to collect the sacks. When heavy fighting broke out again, she moved from our hut to the refugee camp. People were getting shot on the way from their huts to the toilet and she didn't want to get caught in the crossfire. The brick walls at the camp protected her from bullets at least. After moving to the camp, she started getting weaker and couldn't carry sacks of vegetables, especially with the children. So she started selling tea and *bur*. She had a small room in the university building, about 4 x 4 ft, and a *burjiko*, which is a little clay oven in which you put live coal, a kettle, a thermos and some cups. I really admire my mum. She was a hard worker. She wouldn't sit in one place and cry about things. My mum said that everywhere you go militiamen have set up *isbaaros*, and you have to pay them to cross unless you are a member of their tribe or you know them. Some of them are only fourteen-year-old boys with guns. They will frisk you to make sure you're not carrying any money or ask you to take off your clothes, even if you are a woman. They will threaten to kill you. You have to pray and say 'please let me go, I don't have enough money'.

My mum and I had six days together. Sometimes we talked through the night. I gave her what money I had and we started to make plans. Shall we go to Eyle? She was against it because you couldn't earn money there. She said she would only go if she had saved enough. She was hopeful that things were going to change. The new government would be better. When I told her about Daahir, she cried all day. She couldn't believe it. She had also worked for that family and had always thought of Daahir as a quiet and polite man. I asked her what she thought about my going to Nairobi. She said, 'you have nobody to help you. I lost you once, I don't want that to happen again.'

On the sixth night, at about 9 p.m., we heard noises, men with guns walking down the long corridors. We had done all our work, eaten our meal, the children were asleep and we were chatting. I looked out and saw four men. It was Daahir and three others. At first I didn't see him because it was quite dark. There was no electricity, but many of the rooms had a *feynuus* which cast some light into the corridor. The other men were in front and their faces were scary. Next to my mother's room was her friend's room. She was single and would sometimes go out with men so the room was empty. I told my mother that whatever happened I would come back and look for her, and quickly slipped into the empty room. I had to distance myself from my mother for her own safety. I made a gesture to my mother to stay there. I didn't want Daahir to see her because he would have recognized her and might have done something to her. My mother suffered, seeing me go into a dangerous situation and not being able to help because there were even younger children to think about. I could hear some people asking them 'what do you want?' But they wouldn't say who they were looking for. My heart was going boom, boom, boom.

There were no doors to the rooms, just pieces of cloth across the doorway. But one of them had seen me go into the room and called out 'come here, who's with you?' I said 'no one'. He pushed me roughly back into the room, grabbing and pulling at me. The men had recognized me because I used to cook for them. Then Daahir came in and asked, 'why did you run away?' He grabbed me. I said, 'just let me get my stuff and I'll come with you', but he thought I was trying to run away again and pulled me back. I was trying to find a way to say goodbye to my mother. One of the men hit me on the head with the butt of his gun really hard. My head throbbed. Then he kicked me in the legs. It was such a strong kick that I could hardly walk. They dragged me to the jeep and made me sit on the floor at the back. Daahir sat in front with the driver, chewing *qat*. I got a swelling on my head. On the journey home a lot of things were going through my mind – the death of my father, the way I left my mother, how Daahir knew where to look for me. Maybe it had been that family friend. I felt a bit better that my mum knew where I was. It would be easier to escape next time.

The old woman didn't talk to me from that day on. She must have felt that I had let her down by looking for my family. How inhuman they were – I could never hold somebody against their will. If they had been nicer to me I would have come back and even brought my mother to work for them. The daughters became more violent than before. Daahir said 'don't you ever, ever do such a thing again'. Now I wasn't even allowed to go to the farms to pick up food like I used to before. Nobody would talk to me, not even the farm people, who thought they would get into trouble.

Daahir came to my room again on the third night after I returned. I was braver now. I had recharged my batteries. I knew what had happened to my family. Before, I never said a word. I had no hope. I used to just cry. Now I started talking to him. I would say, 'you're really rubbish, you're not a good Muslim. You take money from people and that's what you live off.' He would say it was business, you sell things to people and you get money for it, there was nothing wrong with that. 'You're going to burn in hell', I would say. 'I'm not responsible for any of this but you are. Why don't you marry someone instead of doing things like this?'

In September 1995, Daahir took me to a priest. I think somebody else in the family knew about us although no one would question him as he was the man of the family. I think his sister saw us. She would call me *sharmuuto*, prostitute. She thought that I had attracted her brother and that I should have done something to keep him away. How can you stop a man who is raping you? Maybe she talked to him. I don't know. But one night, at 9 p.m., he gave me a *baati* and a *garbasaar* and told me to get dressed. He wouldn't tell me where we were going. I was convinced that he was going to kill me. Usually when they are going to kill you, they give you a set of new clothes, take you somewhere and make you say *shahaada*, 'There is no God but Allah and Mohammed is his prophet'. In Saudi Arabia, before they execute someone, they make them say the *shahaada*. Everyone was sleeping. As we walked through the house, I could hear one of the children crying. Only the men who guarded the house were up, listening to the radio. I kept asking Daahir where we were going. He was driving and wouldn't say anything. We drove for twenty minutes or so. I didn't have a watch. I used to go to Farida's room to look at the clock. I didn't have a calendar and it was actually quite hard to keep track of time.

We came to a place where a man was sitting cross-legged. He had another man with him. They made me sit at the back. He said things in Arabic and although I knew some Arabic I couldn't understand him. It wasn't the Koran. It was what you might say during a *meher* – the vows between the bride and groom – but I had no idea as I had never been married. Daahir shook hands with the old man and said 'this is the woman', and they all looked at me. I wasn't given a ring.

This man was not a proper imam or sheikh. It wasn't done in the proper religious way. Usually you have to ask the girl if she agrees to get married. I would probably have said yes. But the thing is that he never asked. You have to ask how old is she, if she knows this person by name, how much is her *meher*?[7]

When we came back, he said 'now you are my wife'. No consent needed. Now it was legalized rape. Now I couldn't even say that he was not a good Muslim. With the permission of his God he was free to do as he wanted. I was still the servant. I still slept in my old room. I didn't move into his bedroom. He knew about the beatings that I got from his sisters. He would say 'don't do things that make them angry'. Or he would say that he would talk to them, but he never did. I had no family, no chance of getting married properly, of picking up my life. I used to think of my boyfriend sometimes and cry. Life would have been so different if this war hadn't happened. I would have got married to someone I loved. I didn't want to live, but I didn't want to die either.

When Daahir was at home, he would come to my room every night. There was no talking. Sometimes I would be sleeping and he would come in, lift my skirt and have sex with me. I would just pretend nothing was happening. Sometimes I would fight back, but he would hold me tight. At first, I used to go to the toilet and wash myself, then I stopped doing that because his sisters might see me. They didn't come to my room and ask me to heat milk for the children any more. I would say to him that if his father got to know, I would be killed because I was bringing shame to the family. His family would say there are so many girls out there that he could marry. Why did he want to have sex with me? An Eyle girl? I think he didn't want the hassle of marriage. This way he could have sex whenever he wanted and no one complained. He would have had to take care of a wife. Maybe she would have been horrible to his children. As it was, his children were very attached to me. His little boy would study the Koran only if I put him on my lap. He would cry when the Koran teacher came.

Things were getting worse. Neighbours started to leave. Some of them left for Europe. Daahir didn't want to leave, but the shame of our relationship was becoming a burden for him. If his sister told the militiamen about me, they could have killed me. Although he was the most powerful in the group, they were older than him, and age in our society gives people power. They could have persuaded him that what he was doing was wrong. And when they have guns in their hands and qat in their mouths, anything can happen. Some time in 2000, he said, 'I will help you to go away if you want. Are you ready to go?' 'Where do you want me to go?' I asked. And he said, 'Europe. I've got some money. I can pay for it.' He said, 'don't think of escaping or of looking for your family'. He said he wanted me to sponsor his children, I could tell the authorities that I was married to him. He would then come to Europe with his children and leave them with me. I looked after them like my own brothers and sisters and they would have a better future there. Their aunts were too busy to look after them. In his situation he couldn't look after them. I told him that I would sponsor his children. I had never rebelled. I hadn't told anyone about him. Maybe he felt I could be trusted. He said that he would pay an agent to take me to Kenya. 'If it goes wrong,' he said, 'just come back.'

When it happened, I wasn't expecting it. I had been in this prison for eleven years. Then one day he said to his sister that I was going out to buy something for him. He told me I had to go to this particular shop in Afgoe market and ask for Hadija. It all happened very quickly. I took nothing with me. Again I thought he was going to kill me. I wore a dress and a pair of trousers underneath. I didn't have any money because he didn't want me to run away. I found the shop and told her that Daahir had sent me. She said 'we will leave just before dawn'. I didn't bother to undress, I just lay down, but I couldn't sleep. I was thinking about the future. She came into the room in the middle of the night. I just got up and went as I was. We got on this lorry which was carrying sugar, bananas and fruit to Kenya. There were five of us, her and me, two other women and a child. We travelled for three days.

We would stop at lunchtime for a break. There would be a little shack or people like my mum selling food. Every time I ate I felt like throwing up because I was so tired. At night we slept on the ground next to the lorry.

At the border we met Ismail, who travelled with us. They were all speaking Swahili, which I couldn't understand. It wasn't difficult to get into Kenya. The soldiers at the border knew the drivers, who showed them all our papers. The way that Kenyan soldiers talk and hold their weapons is quite scary. I was always scared of soldiers anyway. We went to a small hotel in a border town where there were a lot of Somalis. The day after we arrived, Hadija took me to the shops and bought clothes and shoes for me. She told me it wasn't very safe and that I should stay inside the hotel. She said that sometimes Kenyan soldiers came to the hotel and asked for *kipande* (papers). You had to bribe them, otherwise they could take you to prison and hurt you. She was an unusually nice woman. She left the morning after.

Ismail and I went to Nairobi where he had rented rooms in a small hotel. We stayed there two months. He said that if I wanted something, I had to ask him and he would get it. I was allowed to go to the shops downstairs to buy food, which I would take back to the hotel room. Ismail would give me the money. Sometimes he would take me to Somali restaurants. He never tried anything funny with me. He was very correct and professional. The thing that I didn't like about him was that he wouldn't explain anything. He would just say 'don't worry'. If I asked when we would travel, he would say, 'you will go soon'. They don't talk to the people they are escorting because it is dangerous for them to have too much information.

I met some Somali girls who had applied to go to America. The girls told me that people paid a lot of money to get to Europe. Their cousin had paid $4,000 to get to Holland. That's the first time I found out about these things. On one occasion, the girls had a party. The party had finished at about 9 p.m. and we were still chatting, when Kenyan soldiers with their boots and guns knocked on the door. Some people tried to jump from the window because they knew the soldiers would want money. They were asking for *kipande* – I had to hide because I didn't have any papers on me. A soldier came into the middle of the room and frightened the girls into giving him some money. He said he wanted the radio they were listening to. They gave him that too. It was shocking. Their soldiers are horrible to Somalis.

Ismail bought skirts and trousers when I told him that I didn't have enough clothes. Then the chance came for us to fly to Britain. He said I could claim asylum in Europe by saying that I was running away from war. But that's not good enough, as I later found out. To get asylum, you have to be fleeing from persecution. That's why they refused my case. It's not enough to belong to a minority. Ismail had made a false passport for me. The photograph looked a little like me. I only saw it once. It was Kenyan I think because it was blue in colour and Somali passports are green. But he held all the papers.

The day we were going to travel, he told me to change the way I covered my head and try and look like the person in the passport. We went to the airport at night by taxi. We were harassed by every single soldier on the way, asking for money. We travelled by Kenyan Airlines to Rome. People advised me not to talk about my stop in Italy because the Home Office would ask, why didn't you apply for asylum in the first safe country that you reached? Why were you trying to reach Britain? One of the reasons why people choose Britain is because they know the language. In Kenya you can't claim asylum. Anyway I didn't like Kenya, especially the soldiers. I would rather go back to my country.

We stayed in Rome with this Somali woman, a friend of Ismail's. She was a fantastic woman. She had a washing-machine for clothes. She asked me if she could wash clothes for me and I said, 'oh no, I'll wash my own clothes'. Then she showed me how to use the washing-machine. I was expecting to wring the clothes dry when they came out of the machine, but the machine did that too. It was nice and clean everywhere. When we went out to buy milk, we were not scared walking the streets. When you see all this peace, you feel relaxed. I slept well after a long time. I cannot explain what freedom from fear feels like. For so long I had worried about who was going to come knocking on my door. I was lucky that I didn't go mad. I used to shake and drop glasses sometimes. I am no longer like that. I don't remember breaking any glasses in England. Food was plentiful, but I had been starved for so long that if I ate more than once a day I felt sick.

Yeah, there were things I had never seen, like escalators and lifts at the airport and coffee-making machines. I was scared to ask questions because I didn't want to look stupid, but Ismail told me you use the lift to go up and down. Then we went to Milan by train. I'd never travelled by train before. Ismail said he had money in Milan that he wanted to collect. I met some Somalis who ran a centre in Milan. What was nice was that no one cared about your tribe and who you were. From there we travelled to Belgium. We stopped twice and changed trains. We started at 4 a.m. and reached Belgium on the evening of the second day. I think we crossed Switzerland and France. I wasn't as informed then as I am now. Immigration officers would come on the train and check our papers. I was supposed to be Ismail's wife or daughter, I'm not sure which. The passport belonged to Saeeda, a Somali woman who lived in Belgium. I think she was going to get a British visa for me. That's why we couldn't come directly to Britain. Ismail probably paid her to use her passport. Sometimes they steal passports, take the photograph out and stick yours in its place. But the machines at the airport can discover that now.

We stayed with Saeeda in Brussels. We took a cab from the station and travelled through the centre of Brussels. It was beautiful. There were flowers and lights everywhere. I wanted to stay there, but Ismail said he had promised to take me to England. I would love to go back to Brussels one day. It was a happy time after all that sadness. Now all my tense (*sic*) was gone. I forgave Daahir even though I lost something so precious as my virginity through rape. That will hurt me forever. For women, the first time that they lose their virginity is an important moment. When I was younger, and used to think about the year 2000, I used to imagine that I would be a mum. I didn't see myself as a career woman, but I always liked the idea of working as a teacher or a midwife. These are the only jobs I ever wanted to do. When I saw my mother give birth to my younger sister, I was fascinate (*sic*).

We arrived at Heathrow airport early in the morning. Ismail showed our passports and we entered without a problem. We went by bus to an empty house in Hounslow where we stayed the night. In the morning, he said he was going to take me to a Somali place in Southall. Ismail said, 'this is the place where I agreed to bring you. You are in a free country. You can claim asylum. You see that police officer there, go up to him and say that you are claiming asylum. If you see me somewhere, you don't know me. I will not recognize you, I won't even say hello to you.' He gave me nearly $100. He said 'this is your money, use it and you'll be fine'. It had taken me more than three months to get here from Somalia. Once I got to England, I didn't want to know anything about Daahir. I never phoned him.

In the UK, a person is recognized as a refugee when their application for asylum has been accepted by the Home Office. When a person has lodged an asylum claim and is waiting for a decision on their claim, s/he is called an 'asylum seeker'. An asylum seeker is fingerprinted and photographed and given an Application Registration Card (ARC) by the Immigration and Nationality Directorate (IND), which is issued to all those who apply for asylum from outside the European Economic Community (EEC) at a short screening interview on first application. After that (if they are not detained in a fast-track process), they are called for a longer interview, before which they may have to fill in a complex twenty-page form in English, a Statement of Evidence Form (SEF), giving their reasons for seeking asylum and providing evidence of their claim. The IND is supposed to make its written decision within two months. Its decision can be appealed.[8]

The IND assesses claims on the basis of an asylum seeker's history, taking into account their credibility, the current political situation in their country, evidence of the country's human rights record and, if applicable, medical evidence of torture and abuse. The asylum appli-cant will be granted refugee status if they can demonstrate that they have a 'well-founded fear of being persecuted for reasons of race, reli-gion, nationality, membership of a particular social group or political opinion ...', as stated in the 1951 UN Convention on Refugees also known as the Geneva Convention.

However, since August 2005 refugees will no longer be granted Indefinite Leave to Remain (ILR); they will only be granted limited leave, initially for five years. At the end of five years their case will be reviewed to see whether the situation in their country of origin has changed and they are no longer in fear of persecution. Refugees could at that stage be faced with removal. Refugees have full entitlement to family reunion, welfare benefits, housing and health care, and the right to work. Asylum seekers do not have the right to do paid or voluntary work while they are waiting to hear the outcome of their application. This can easily take up to twelve months, although the government has put in place measures to speed up applications.

If the asylum application is initially refused, the applicant usually has the right of appeal. If applicants do not meet the criteria of the Geneva Convention they may qualify either for 'Humanitarian Protection' or 'Discretionary Leave'. Humanitarian Protection is granted where the Home Office recognizes that there is a real risk of death, torture, or other inhuman or degrading treatment, which falls outside the strict terms of the Geneva Convention but which comes within the scope of Article 3 of the European Convention on Human Rights (1950) (ECHR). Applicants are given the right to remain for five years as above.

The Home Office can grant Discretionary Leave to those who do not qualify for refugee status or Humanitarian Protection but cannot be removed. This may be because they have a serious medical condition, making travel or return dangerous, or because removal would contra-vene their human rights, such as the right to family life. Discretionary Leave is normally granted for a period of three years. Those granted Humanitarian Protection or Discretionary Leave are entitled to the same benefits as refugees. Those on Discretionary Leave are normally eligible to apply for ILR after six years but their cases will be reviewed at both the three and six year stages.[9]

In most cases, all financial support for an individual (without children) who is at the end of the asylum process, and has no further rights of appeal, will be stopped twenty-one days after their asylum claim is finally refused. Refused asylum seekers can obtain basic support from the Home Office if they can show they are co-operating with steps to remove them from the UK, are unable to leave the UK, have an appeal pending in the High Court, or have made a fresh application for asylum.

Ismail took me to the *hawala*, the money-exchange place where the Somali community sends money back home. It was full of men. He said, 'sit here, maybe you'll find somebody you know'. I started to cry. When you're new to a place, you want a guide. I never expected that I would have to worry about where to sleep, how to get a job, how to start a new life. I could cook, I could keep children, clean house, whatever. I was ready to work hard. I had a small bag with me with a few essentials in it and a walkman that the woman in Italy had given to me.

I finally asked the man who worked in the *hawala* if he knew anybody from the Hawiye family that I worked for. He asked if I was new to the country and if there was anyone else I knew. I said 'no'. Then this woman Leyla came. She was sending money home. She sat in front of me. She gestured to the man who worked there, as if to say, what is wrong with her. He introduced her to me. I told her that a man had dropped me here. She said, 'they always do that. But if you don't have any family, it's going to be really hard for you.' Leyla took me to her flat in Hounslow. She was divorced and lived on her own. She was a businesswoman. She would buy wholesale clothes, things for the hair, henna from Dubai and sell it to the big shops. Below her house was a Somali shop and she said that the owner, Elmi, would find a solicitor to help me apply for asylum. I had no papers. Ismail had taken the passport back with him. I started cleaning and cooking for her.

A friend of Elmi's took me to an Indian solicitor in Hounslow. She translated for me, though I don't think her English was that good. What she said to the solicitor was different to what I told her. For example, in my statement it said that my father died in a random shooting, but actually he was hunted down and killed – now my English is good enough to see the mistakes. That makes all the difference. She also advised me not to talk about the rape because it would bring shame on me. But actually that would have helped my case. The solicitor didn't explain anything to me. His wife prepared my statement. She handwrote it and asked me to come back the following day when it was typed so that we could go through it together to check it. This statement was sent to the Home Office. It took me one week to claim asylum. I arrived on 15 July 2002 and claimed asylum on the 22nd. I was told that I had waited too long, but it took that much time to get everything organized, to find a solicitor, to prepare the statement. I was lucky to have found someone to help me so soon. My basic argument for claiming asylum was that I was fleeing war, that as a woman I was in danger of being raped, and as a member of a minority tribe there was no one to defend my interests.

Elmi found someone to travel with me to the passport office in Croydon – an old couple who were going the following Monday to renew their visa. They said we should leave around 4 a.m. in order to be at the front of the queue. At Croydon, they took prints of our fingers and our eyes and gave me an ARC card with all this information on it. I finished at 5 p.m. The couple had gone by the time I came out. I called Elmi and he gave me detailed instructions on where to go and what to ask for at the ticket office. I wrote down everything. He said, 'when you get to Hounslow wait for me or Leyla to come and pick you up'. I don't remember the exact route but I think I had to change at Victoria. It was really hard. Even the phone booth was a new idea to me – putting coins in the box as you talk. When I got to Hounslow, Elmi clapped when he saw that I had arrived safely. 'I can't believe it', he said.

Leyla advised me not to claim housing benefit because asylum seekers under the National Asylum Support Service (NASS) get sent to remote parts of the country where there is racism, where I might not find other Somalis, and where I might not find a job because I was an asylum seeker. I didn't want to live like that again, being constantly scared that someone was going to hurt me. She said, 'you can stay with me until you get your "stay"'. I felt safe with Leyla. She also advised me not to talk about the rape.

About ten days after I moved in with Leyla, I started getting benefits, approximately £37 per week. When Leyla needed anything from the shops, she would ask me to buy it. I would spend all my money. I ended up spending £5–6 on groceries every day. If there wasn't any food in the fridge, I would go to the shop downstairs and buy a banana for lunch, or I might find beans in a can. She had only one key and she would often take it with her, so I wouldn't be able to go further than the shop downstairs. I wanted to save some money because I never knew what might happen to me. If I could have sent £5 every week to my mum, she would have been able to live on it and look after all the children without having to work. She had been earning enough to buy food only for that day. But you have to put some money aside to buy flour, rice, coal and oil in bigger quantities.

After six weeks with Leyla, she introduced me to Amina, who was seven months pregnant. Leyla asked me to stay with her and help her cook and shop. She was married, but her husband was having an affair with another woman so she was mostly on her own. Leyla was obviously fed up with me. Maybe she thought Amina had greater need of help. I don't know. Leyla said I could continue to use her address for all my letters, which I do to this day. She never treated me badly, like the others. I moved in with Amina. She too would say 'let's do some shopping' as soon as I got my money. I stayed with her for a year and I enrolled at a college to learn English. The college paid half my fare. The other half I paid from my benefits. I was supposed to go to college four days a week from 10 to 4. Once Amina had the baby boy, I would look after him in the mornings, because she wouldn't wake up early, and hand him over to her before I left for college. When I came back from college, I would do all the housework. Then, at least once or twice a week, I wouldn't be able to go to college because she would say, 'I'm going shopping, can you look after the child?' She wouldn't come back for six hours. Although she'd apologize, it didn't stop her doing it again and again. She had a habit of collecting all the dirty clothes and throwing them on the ground, then she'd tell me very rudely to wash the clothes. I couldn't say anything.

At one point, I didn't claim benefits for four weeks because the system changed and I didn't understand how the new system worked. I wouldn't eat at college because everything was so expensive – I didn't like to spend £2 on every meal, so I'd take a banana from home. Often when I got back to the flat there would be no food, especially when she had made up with her husband. Whenever Amina got angry, she would say she wanted a divorce and he would say '*talaq, talaq, talaq*', three times, which means 'I divorce you'. This doesn't have to be done in the presence of the imam. This guy also had a child by another woman. In this country they don't have to be rich to afford two 'wives'. If they don't work, they live on benefits. Then they would get back together and he would say 'rajatù', which means 'I am having you back'. On the days that he was there she would want me to go and stay somewhere else. I found that really difficult because I hardly knew anyone.

During the summer, I would wander the streets until 11 p.m. when it would become quite cold. Sometimes I would sleep in a small room on the ground floor of Amina's building where all the gas and electricity meters were installed. People would leave cardboard boxes lying around and I would flatten these and sit on them and try sleeping for a couple of hours. This space was sometimes used by homeless men. I would not be able to sleep wondering if they would come there that night. The rubbish bins were kept just outside this room so the smell would float in from time to time. Sometimes I would go and sit in the corridor outside her front door. If her husband came home late, after three or four hours, he would let me in. Once I slept on a bench in the garden of a pub near by. I can't really call it sleeping because I was always frightened that somebody would find me. Another time

I walked and walked through the night. Finally, I got so fed up that I went to a mini-cab firm that Amina used to use and begged the man to allow me to sit on the sofa. Even though he recognized me, he was really rude and said, 'go away, do you want me to get into trouble with my boss?' I sat outside Amina's door until the morning, when she came out to throw out the rubbish. She would then apologize, saying, 'I didn't hear you knocking' or 'why didn't you ring?', although she would often pull the phone out of the socket.

Amina would want me to do all the jobs before her husband, who was a shopkeeper, came home in the evening – wash the floor, do the ironing, do the beds. She didn't want to let him know that I had cooked the dinner, so I had to finish cooking well before he came, and she would serve it to him. I would work from 4.30 to 9 p.m. – sometimes I didn't have time to pray. The kitchen and sitting-room were together so I couldn't go to the kitchen while he was in the sitting-room. Sometimes he watched TV until midnight and I would get really tired waiting for him to go to bed. I would eat if there was something left. It is the custom that a woman must not eat food before the man. She would ask me to cover my body with the *garbasaar*, not just the *hijab*, when her husband was around.

The Home Office sent me a date for the big interview at Croydon. I went alone this time. They had sent me a ticket for my travel. I thought the interview went well. But, in September 2002, they turned down my asylum application. I still had hope because they said that I could appeal against their decision. The solicitor said my case was very weak. A neighbour advised me that I should have told them about the rape. The solicitor said that I should have told him this at the beginning as the government would think I was lying. I said I had felt ashamed and the translator had told me not to say it. I thought she was right because she had been in this country longer than me. The solicitor said that he would represent me strongly on my original case. He said that the Home Office didn't believe I was from Somalia, so for the appeal I had to find people who knew me back home. I had answered all the questions about Somalia correctly. If I was not

Somali, I wouldn't know all that, would I? And surely their Somali translator would have told them that I was really Somali.

At the interview, Farhia was asked to name the capital of Somaliland, which had declared independence from Somalia in 1991 when she was imprisoned by Daahir's family and had even less access to news and none to calendars. She said it was either Hargeisa or Burao (Hargeisa is correct). She also did not know the capital of Puntland, a semi-autonomous region of Somalia. She was able to say what had happened to General Aidid and who succeeded him after he died, to explain who the Reer Hamar are, to name the principal rivers of Somalia and the main hospitals of Mogadishu. The letter of refusal says, 'The Secretary of State is not satisfied that you are a Somali as you have claimed because your knowledge of Somalia is not convincing ...'.

Leyla and the others could not testify that I was Somali because the solicitor said that the court does not value individual opinion. They need an organization. I went to a community centre, where I met Ali, the manager. I told him my story. He wrote a letter for me. He told me to get letters from other places as well. I found two young men who knew me. One man I met at a community centre in Hammersmith and Fulham. He used to buy meat from us back home. He tried to get the manager of the centre to write the letter, but she was rude and unwilling. She was from the Reer Hamar tribe. She kept us waiting for three hours. Once people see that I'm Eyle, they don't want anything to do with me. I was so angry that I went home. After two days he managed to get a letter from her and offered to come to court. I met the second guy at a bus-stop. His family used to buy rabbit and eagle from us. He said, 'I remember your smile, you've really grown up'. He offered to have tea with me, a Merehan guy and an Eyle girl! In Somalia he wouldn't have wanted to be seen with me. I asked if he would come to court. He agreed. The solicitor said, 'now they can't argue that you're not Somali'.

*

However, the main ground for refu
lawyers had not established a well-founded
the terms of the Geneva Convention. The Secretary
that your inability to seek the protection of your national a
due not to having a well-founded fear of persecution, but rather
general state of lawlessness which prevails in some parts of Somalia at
present'. Despite acknowledging the war situation in Somalia, the letter
goes on to say that the Secretary of State 'is of the view that the fighting
and disturbances were indiscriminate, that individuals from all sections
of Somali society were at risk of being caught up therein and that the sit-
uation was no worse for the members of the Eyle clan than for the
general population ...'.

We appealed the case in January 2003. Elmi came with me to the solicitor. The solicitor said that you have to pay £250 for a barrister. I asked
him, 'what if I get refused again?' He said that he would need more
than £700. I started to worry. I didn't even have £250 because I used to
do the shopping for Amina's family with my benefits. I asked Elmi if
he could pay the solicitor and I would pay him back every week. He
agreed. I asked Amina if I could pay her £20 per week and save £15 for
the solicitor. I also needed money for the bus-pass to go to college.
Education was important to me. I said to Amina, 'I will do everything
you want me to do, but I want to go to college'. She agreed. Amina was
pregnant again. Her baby was only three months old and she couldn't
cope without me. The child would come to bed with me since she
wasn't breast-feeding anymore. I would bathe him – he was more
attached to me than to his mum. Sometimes she would say, 'you
know, my child thinks you are his mum'.

At the appeal, one of the questions that my witness was asked in
court was how old I was the last time he saw me. He said, 'she was very
tall, so I think she was eighteen'. I was fourteen actually. The judge
thought he was lying. The second guy's testimony also created misunderstandings. When the judge asked him what they used to buy from
us, he said 'elephant' when he meant elephant tusk. The judge said,

...missed the whole case. He
...ot allowed to work.

...issues of credibility. It is easy to see
...ound implausible without the detail to
...at get lost in translation. The judge said,
...ilability of such game in close proximity to
...was an objectively verifiable fact. He thought it
...ould have found her mother so easily on her one
day o... ...gees are as poor as Farhia's family, they cannot afford
to travel j... ...university was nearest to their squatter camp and the
obvious place for Farhia to go in search of her mother. The judge wanted
to know how she was traced so readily by Daahir. He did not believe that
Farhia 'would have time to hide her mother but not herself'. There was
also a gross factual error in the judgement that all her siblings, except for
the youngest two, had been killed along with her father. Farhia has
never said that.

We can see why Daahir's secret marriage to Farhia may have confused the judge without the benefit of a fuller narrative. He says, 'I find
it implausible that the alleged son of the alleged family would undergo a
marriage ceremony with the appellant for purposes of non-consensual
intercourse with someone held by his family as a slave and whose
mother he or his family was prepared to kill'.

The judge was seriously exercised by the fact that Daahir spent a
large sum of money to smuggle Farhia abroad: 'I find this expenditure
improbable on the part of a man who the appellant says treated her in
the way described above'. He could have sent her back to her 'mother's
household'. Farhia says that, apart from the fact that she was an insurance policy for the future of his children, she cannot explain why Daahir
helped her escape, but that is what happened. The truth often slips and
slides in our hands. Everyone with money was going to Europe and she
feels that must have influenced him. He was not in a position to leave at
that point because his father was ill and he was responsible for the whole
family.

The judge quoted from a Country Information and Policy Unit (CIPU) report on Somalia, October 2002, to argue that Farhia was not facing particular human rights or security problems in Mogadishu, because the situation had improved. The CIPU, under the Home Office, provides country reports, which are used by immigration officers and the judiciary as the basis for assessing asylum claims. These reports have come in for extensive criticism for the partial and misleading way in which they quote from source material in order to support a particular view. Unfortunately for people like Farhia, the IND and the tribunals rely heavily on them.

The solicitor said the judge wouldn't even let me appeal his decision. He had dismissed my case on asylum grounds, human rights grounds, everything. I felt really desperate. I was so closed up inside that all I could say was yes and no. I thought that people would see through me and understand. You have to explain about tradition and honour and how women are judged. The judge was talking about 'my mother's household'. It didn't exist. It was a war situation. I hadn't said enough to make them understand. I felt the solicitor had not done a good job in explaining things.

The last straw was when the solicitor wrote to me saying that he would appeal again but I had to tell him why I couldn't go back to Kosovo! That's when I realized that he was really inefficient if he couldn't even remember which country I came from. The guy who had acted as a witness helped me to change solicitors. He said, 'the judge didn't like you. It was only his opinion.' The new solicitor said that there wasn't much he could do apart from a new representation asking that I be allowed to appeal.

In April 2003 my benefits stopped. The Home Office sent a letter saying that I must leave the country. I didn't know what to do. I thought I had come to a safe place. I told Elmi that I didn't have the money to pay back the solicitor's fee. He said, 'pay it back when you have the money'. Amina stopped giving me food. She knew that I had nowhere to go. I was still doing all the work. I would look for coins fallen on the ground. Sometimes I would go to Leyla's house and ask for money. She would give me £10 and tell me that I would have to do something for her. I would take stock to the shops she supplied. I used to lose consciousness because I was always hungry. I was weak and dizzy. I couldn't see when it was dark, and I constantly wanted to vomit although nothing came up because my stomach was empty. When a GP surgery finally accepted me, the doctor said I had anaemia and that I should eat a lot. I would go to the supermarket and steal food. I would get a yoghurt or milk, just open it and drink it in the shop. I didn't know that I could have been spotted on the camera. He gave me sleeping pills for my depression and pills for heartburn.

I had been relying on getting my stay. I felt robbed of my future. I thought there was nothing else that I could do except jump in front of a car. On the way from the GP surgery to Amina's place, there was a junction with the A4 in Hounslow where cars travel really fast. The lights were green, I could see the cars speeding towards me, I stepped into the road, but I slipped and fell by the kerb. The fall broke the moment. I sat on the kerb and cried. Gradually I calmed down and went back to Amina's. That evening, I sat in my room with all the sleeping pills heaped in the palm of my hand. I wondered how I could take them all in one go. If I took them one by one, I worried that they might start taking effect before I had finished the lot. Then they would rush me to hospital and pump my stomach out. Instead of dying, I might end up with some other problem. That thought stopped me from going further. On another occasion, by a junction in Staines, I tried to cross the road when the lights were green. I had woken up early, sorted out Amina's children, and gone to do some shopping for her. I remember it was a windy spring morning. My mind went blank. The lights turned red. I crossed the road and went to the shops. It was only after talking to the counsellor for months at SBS that I no longer felt like committing suicide.

Meanwhile, I needed money to live. Even travelling to college was expensive. I had become friendly with this bus-driver who often drove the bus that I took in the morning. Sometimes there would be no one else on the bus and we would talk. He would shout 'do you go to school here?' over the noise of the engine. Sometimes I would sit near him. He would joke and chat and ask if I was married. When I told him that I had lost my appeal and wasn't getting any benefits, he promised to get me a year's pass to travel free on buses and tubes. He was allowed a pass for his wife and, as he wasn't married, he would get one for me. After a couple of months he asked me for my number. In the beginning I said 'no'. I know how it all ends up.

One day I met him in Hounslow market. He asked me to have tea with him. I couldn't because I had to rush home. He asked me for my number so that we could fix a time. I had a very old mobile which belonged to Amina. She would give me £10 to top it up. She always wanted to know where I was so she could control me. She would ring to find out when I was coming home, or if I could buy something on the way home. He walked me to where I live, which I didn't like. He rang me one day and asked, 'can I see you tomorrow?' I asked Amina if it was OK to go out for one hour. He would come to my college and drive me home. He said I should get married to someone with a British passport. In another conversation he told me that he was a British citizen and he earned a lot of money. But his behaviour was not respectful. He would put his hand on my thigh when he was driving. If he was hinting about marriage, he should not have done these things. I think he told me all this so that I would give in to him. One time he bought chicken and chips, which we ate in the car. Then he said he wanted to show me where he lived. I knew what was coming.

It was embarrassing to ask for money. Before we got to the house, I said, 'are you going to give me some money?' 'Why do you need money?' he asked. I said I wanted to buy things. I had never done this before. He gave me £20. We went upstairs to his flat. He told me to go first. He followed, touching me up from behind. He said he shared the flat with some other men, but nobody was in. He showed me his room. I didn't go in. I remember opening the door to the flat. I didn't want it to be closed. He started touching me and saying horrible things. I can't bring myself to repeat them. He lay down on the bed and started unbuttoning his trousers. I said, 'no, no, no'. He started hitting the walls again and again, shouting, 'you took the money, I thought you wanted to'. I didn't want to give the money back and I didn't want to do anything, so I started to walk away. He came after me. On the stairs he started to kiss me and touch my breasts. I didn't stop him. He said, 'you tricked me'. I said 'you touched me'. I was scared that he might punch me. He knew where I lived. He might tell Amina.

It was night-time. I started to run. I thought I knew the way, but I didn't. My heart was pumping. This man came after me. He asked if I knew the way. I said 'yes'. He said he would drive me, but I didn't want to get in his car. How can you fight with someone who's driving? He still hoped to see me again, he said. I walked a lot. Then I realized where I was and took the bus. At home I started to cry. That £20 caused me a lot of pain. He would call and ask if I was going to pay him back in kind. He offered to pay again. I started going out with men – they were all Somali – I would take their money and not do anything. I can't count the times it happened. It was a dangerous thing to do. Some of them tried to force me. But I never slept with them. It's not my fault but you need to eat. It's one of those things in your life that you wish to cancel. This is something I don't like to talk about. Yes, Elmi was one of them. Let's just say that he liked me and he used to give me money. Meeting these men took me right back to the pain of being with Daahir. Only in one sense was it easier – there was no danger of losing my virginity.

At college, I had made friends with a girl from the Reer Hamer tribe. Sometimes I would stay with her when Amina wanted me out of the house. My friend advised me to find a place of my own. She told me about SBS, that they helped homeless people. I knocked on their door. I was crying. I didn't want to go back to Amina. SBS said that I was not entitled to a place. I was really angry with everyone. It's like saying that you're not entitled to live. You can't work. You don't have any relatives. Basically, you can die on the streets. I even thought of going away to Holland or some European country or claiming asylum at some embassy, saying that Britain has refused my case, please can you help. Meena, one of the co-ordinators of SBS, would sometimes give me £10 to buy something to eat or give me apples or leftover food. Once she gave me £60 for six weeks. I went straight to Elmi and gave him £30. I had to return his loan because things hadn't worked out the way he wanted and he kept asking for his money.

Southall Black Sisters was set up in 1979 as an advice, advocacy and campaigning group for local women who were escaping domestic violence, although this was not the only issue that the group dealt with. Homelessness, welfare advice, and immigration issues, for example, form an important part of its work. It also provides counselling services for women with mental health issues, and support group activities, including daytrips and short holidays, for its most vulnerable clients.

The moment I finished college I found a job in a shop in Southall through a friend of Amina's. The owner of the shop liked me and asked me if I would work in her shop. I told her about my situation. She sold curtain material, clothes, children's shoes, lots of stuff. She paid me half of what she paid other people – £50 for a week, and for her a week wasn't five days, it was eight days. I worked sixteen days and she paid me £100. She also paid for a weekly bus-pass. This money was not enough to live on. To travel from Hounslow to Southall, I had to take two buses. She asked me to open the shop between 9 and 9.30 a.m. but sometimes I opened the shop at 10. Before I went to work, I had to prepare breakfast, get Amina's child ready, do the laundry and clean my room.

Before the owner went away to Dubai to buy stock, she trained me for three days. She said 'I trust you, you're nice with the customers'. I used to keep all the money underneath the counter. At the end of each day I had to write down how much money I had earned and how much I had spent. She said I could spend up to £2 for lunch everyday. I would buy bread with some salad and meat or samosas. When she came back, I worked for another week and then she asked me to stop. I haven't been paid for that last week to this day. Shop work is difficult because people want one thing, then another, and you end up getting everything down and then having to fold it all up again. When I got home, I couldn't feel my legs.

At the shop, I met Medina, a friend of Amina's who asked about my situation. I told her that I didn't know when Amina's husband would come home and I would have to find somewhere to sleep that night. She invited me to stay with her. She said, 'I live alone and you will be company'. When I left Amina's, I told her she could call me whenever she wanted to. She got offended. She said, 'people can be horrible, why are you leaving me, how're you going to cope living in Croydon? Sometimes you don't have money for the bus.' But Amina hadn't been nice to me. Whenever she felt like it she would ask me not to come home. If somebody said to you, don't come tonight, what are you going to do?

Medina treated me badly too. She used to order me around to increase her status in front of her friends, snapping her fingers at me. I started living with her while I was still working at the shop. I didn't get home until 9 or 10 p.m., even though I'd closed the shop at 7. The owner had told me to close at 9 p.m. because there's a lot of people in Southall in summer, but I told her that I was living too far away. I think that's why she didn't want me to work for her any more. Medina would complain about how late I came home. She was bored because she didn't have anything to do all day. She was on disability benefits because of back pain. In Somalia, militiamen had tried to rape her. They beat her and threw her from a car and her legs were broken. They didn't heal well and she couldn't walk properly. She would stay in bed till 11 a.m. Sometimes she would go to her aunt's in Clapham, but she wouldn't call me to let me know. I didn't have keys to the flat. She kept saying she'd get some cut, but she never did. You can't force someone to give you a key. I would get to Croydon and call her from a phone box because I couldn't afford to use my mobile. She would ask me to go to her aunt's. I would have to take two buses. I would fall asleep there. In the morning when I was at the shop I would walk around like I was drunk. Sometimes I would fall sleep on the bus and I'd wake up not knowing where I was. I was homeless. When I see homeless people I realize they're in the same situation. You don't know what's going to happen to you, you don't care and you just want to die.

Medina and I would be together all day when my job ended. We would go to her aunt's house to help with her daughter's wedding. That aunt always says that she will never forget the way I helped out. That was a good time. Everybody was focused on the wedding. For some time I forgot about my situation. The girl was lucky that she had her mum around to do things for her. For two weeks we worked very hard, washing and cleaning and putting everything away. Preparations went on for nearly a month. Medina would tell all her friends and family that I was an asylum seeker. I didn't usually mind that, but sometimes I would start crying and wondering when all this would end. Everybody else had a normal life. I remember one old lady who gave me £70. I was too ashamed to take it. She gave the money to Medina and asked her to buy something for me.

That summer SBS took me and a few other women to Edinburgh for four days. It really helped me with my depression. We went for a massage and a sauna. It was my first time in a sauna and the first time that I wore a swimming costume. We went to see Edinburgh castle. I wish it had been more than four days. But there was always somebody to listen to you, which really helped. In September, Meena changed my solicitor because the other guy wasn't doing anything at all. I told the new solicitor everything. She said she needed new evidence in order to make a fresh application to the Home Office.

I used to ring Halima, my mother's friend, who lived in Medina, to get news of my mother about once every two weeks. They had been friends from before the war and she was financially much better off than us. My mother had told me to call her if something terrible happened and we were parted again. She would give her savings to Halima for safekeeping because they would have got stolen at the camp. Halima told me that my mother had disappeared. Daahir and some militiamen had gone to look for me at the camp. I think Daahir didn't want anyone to suspect that he might have helped me escape. The militiamen asked her where I was. One of them was holding a gun and kicking her, saying if she didn't talk, he was going to kill her. Daahir was trying to defend her. While he was doing that, the gun went off and Daahir was injured. One militiaman slapped the other guy, saying 'you fool, look at what you've done'. They collected my mum and the children and got into the car. Nobody knows what happened to them. I asked the British Red Cross to try and find her. They could not. I think about my mum all the time. The solicitor said that I could argue that I had no family now so the Home Office shouldn't send me back.

A London law centre is now representing Farhia. They have written to the Home Office asking that she should be allowed to stay here temporarily on an exceptional basis. They have cited medical evidence of the depression from which she suffers and the dangers that she would face as a single woman in Somalia which would be a breach of her human rights. The letter states, 'that it is unlawful to leave my client in a limbo situation, where she cannot return to Somalia but has no status in the UK'. It was written in February 2004. Farhia has not heard from the Home Office to date.

The solicitor told me that until I get a response to the letter, they cannot remove me. I have to go once a month to sign on at an immigrant reporting centre. In the beginning, I could not bring myself to go. I had heard that sometimes people go there and don't come back. On three occasions I was late by three or four days. Each time, the policewoman would ask me why I hadn't come on the given date. I said that I was ill. She said I have to get a doctor's letter. On the third visit, I said I had forgotten. She said that if this continued, she would make me come every week. I said that it was too far to walk and I couldn't afford the bus fare. She said that was not her problem. Then

I started going on time. I am still scared that they might detain me and deport me. But the solicitor said that they can't do that without informing her first. They know that I am here. So I am not underground. I think I am a failed asylum seeker, but not an illegal immigrant.

Things were not going well with Medina. When Amina called me in September 2003, crying that she had had a fight with her husband, I went to live with her again. They had divorced. He wasn't coming to see their child. In October she had her second child. I stayed all October with her, then Amina was moved to a flat which was very far from the shops. Even to buy the smallest thing in the world like salt she had to walk ten minutes. She really needed a car to do the shopping, that's why she decided to get back with her husband. I thought, what do I do now? I had become quite friendly with that old lady who had given Medina £70 for me. Whenever I felt that Amina wanted to be on her own with her husband, I would go and visit the old lady. She would cook for me. I had been helping her because she didn't speak English. She would call me the day before and ask me to go with her to the housing office and other places. She would give me some money. At first, I wouldn't take it, but she would force me to. She said I could stay with her daughter Suad. For the next few months, I moved between Medina, Amina and Suad's places.

I finally moved in with Suad in August 2004. Suad is very good to her mum. Her mum wanted to help me so she obeyed. Suad has grown up with a lot of money and, like the others, she also expected me to do a lot of work. Sometimes we would go to an internet café near her mum's place and talk to Abdi who ran it. Suad's mum used to cook for him after she realized that he was often on his own in the shop and could not go out to buy food. One day Abdi said he wanted to take us out for a meal. Then he asked me out on my own. So many beautiful women used to come to his shop I never thought he would be interested in me. I didn't like him in the beginning – he wasn't handsome like my first boyfriend. He's tall and very dark-skinned, but he's so nice. You can tell him anything and he will keep it secret. He will always give you good advice. He was born in 1968, but he looks more mature than his age. He's so liberal that he doesn't like me wearing the *hijab*.

Although he is Reer Hamar, he is not put off by my tribe. He doesn't judge people by their clan. He finds humanity in people. I thought the question of tribe would come up with anyone I met. When he talked to me, I felt human. Having him in my life has made me feel protected. You have a stronger hand when you negotiate. When you are alone, everybody thinks they can take advantage of you. He is the only one who hasn't tried to take advantage of me. He was very straight with me and told me that his wife had left him, things just didn't work out. Yeah! I didn't expect him to propose.

I met Abdi at the beginning of the year and we got married at the end of September 2004. One evening after spending the day at SBS, Abdi said he wanted to marry me. 'What do you say?' he asked. I said 'OK'. He gave me money to buy some clothes. His friends took me to the hairdresser and they did henna on my hands. In two days I was married. I invited a handful of people. All of Abdi's friends came. For one day I felt really good. I got married in the religious way. Actually, I didn't want that. I wanted to get married properly, get my papers and my stay. I don't know why he won't marry me properly. Maybe he is still married to that other woman. Maybe he is using me. I want to believe that that is not true. There is also another problem – I cannot marry him properly without a passport. We would have to go to a place in Scotland where you can get married without a passport. As we are still not living together, I don't know whether he disappears to meet someone else, but I didn't want to live with him when he was living in a small room in a flat full of men. When you went to the kitchen, there were men. When you went to the toilet, there were men.

Suad asked why I didn't live with him now that I was married. She wanted rent now. She thought I had a job because I used to go to SBS so regularly. My husband asked her how much she wanted. She asked for £50. Her mum wouldn't let her take money from me. Suad thought I had complained to her mother. I explained that I don't earn money at SBS, I go for counselling to help with my depression. I have been doing that for more than two years. That's why I am able to talk to you now. Before that, if anybody asked about my past, I would just sit and cry. It still hurts. I haven't reached the point where I have told my story so many times that it has become just words. The words still have meaning. I go to SBS for support group meetings and to learn how to use the computer. Abdi supports that because he thinks it is important to get an education. Money doesn't make you a more intelligent person. As a failed asylum seeker I am not allowed to study. Meena organized English classes at SBS and I did four months of English there. However, in September 2005, I found a way of going back to college. Suad's friend runs a small community college where they help students with GCSE biology, chemistry, physics and mathematics. I told him I wanted to be a nurse. I'm not enrolled there, but I am allowed to join the classes. When we finish at 5, I teach some children the Koran and Somali writing till 7 p.m. That's the way I pay back.

It took Abdi so long to move to his own place that I went to him and asked what is marriage for if we can't live together. I don't know how much he earns. I never ask him and he doesn't tell me. I think he earns about £200 per week. He has worked in that shop for so long now, I think he has a share in it. It's not a salary. He gets some income from selling telephone cards in bulk. He gives me roughly £20 to £50 per week. Depends on how much stuff I need to buy. Now he's got a one-bedroom flat in Shepherd's Bush. My college is in Clapham, so I will move to Shepherd's Bush when my college finishes in June.

I thought life would be better in Europe. I thought that they encourage people to develop themselves here. But I think there is wrong everywhere. There are selfish people everywhere, who won't help you even if you're dying. There is something written into everyone's destiny. I have been unlucky. You might wonder why I am religious because religion hasn't improved my luck. But prayer helps me overcome my misfortune. There is a saying in Somalia, that the chicken eats dung but it knows how to clean its beak well. Hopefully, things will get better. The support of SBS, the counsellor, Abdi and the old woman's family make me feel better, and maybe one day I will get my stay. We are trying for children. My dream is to become a midwife. Who knows? Even that might come true.

Farhia Nur moved in with her husband in the summer of 2006. She has changed solicitors once again, on the advice of SBS. The new solicitor says that there is not very much she can do because the Home Office already has her application. She is going to send additional information: a supportive letter from SBS, a letter clarifying the misunderstandings on which the tribunal based its decision, an expert report on the situation of minority clans in Somalia and a report from Farhia's counsellor. The solicitor felt that it would help her case if her husband submitted his documents and declared his intention to marry her. He says he cannot divorce his wife because it would make her very vulnerable. She is part of his family, possibly a cousin, and there is a lot of family pressure against the divorce. Farhia feels badly let down by him because he will not support her application to remain in this country. He tells her everything will be fine and that she does not need to worry. Farhia is very grateful for the shelter that he provides, but feels trapped by the fact that she cannot work or study. She says that sitting at home and eating is killing her slowly. It is not the life for her. She is very depressed. She is seriously considering going to another English-speaking country like Ireland and starting all over again.

NATASHA BULOVA: On the Run

*'Natasha' was rescued by the Metropolitan Police in June 2004
when they raided a massage parlour in Sudbury, London, although she
always refers to the experience as being 'caught'. She was a young
woman of just seventeen at that point and had worked as a sex slave for
seven months.*

*We meet for the very first time at the British Library in April 2006.
She is forty minutes late – a teenage disregard for time that delays all
our meetings. It is ironic that she chooses to call herself 'Natasha'
because the name appears to have become synonymous with Eastern
European sex slaves, no matter what their nationality. Victor Malarek,
in his book* The Natashas: The New Global Sex Trade, *quotes a
Ukrainian woman who bitterly recounts the way in which all the men
would call her Natasha, a sexual fantasy that dehumanized her and
quashed her individuality in one stroke. Although now nineteen,
Natasha looks like a chubby, fresh-faced schoolgirl with short black hair
and blonde highlights. The Russian translator, Elena, who has known
her ever since the police arrested her, tells me that she used to be slim
with her long hair tied back into a pony-tail and looked even more
childlike than she does now. Natasha smiles shyly and manages to look
both lost and hunted at the same time. She does not make eye contact
except fleetingly – she says it is a habit she developed when working as a*

prostitute. She hated the clients so much she never looked at them and now she has trouble looking anyone in the eye.

We take frequent cigarette breaks. She does not speak in sentences, only single words. A general question about her childhood draws a blank stare. Finally, she responds with a question: 'what precisely do I want to know?' When I ask her to describe where she lived as a child, I have to break it down into questions like, was it a flat or house, which floor, how many bedrooms, what kind of area? I get only what I ask for, as if she is worried that I am trying to trip her up. It is hard work. I ask her if she is normally a chatty person and she says, 'yes, but I don't like to talk about my feelings and there are some things that have happened that I try not to think about'. It is three hours into the interview before she casually mentions a paternal grandmother who lived with them, despite the fact that we had been talking about her family at length. Although she happily agreed to do the interview, I get the feeling that if I don't scratch away behind the headlines, the substance of her story will remain buried. Perhaps it is her only way of coping.

Natasha is a casualty of the mass unemployment that occurred after the break-up of the Soviet Union in 1991. The sweeping away of Communism and the introduction of democracy and the market economy, much heralded in the West and perhaps much anticipated by the Soviet people, led to disappointment, hunger, crime and corruption. Women suffered severe and disproportionate cut-backs in employment opportunities in the mid-nineties. Although the situation has improved, it has merely corrected the imbalance created then.

As a consequence of the economic situation and the desperate short-age of work, women have been forced to take sometimes radical steps. There are, for example, significant numbers of highly-qualified Russian women reduced to advertising themselves as potential wives on websites appealing to Americans or Europeans. Virtually any Russian website will carry an advert for Russian brides. When I look up Samara, Natasha's home town, the very first site I click on provides not only rooms for the night but Russian brides. The owners of the bed-and-breakfast claim to be promoting them from the goodness of their hearts because so many of the people who come to stay want to be put into contact with Russian women. There are pictures of very attractive women, mostly in their thirties, some posing provocatively, all of whom are personally known to the bed-and-breakfast owners. Men are invited to write to these women with the promise that their letters will be passed on. Charges for this service are incurred only if translations are needed, but most of the women speak English.

If educated women seek to escape in this way, it is hardly surprising that the deteriorating economic situation and relaxation in travel restrictions create conditions where disaffected and unskilled young girls like Natasha fall easy victims to traffickers promising life as waitresses and dancers abroad at attractive salaries.

I left home on 5 November 2003. I didn't take much with me because everybody was at home and they would have got suspicious. Just a small bag with knickers and a toothbrush. I thought I would be able to buy things when I got to Spain. Even so, my grandmother stopped me and wanted to know what I was taking from home. She tried to open the bag. I thought, oh my God, if she opens it, that will be it. I pushed her away because she was standing next to the door, and ran. My friend Marina came to my building to pick me up. The train to Moscow was due to leave soon at 7 p.m. Two of our friends came to the train station to say goodbye.

We arrived in Moscow the following day after a fifteen-hour journey. Neither of us slept all night and we didn't eat or drink because we had no money. We couldn't even get a pillow because you have to pay for it. You can't sleep sitting up and the train was packed. Luckily, we had slept during the day. I was suffering because I hadn't said goodbye to my mother. I thought I must call her as soon as possible because she will worry if I go missing for two days. I had run away from home before but she always knew where to find me. I'd never been out of Samara, though, apart from visiting some villages in the surrounding area. I thought Moscow would feel intimidating after Samara, but it didn't. I took it for what it was.

Olga met us at the station and took us to the hotel in her car. She paid for the hotel. It was a good, clean hotel. I called my mother as soon as we arrived – she was crying, but I wasn't because I was very happy to have escaped. I called her twice more during that month. I told her I was going to stay in Moscow for a bit with some friends. She wanted to know my address, but, as she said that she had already been to the police about me, I didn't tell her. The police would have taken it seriously because I was underage. My mother asked me why I didn't tell her I was going – 'you wouldn't have let me go if I'd told you', I said. She had no choice but to accept it.

Olga promised to take us to the French embassy in two days. We thought that was odd because we were supposed to be going to Spain, but she said that it made no difference where we got our Schengen visa, that it was easier to get a French visa and then we could go anywhere in Europe. Meanwhile she gave us 1,500 roubles to spend! Although it was a lot of money for us, it didn't make me suspicious because I thought that it was nothing for them, and that we would have to pay all this back once we started working. We went to see the Kremlin, had food and drink. We even bought big Cuban cigars and smoked them in the hotel. We thought we were so cool. At the French embassy, they asked us if we could speak French. I said yes because I had studied it a little at school. The woman started speaking very fast as if I was French. Of course, I didn't understand. She wanted to know why we wanted to go to France when we couldn't speak the language. We told her we were just going on holiday as we had been coached to say. Olga provided us with some documents which showed that we had a reservation for a hotel in some town. We said we were going for two weeks. That was weird too: that we were only applying for a two-week visa. Olga said we could extend it once we were there. We had to wait two hours for a decision. We were refused. We felt really bad when Olga said that we would not be able to leave Russia for six months because there was a stamp in our passports, something like 'visa denied'. We would have to wait a month for Olga to clean up the passport and get rid of the stamp, which would cost her more money.

She said there was no point in going back to the embassy because we were so useless. Then she passed us over to Sergei and returned to Samara. She said we didn't need a nursery teacher to take care of us all the time.

Sergei looked after us for the next month. He moved us to a two-roomed flat in the centre of Moscow where there were four other girls. Marina and I slept on the floor. They had the beds because they were there before us. We had one pillow and an old single mattress between us. They told us constantly, don't worry, it's only temporary, it's because you were refused a visa, everything's going to be all right. We believed him. We were forbidden to go out because we didn't have registration. In Russia we have a *propiska* system. You have to be registered in the town where you live and you have to get a *propiska* when you go to another town.

A propiska *is a permit issued by the authorities that registers the bearer's place of residence. It is a legacy of the Tsarist government's internal passport regime, implemented to control population movements throughout the Empire, particularly to manage urbanization in the late nineteenth century. Restrictions on peasants' movements were lifted in 1906 and the entire internal passport system was abandoned shortly after the 1917 Revolution. In 1932, however, the Soviet government aped the tsars by reintroducing internal passports.*

Under the Soviets, internal passports were issued at the age of sixteen, subject to renewal every five years, with a propiska, *or residency permit, stamped inside. No change in residence could be made without official permission and failure to register was subject to fines or imprisonment. A valid propiska was required in order to work, get married or gain access to education or social services. Individuals were required to present their passports and* propiski *for internal travel or on demand by authorities or employers.*

Propiski were particularly difficult to obtain for certain places, such as Moscow. Many people, including ex-convicts, political dissidents and Romany gypsies, were refused propiska *virtually as a rule. Because these*

documents were so difficult to get, and were sometimes arbitrarily with-
drawn, bribery and fake marriages became common methods of
circumventing the law.

Propiski were officially abolished when the Soviet Union collapsed in
1991. However, Moscow is one of the regions in Russia that continues to
operate the system.[1]

They said that if the authorities came across us there would be a big
fine to pay or we would get arrested. If a policeman comes across an
'illegal' he can ask for a bribe. It's an extra source of income for the
Russian police. I was never stopped in Samara, although I was registered there. The problem is that nobody wants to come to Samara but
everybody wants to go to Moscow.

Sergei brought us cigarettes and food every day. The girls cooked.
Sometimes we ate with them. We became friends. They were waiting
for visas as well. Two were planning to go to Madrid, one to France
and one, a professional dancer, thought she was going to dance in
London. One was a professional masseuse and two girls were going to
work as waitresses in Spain like us. The only thing that kept us sane in
that month was television. We were bored to death. We did go out, but
luckily we didn't get caught. Sergei didn't know. We knew that he only
came early in the morning or late at night. We spent the whole of
November there. At the beginning of December, Sergei took me into a
separate room. He told me that I would have to go first because my
visa had come through but Marina's hadn't. I wanted to wait for her.
The visa for Spain was valid for only one week so I had to go, but
Marina would join me five days later.

I don't know why he chose me first. Marina's taller and slimmer
than me. She looks like a model. Marina said she would be very upset
if I did go. *I* didn't want to go. I said we would meet again in five days
and everything will be like before. She calmed down finally and said
goodbye. In the morning a car came and took me to the coach station.
They stopped off at some cul-de-sac and supposedly got permission
from my parents to leave. I don't know whether they needed another

letter by law. I remember I made a joke about how quickly they could get everything they needed. Sergei gave me €100 and put me on the bus to Frankfurt, where György would meet me and take me to Spain. He said it would take one day, but it took two days. I didn't even have a book.

Nobody met me at Frankfurt. I thought I was going to go crazy. I waited for five or six hours before György turned up. He was rude and rough. He was Greek and he spoke Russian with an accent. He was dark with black hair, not very big but solid. He looked like he was from Georgia with his hooked nose. I fell asleep in the car and when I woke up I saw a sign for Brussels. I asked him why we were going to Brussels. I knew my geography, I had got a distinction in it at school. He said the person who was going to have you in Barcelona refuses to have you now. I asked him what he meant: who wants to see me in Brussels? 'The guy who's going to be your pimp.'

What?!! I nearly jumped out of the car. It wasn't what I had agreed to do. He said, 'nobody's asking you what you agreed to do'. I told him that I wasn't going to work like that. I was thinking of running away. After that, it was total silence in the car. I decided not to irritate him. There was not much I could do on the motorway. I thought, I'll run away when we arrive. Surely they are not going to keep me captive. I started to think where I could run to and how unreal it was – I had no money. My mother used to tell me that I was always trying to run away. Even when I was very little, I ran away from nursery, the same nursery where my mother worked. I climbed over the fence and off I went. I was found five minutes later wandering about. I didn't try to escape the nursery again, but at school, from the age of thirteen upwards, I did it often. Once in winter I ran away from school to ride a sleigh. I made up a story that I had a headache. I got into trouble with my mother then. But she never hit me. She didn't even shout at me. I don't think she's capable of shouting. She didn't let me go out afterwards for a week. Of course, because she was at work herself she couldn't enforce it.

My mother is the only person with whom I have a good relationship. She was always talking to me and helping me, always asking if I needed anything. Even then, I didn't open up my heart to her – I only did that with my best friend, Marsha. I have a photograph of my mother on my mobile. She's not tall – quite chunky, like me. She has short, curly hair. My father is not tall either. He's got a beer belly and now he's almost bald too. He's forty-two and my mother is forty. I don't know how to describe my older sister, Sveta. We don't get on.

I used to run away from home because my father would drink, get hysterical and beat me up. I would go and stay with friends. My best friend, Marsha, lived on the eighth floor. We lived on the first floor of a twelve-storey building, in an ordinary flat with two balconies. One balcony was attached to the kitchen and one to my parents' bedroom. You could see my school and the shops from one balcony and from the kitchen you could see the forest.

My father was violent to my mother as well, but for some reason he didn't touch my sister, Sveta. He was constantly arguing with my mother. I just happened to be around at the wrong times. Sometimes I would get bruised. Sometimes he would go into a *zapoi*, a spiral of drunkenness, a binge from which he would emerge after a whole week. There is no similar word in English. My mum would send me a message that it was safe to come back. My best friend's parents knew about it and they let me stay. I don't know how he managed to keep his job. My father worked in an industrial factory cutting sheets of metal. Sometimes he would go to work and sometimes he wouldn't.

Elena, the translator, interjects to say that being drunk at work in Russia is a very common thing. She says it is tolerated because otherwise they would have to fire the whole workforce. Alcohol is known popularly as the 'green snake'. A substantial percentage of manual workers have drinking issues. This is another problem which has grown in the post-Soviet era. A recent report says that daily alcohol intake by men increased fourfold between 1991 and 2000 and sicknesses related to alcoholism grew by almost 50 per cent in the same period.[2] Russia has the highest level of alcohol consumption in the world. According to the Daily

Telegraph around 24 pints of pure alcohol a year are consumed per head: man, woman and child. An estimated twenty-seven thousand Russians die every year of alcohol poisoning, quite apart from other drink-related complaints.[3] Russia cannot afford this loss of manpower when its population is in sharp decline.

It was almost like my father had fits. He would come home drunk and he wanted to take it out on someone. When he was sober, he never asked me about my studies and how things were. But when he was drunk, he would tell me that I was a low-grade student and he would beat me up. When I grew up, I tried to defend my mother and I got beaten up as well. I couldn't watch the way he was abusing her; it was too horrible. I wanted revenge. I wanted to get my friends to beat him up. There were boys I knew who were older than me at seventeen or eighteen, they were quite big, and I hoped that they would give him a good hiding. It never happened, of course.

There was one incident when some money got stolen from our flat. I don't know how and I don't know who. That day I didn't have my friends round, and I didn't steal it. I was asleep in the morning. He was sober when he burst into my room, threw my duvet cover on the floor, threw me on the floor and started kicking me. I was screaming, 'what's going on?' He screamed back, 'where did you hide the money?' He thought I'd stolen the money because I wanted to run away. He beat me up quite severely. I had a broken rib and problems with my spleen. My nose wasn't broken but it was so swollen that it was massive and my lip was torn. I spent about three or four days in hospital. I told the doctors that I had a fight with my girlfriend because it would have made it worse if I had told the truth. I wanted to call the police but my mum wouldn't let me. My sister didn't come to visit me. I haven't got a clue why.

Once, when I was twelve years old, I was watching TV in the living-room and they were shouting in the kitchen. I saw him hitting my mother with his fist. I was really shocked. I went to the kitchen and started screaming 'leave her alone'. He pushed me to one side and just carried on. I went to my grandmother to get her to stop him. She told me not to interfere. I tried to discuss it with my mother afterwards. She wouldn't talk about it. She used to get bruised, but nothing was broken. He didn't hit her on the face so she could go to work. I used to tell my best friend about it but I doubt very much that my mother spoke to her friends at work. When I spoke to her on the phone recently, she said that he's got better. Of course, she could just be telling me that so that I don't worry because I am far away. I asked her if she would like to come here. She said that she couldn't leave things behind. My sister has a baby now and my mother feels that she won't be able to cope on her own, although she lives with her husband and his parents.

I've got loads of feelings but I don't know how to describe them. I always knew that I was a normal person, despite my family. Sometimes I felt worthless, sometimes I felt I was to blame. And I was constantly thinking what I could do so that my mother and I didn't have to suffer like this. When I couldn't make things better, I used to feel a sense of failure. The flat was his so we had nowhere to go, and there was no way we had enough money to make it on our own – not that Mum would have left anyway. At school people would sometimes make fun of me. He would walk around the area drunk, shouting and screaming. Everybody knew that he was my father. It was very embarrassing.

I always wanted to leave Russia. From the age of ten or twelve I wanted to go to the USA. I don't know why. Maybe because of the movies. I was young and silly. Everything seemed warmer, prettier and nicer there. I loved *Beethoven*, the movie about the cute, dribbling dog. I really liked the family in the film. There was a big difference between my family and that family. In the film, they were doing things together. They were friends. I had this crazy father. My sister didn't talk to me. She was constantly sulking. I think she didn't like me. She would tell me, 'you are not my sister'. I would ask her why she said things like that. I introduced her to one of my friends when she was seventeen – and then she went and married him! I was really annoyed.

After I introduced them to each other we started to socialize more, because he was my friend, but I still had the feeling that she didn't like me, and it made it awkward between me and my friend. About four months later I found out that she was pregnant. And he didn't want to marry her, the bastard! People don't frown on lone mothers, but it would have been hard for her to bring up a child on her own. My mother would have supported her. I gave him a really hard time before he agreed to marry her. I went to the wedding. She was eighteen when the baby was born. I think she's happy but I doubt if she feels grateful to me. When the baby was born, I wasn't allowed to go anywhere near it. She said, 'if you pick her up, you will drop her'. She didn't trust me.

We were quite poor. In Russia many people are poor. My father drank all his money away. Never mind him not giving my mother money, sometimes he would even take money from her. Of course, if we had two salaries coming into the house we would've had a better life. Sometimes we didn't have money for food. I ate at my friend's house. One time my mother tried to borrow money for three days and nobody would lend her any. Russian culture is different and they don't like to lend money. Maybe they thought that the money would be used to buy alcohol for my father. We would often eat pasta. We rarely ate fresh meat. We would eat some sort of soup and tinned beef. We never bought fresh vegetables and salad. Sometimes in the summer we would get our vegetables from the allotment. My grandmother used to look after the allotment, which was outside the city. In the summer she lived in the allotment in a tiny wooden hut. She was energetic even though she was seventy. Sometimes she would cook, but she never tidied or cleaned up. She wasn't at home during the day because she worked in the market. She would sell chocolates in the winter and sunflower seeds and vegetables in the summer. She would bring her unsold chocolates home but she never gave them to me. She said it was business. In the evening she would come home, watch a soap on TV and go to bed.

I don't know what my grandmother thought about my father's

violence. She didn't interfere. We didn't have a good relationship. She always thought that I was being naughty. But when he was trying to beat me up that time, she did try to defend me. She hated my mother. She wouldn't talk to me about it. When I was sixteen, she said, 'your mum is not as good as you think. She had a child before she married your father. That's why I never wanted him to marry her.' I was shocked by the news that Sveta was not my real sister. Then I found Sveta's birth certificate which showed that she was born in a different city and the father's name was different. Maybe she was jealous of me because I had a father and she didn't. Yet my father treated her better than me. My mother was nineteen when Sveta was born. I was too embarrassed to ask my mother about her earlier relationship. I was only seventeen when I left home.

I shared a room with my grandmother from the time I was in nursery. My grandmother snored like a trooper. We had two bed-rooms. To start with, my sister was in the same bedroom as my parents. Then she moved in with my grandmother and I got kicked out into the living-room. From the age of fourteen, I slept on the sofa in the living-room. I would like to ask my parents how come my sister, who wasn't even their child, slept in their bedroom and I didn't. When I was five, I was moved out. Nobody asked me if I wanted to go.

I started smoking at fourteen. I remember a New Year's party at school when I got really drunk. We were not allowed to have alcohol but we bought a big gin-and-tonic bottle and drank it behind the teacher's back. I was really, really drunk. Everybody laughed at me and said that I took after my father. I didn't vomit, but I couldn't walk in a straight line. Life is more colourful when you drink, and you feel happier, but I didn't want to drink like him. My friends would usually buy the cigarettes and the drinks. Their parents had more money because they were not spending it on alcohol like my father. I didn't get any pocket-money but sometimes I would be given a few roubles to go and watch football. I loved football. We had our own football team which played in the premier league.

My mother always said that what I wanted to do with my life was my choice. She told me not to be so trusting. She was worried that my friends might lead me up the wrong path. She used to say, 'if you start drinking, you can get hooked and become like your father'. But drinking wasn't a problem – I'd only drink in company. I was offered drugs but I always refused. She had no ambitions for me, but I had lots of dreams. To start with, I wanted to be a good chef – I still can't cook but I would love to learn. Until recently I wanted to be a lawyer. I don't know why I like the law. I enjoy winning a good argument, I suppose. Of course it involves a lot of reading, which put me off a bit – I've only read twenty books in my life. When I was little I used to like to read, but I prefer the telly now. I want to earn good money – I have dreams like everyone else. I also dreamt about having a different father. I thought why was I so unlucky as to have this man as a father? That was when I was about ten. When I turned fourteen, I dreamt about my parents getting divorced.

I had my first boyfriend at fourteen. We only went out for two weeks but I lost my virginity to him. We were studying in the same school. He was one year older. He had a cute face, like a rabbit's. He started dragging me along to discos. I never learned to dance properly so I don't really enjoy dancing. We would go to the park or to his place. I broke it off because I got fed up with him. He was boring. After that I didn't really want to go out with anybody. A year later, at fifteen, this guy moved into our block. We went out for a month, but I found him boring too. I wanted someone who could entertain me. I wanted somebody attractive – having a handsome boyfriend raises your status with your friends. Then I met this twenty-year-old guy, Valeriy, while I was still with my neighbour. I went out with him for four months. I think I was in love with him. But he had to go into the Army. We have compulsory national service in Russia for two years.

We used to write to each other. I was waiting for him to come back home, but then I left Russia while he was away. He didn't know that I had gone. When he got back, he came to my place with a big bunch of roses and a bottle of champagne. My sister opened the door and said that I had gone to Moscow. That's what I had told her. When he found out, he threw away the flowers and the champagne. He wasn't that attractive, but he was really helpful and kind. We always had a good laugh, so I never found him boring.

Before the age of twelve, I had only distinctions at school. After that, I had passes, passes. It was something to do with my father. I was nervous all the time. I did four subjects for my final exams: algebra, Russian, French, and, let me try to remember, yes that's it, geography. The first two are compulsory, the other two you can choose. I got a merit in Russian and French, a pass in algebra and a distinction in geography. I think I did pretty well given the situation at home. Looks like I'm a survivor, doesn't it? It wasn't easy. I think my early life has made me more irritable. I am irritated by dense people who don't understand even if you tell them something ten times. I also worry about things too much. Sometimes I cannot sleep. I get angry about little things. If somebody rings me early in the morning, I get grumpy. Yes, I can be grumpy!

I left Russia with my friend Marina. We had been friends since the age of eight. When we turned fifteen, we were inseparable, although she wasn't my best friend. Marsha was jealous of my relationship with her and we ended up having arguments about Marina. Marsha would say 'that Marina is a fool'. My family didn't like Marina either. They thought she was a bad influence on me and that she dressed provocatively, that her skirts were too short and her tops too revealing. Working abroad was her idea. She always wanted to do something risky. Sometimes we'd go mountain-climbing. And once we ended up literally hanging off the edge of a cliff without any equipment. I was fascinated by her sense of adventure – I recognized it because I have something like that programmed in me too, except I'm a bit quieter. She was always the one who would say 'let's go'.

I remember one time in spring when the ice began to melt on the river Volga. We decided to walk on the river. It broke when we were in the middle and my leg sank into the water up to my knee. Freezing cold outside, freezing cold water! Everything got wet straight away. Somehow we managed to get to the bus station and go home. In winter it can go down to −20°C. Marina was one year older, so she left school before me and went to college. I tried to carry on with school, but at one point I was off for a month. First I had flu, and then I was just playing truant. I lost my sickness certificate and got expelled. The school day started at 1 p.m. and finished at 6 p.m. In the morning, I slept. I didn't help my mum. I regret it very much now.

When Marina finished her college course, we looked for a job for six months. She also came from a poor family. Her mother had died and she was living with her father, sister and grandmother, five minutes away from us. I wanted a job so that I could rent a room and live away from my father. But we were not able to find anything apart from washing lorries. It was a long day from early morning to late in the evening. Every muscle in my body ached. We earned 60 roubles a day, about £1. We could work as many days as we wanted. If we worked five days a week we would earn roughly 1,200 roubles a month but the cheapest one-room flat would cost about 1,000 roubles so that was never going to work. We did that job for one week and then ran away.

One day we saw an advert in a free newspaper, the *Samara Weekly*, which comes through your door. The ads were mainly for people who have driving licences. There wasn't anything for us. Then Marina came across this advertisement that said 'Work abroad'. Many countries were listed. I was surprised that there were Asian countries like Thailand on the list. She called them and spoke to a woman who told us to meet her the next day. We were not given a definite time but simply to get there before they closed at 5 p.m. We couldn't believe our luck. We thought we haven't got anything else to do. Let's just go and see what happens.

It was summer. We wore jeans and T-shirts. We didn't bother dressing well for it because we didn't expect to get the job. Public transport's cheap so we went by trolley-bus to the centre of town where they had an office. It took us about half an hour. It was tucked away in a tiny street that was not big enough even for cars. The office was on the first floor. It was small and dirty and had a broken staircase with one step missing. It was more like they were looking to employ people to wash cars, rather than to work abroad. This woman, Olga, who was about forty years old, was quite nice. She asked us what we could do. We said we don't really have any education. She said you don't need education to work as waitresses or shop girls. There was work available as waitresses in Spain. I did wonder about the question of language, but she didn't say anything about that. It didn't make me suspicious.

We asked about how much we had to pay. We knew we had to buy a ticket and get a visa. She said, 'you're very young, you don't have any money, so don't worry about it. When you start working, you can start paying.' Our interview lasted half an hour. We filled in some paperwork, maybe an application form. We asked how much money we could expect to earn and she gave us a figure which I think was two to three times the average Russian salary. Even then we didn't really believe it. I was underage. To get a Russian exit visa, I would need permission from my parents. I didn't know how I would swing that. We said we would call her later and we left.

I wasn't really keen, but when we came out Marina started convincing me to go for it. She was on a high. She said, 'this is our chance'. We met up that evening and discussed it at length. In the end I agreed because she said if we don't get on we can always come back. Sure. If only I had known! We called Olga. She said that we have to bring such-and-such documents. I had to bring more documents than Marina because I was underage. I needed a passport-sized photograph of my mother and a letter signed by her and the director of her nursery school to confirm that she was employed there. What was I going to tell my mother? I made up this story and I can't believe that she believed it. I told her that I wanted to go away with Valeriy to Bulgaria for a one-week holiday and I needed an external passport. She didn't want me to go, but after two weeks of walking around looking sad and not eating I managed to convince her.

Olga called us all the time. My mum didn't get suspicious because lots of people called me all the time. Interesting thing was that Olga asked for a 'full body photograph' right from the beginning. We asked her why she needed our photographs when we were going to work as waitresses. She said that they wanted pretty waitresses, not fat or ugly ones. How stupid we were!!! She also sent us to have our passport photos taken and paid for all the paperwork and photos. She gave us 50 roubles for the photos. Over a period of three months we visited her office many times to get money for various things. We didn't see anybody else there. Sometimes she had a woman helping her. Once we saw a guy who was going to Cyprus to work as a builder. Maybe it was an act to show us that it was a genuine employment office. I got all the signatures that I needed, but getting the paperwork sorted out was difficult. Olga submitted the application on our behalf. She called us in November and said the passports were ready. She gave us money to buy tickets to go to Moscow within two days. We had a big, all-night party to say goodbye to our friends. Eight of us went to a café and drank, oh yeah! We told them that we were going to work abroad. I knew that none of them would tell my mother.

Maybe I should have. Then maybe I wouldn't have found myself on a motorway to a life that filled me with fear. We travelled for three hours. We arrived in Brussels. We parked, and walked along a beautiful street. I had not seen anything so beautiful in Samara or in Moscow. We went to McDonald's. György went up to two men and started talking in a language I didn't understand. He asked me to sit at a different table. Ten minutes later he invited me to join them and introduced Poly to me. He didn't speak Russian, only a little French, so we had to communicate by hand signals. György told me that Poly was going to be my pimp. Poly was small and fat. He had short hair, almost bald, kind of ugly. He looked about forty. There was a young guy with him. They were talking for a long time among themselves. György said that they were trying to decide who was going to take me. In the end, Poly got me. I didn't know exactly what a pimp did. György said, 'you must listen to Poly and don't try to run away. I know everything about you and I know how to find you. I will find your mother and I will kill her. If I find you, I won't kill you but I will poke your eyes out and make you disabled.' Of course, I didn't want to have my eyes on a stick! So I went with Poly. He drove a Ford Escort.

He had a two-room flat in not a bad area. The house was pretty and, inside at least, it was clean. There was one big bed. I didn't like that but then, luckily for me, he went out. I was exhausted because I hadn't slept much on the coach so I went to sleep. I woke up in the middle of the night when he came back. That's when he raped me. It is painful to describe it. I was asleep and he just launched himself on me. I struggled to get away, but I realized that it was pointless because I had nowhere to go. Then I just accepted it and that was it. Thank God he didn't hit me. Thank God I wasn't a virgin. If I had been, the shock would have been too much. He was old and ugly. I thought the world had come to an end. But it was nothing compared to what I was going to face later on.

The next day he told me that I had to work. He took me to a big road called Avenue Louise. I think it was right in the centre of Brussels. In the middle there was a tram line. There were big buildings on the opposite side. I had to stand around in the freezing cold. It was horrible. I was told what to do and what to say. If a car stops, you have to tell them how much it costs. Poly wrote it on a piece of paper in French: €50 if it was in a car and €100 in the hotel, plus the client has to pay for the hotel. About 40 per cent of my clients would choose to go to a hotel. Driving to the hotel or the woods was part of the half hour. Sometimes the client would touch you up on the drive. In the half hour they would only get to have sex once, but in a hotel it might be more than that. Rarely did they ask for it twice even then. I had to take the money up front. Most of my clients wanted me to be totally naked. Normally after it was all over we would both get dressed and the client would drive me back to my usual place.

Avenue Louise is a smart street in Brussels which runs from the Palais de Justice all the way to the wooded Bois de la Cambre. It is full of the top fashion houses like Gucci and Armani, hotels and bars. It is a well-known red-light area. The high degree of tolerance given to prostitution in Belgium has been taken advantage of by Eastern European traffickers. No coherent policy of control of the industry exists. In 2002 it was esti-

mated that there were thirty thousand prostitutes working in Belgium. According to a spokesperson from the International Organization for Migration (IOM), 'Among EU [European Union] member states, Belgium is one of the top destinations for victims of trafficking, it is also one of the main countries used for the transit of sex-workers. Most of those destined for prostitution are young women between the ages of twenty-one and thirty and teenage girls under the age of eighteen.'

Prostitution is not a crime per se in Belgium, but the exploitation of another is deemed immoral and prosecutable in a court of law. Sentences can be up to fifteen years. The penal code was recently amended to introduce the exploitation of prostitutes as an aggravating circumstance permitting harsher penalties. The International Convention of New York, combating the traffic and exploitation of human beings, was incorporated by law in 1965 and a further Bill passed in 1994 recognizing and regulating prostitution. Pimping, taking someone to or bringing someone away from a place for purposes of prostitution, as well as acts which lead the under-aged into vice or prostitution, are illegal. The trafficking of sex-workers, however, is the most serious offence.[4]

My first encounter was with a thirty-year-old Frenchman. I felt very strange when I had to undress in front of a stranger. Later it became a habit, especially when I spent entire days hanging around in my underwear. We had to do it in his car. I just couldn't work out what I was supposed to do. He took me to some forest. I was really scared. I asked him for the money first. He gave it to me. Then we got into the back of the car and it all began. I carried condoms and he used one. I constantly came across people who wanted to do it without condoms. I didn't agree. What for? I wanted to stay alive. I didn't want any of their diseases.

I can't remember what else happened on that first day. I was in a really funny state as if I was in some terrible dream. I didn't feel like myself. Lots of things have got erased from my memory.

Oh yes, I forgot, I charged €30 for a blow-job. Everybody complained that it was too expensive. They would say €15 to €20 max., but

I wouldn't negotiate. Take it or leave it. The ones who came for a blow-job were those who didn't have any money – factory and manual workers. Blow-jobs were usually quicker but that didn't make it any easier. I used a condom for that too. And there were times when blow-jobs went on for half an hour. That was a bit of a strain on my mouth.

I was given a mobile. It was the first time I had one and I had to work out how to use it. When I went with a client, I had to send an SMS to Poly saying where I was going and for how long so that he could work out how much money I had made. Sometimes Poly would take the money at the end of the working day, sometimes he would collect it after each session. He would top up the money on the phone. I called my mother once. I was not able to speak for long because the money ran out very quickly. Poly found the number and went mad. I understood some words and he waved his hands around a lot. I said that I called my mother because I missed her very much. He asked why I hadn't told him. Next time I call, he said, I must call in front of him. I couldn't see the point of that as he didn't speak Russian.

I always refused when I was asked to do anything other than straight sex. The pimp never asked for anything else. He was kind of quiet. All he cared about was whether I was going to bring in money. Poly introduced me to a Bulgarian girl who was managed by his friend. I was told that she had been working here for some time and if I had any questions she could help. We were not friends, we just worked next to each other and she would check up on me sometimes. They don't normally encourage friendship between the girls. In fact, most of the time I was persecuted by the other girls. I think there were too many prostitutes on the street. Maybe they liked my patch. I also looked much younger than most of them, who must have been between twenty-five and thirty. Many of the clients came to me because they liked underage girls. Two to three girls would come up to me and tell me to go away. I would call Poly. He would speak to them and then they would go away. I don't know how many prostitutes there were on the street – maybe a hundred. It was a big street and there were prostitutes on both sides. I was dropped off at the same spot at the beginning of the street every evening. I would often hang back in the shadows. The fewer clients I had, the better for me. I wasn't going to get the money anyway. And the pimp didn't get angry with me if I didn't earn enough money. Even when I thought I might be able to pay back the money I owed and leave, I was still not eager to put myself forward, even though Poly was constantly circling the area.

For the first week I worked in my own clothes. Then we went shopping and he bought me a short skirt. I was also forced to wear eye make-up and lipstick, which I hated. Sometimes the men would try and kiss me or show me affection. I was told not to kiss anybody. I would say no if they tried. I was thinking what an idiot I was. It was better to be with my father. I kept thinking about how to escape. It was a constant struggle to stay afloat. I hated all the clients although it wasn't their fault. Some were OK, but some were violent. Sometimes the men wouldn't take me back to my spot and I had to walk back from the woods or the car-park. Poly would usually pick me up if somebody left me there.

I remember one Portuguese guy who came almost every day. He was about thirty-five, dark with a little beard and brown eyes, usual build. He spoke a little French and English. I also spoke a mixture of the two. I could not construct a sentence, I just used certain words. He would invite me to the swimming-pool or to the shops. I didn't even know how to refuse him. He was quite nice. I did think about running away with him, but then I worried that it might be a trap. But I suppose they would have used someone who spoke Russian. I remember too there was a very stinky one. He came only once, thank God!

I saw between three and six men every night for seven nights a week. I worked from 9 p.m. to 3 a.m. Poly would take me home. He would rape me every night. I would wake up at midday. He did let me sleep. I would spend all day at home. I cleaned and Poly cooked. He would make salads, meat, pasta, nothing special. He would disappear and then come back and take me to work. He did not let me go anywhere on my own except when I was working. He gave me the night off on New Year's Eve. We went to a restaurant in Amsterdam and then we stood in a square. That was the only time I was allowed to drink alcohol – one glass of wine. I talked all evening to the Bulgarian girl. She had come with her boyfriend, who was also her pimp. The girl said that it was a good way of making money. I told her that I was not making any money from it. She said 'you have to wait'. She had met her Albanian boyfriend in Bulgaria and they had decided to make money this way. As soon as I told her that I had been trafficked, she went yeah, yeah, and changed the subject. Maybe she was scared that they would overhear us and that her boyfriend would fight with her later, or maybe she too had been trafficked.

On the one hand, I was hoping that the police would find me. On the other hand, I was worried that I was doing something wrong and that I might be put into prison. I was taken to the police station once. I was standing on the street as usual when a man came up to me and asked how much. I told him. Before we got to the car he told me that he was a policeman. There were three more in the car. At the station they asked me what I was doing. I was not able to say much. They asked if I was working for myself or for somebody else. I had been told to say that I was working for myself if I got caught. Prostitution is not illegal in Belgium but they may have been looking for trafficked women. They kept me at the station for thirty minutes. I was very surprised when they allowed me to go. I think they didn't have anything better to do. I wondered if I should have told them the truth. I was scared that I would be deported to Russia where the pimps would find me and kill me. I had nowhere to hide. I would have had to go home. Besides, I owed György a lot of money because he had organized my trip abroad. If he had spent money on me, then I was definitely in danger because he would come looking for me. I was under the impression that György was the main man.

György took Marina to Greece and he brought me to Brussels. I got news of Marina from György when he came to visit Poly to collect his money. György told me that he saw Marina every time he went to Greece. Apparently, she used to scream at the clients. He asked me why I had such a stupid friend. I thought it was funny. I liked the fact that she was screaming at them, but I also thought it was pointless because she was going to suffer for it. The plain clothes police picked her up while she was standing on a street in Athens. She was in detention for a month. Then she was deported. She's back in Samara. I tried talking to her later but she didn't want to talk about it. She is living with a boyfriend. She had a miscarriage. Poor thing! My friends tell me that she's gone a bit loopy. Marina told Marsha that she and I had left together, that I had gone to England with a boyfriend and she came back because she didn't want to live abroad. György said that if Marina is found she is going to be killed because she testified against them in Greece and one of the guys went to prison.

Poly told me that I owed him €3,000. György wanted €2,000 for tickets, visas and all the travel expenses. He wouldn't have spent more than €1000 on our travel. The flat in Moscow wouldn't have cost much because there were a lot of people living there. The €2,000 must have been a buying price for me, but he wouldn't admit it. And I had to pay another €1,000 to Poly. He said it was money I owed him. I was keeping count of how much I was earning every night. It was usually between €100 and €300. It would have taken approximately fifteen days to repay the debt. I did come to a point when I thought that I had returned the debt – about one or two weeks before I got sold on. Then I thought I should wait and earn a little so that I would be able to make a new life for myself. When I asked Poly to start paying me, he said that I owed him another €1,000 for expenses as he had spent a lot of money on me already to buy food, cigarettes and clothes. I suppose he would have said that every time I asked him to pay me.

Two months after I started, I had a violent encounter with a man who tried to snatch my bag. It was quite late. He was the third client of the night. He wore glasses and looked about forty – like a professor. I wouldn't have expected him to be capable of what he did. He had kind of long hair but not long enough to be tied in a pony-tail. He took me to some forest. I quoted him €50. The drive lasted about ten minutes. He didn't just stop on a road in the forest but went off the road into the forest. He looked tense. I thought that was strange. He didn't touch me. I started saying the usual, that he had to give me the money first. He started screaming. I didn't understand what he was screaming about. I realized that he wasn't going to pay me any money and that in fact he was going to take my money. When we stopped, he sat there and looked at me. He grabbed my bag. I tried to get my bag back because I wanted to call Poly. I had all my night's earnings in the bag – about €150. He took a knife out. I went oh-oh. It looked like a kitchen knife. It wasn't very big. I can't remember where he pulled it out from. He held it near my face and said that he wasn't going to pay me but I had to do what he wanted.

We go into a long silence. Natasha says she can't remember anything else. She needs to smoke.

I thought it was pointless arguing with him because his eyes looked crazy. He was shouting that I was dirty, and then he put on two condoms! He threw me onto the back seat from the front of the car. I can't work out how he managed to do that. I remember I hurt myself. I can't remember if he got out of the car and came to the back. I was in shock. He pulled his trousers down, he ripped my knickers off, the bastard, and jumped on top of me. He kept hitting me while he was having sex. I just lay there and cried. I tried to reach out and get hold of my bag which was in the front seat. This was stupid of me. I wanted to phone Poly while he was having sex with me. I knew it wasn't possible, but I still tried. He didn't notice fortunately. The back doors were left open. Usually the doors were closed. The client would sit and I would sit on top of them. He hit me, took my bag, took out the money and threw the bag out of the car window. At least he didn't take the telephone. He threw me out of the car naked and threw my clothes in the mud. I got up, picked up my clothes and started getting dressed. I picked up the bag and the telephone and I called Poly. I couldn't explain properly what had happened. He said I should walk along the motorway and stop at a particular sign. I tried to come out of the forest onto the motorway so I could see where I was. It took me five minutes to get to the road but I had to walk along a little way until I came to the sign. I called Poly. He told me to stay there. He arrived forty minutes later. I just sat by the roadside. Cars passed by but I didn't care. No one stopped.

I told Poly what had happened and I said to him that I cannot work like that. 'I want to live.' I was hysterical. I would cry, stop for a minute, then I would cry again, cry and cry. He asked me to calm down. He didn't just tell me to shut up. Despite being a pimp, he never really treated me badly. I felt safe with him in a funny kind of way. When I told him that I wanted to go home, he said, 'I cannot let you go home, but you can go to another country and work in different conditions'. He said I could go to Spain, France, Italy or England. If I wanted to work from a flat then it was better to be in England. Nobody could take you away and there were usually other prostitutes in the flat. He would introduce me to his Albanian friend.

I stopped working after the 'woods' incident. One week later, at the beginning of February or the end of January, I was sold onto the Albanian guy, Niki Dmitrov, the man who would be my pimp in England. We left straight away. I didn't take anything with me. I have moved several times taking nothing. The most important thing is for me to get out. I can leave things behind because I feel something will turn up. In the car he started telling me about England. We talked in a mix of French and English. I learned my English from my clients and Poly in Belgium – so you can imagine, it's quite colourful! He behaved quite well. It took us two hours to get to Ostend. At his friend's house, we slept in the same bed but he didn't touch me. I was happy.

I liked the way he looked. He was younger than Poly. He had a big face, short hair and was quite fat. I can't describe him in any more detail. In the morning, we went to a hotel where we stayed another two nights. We had to wait until we could find a way to leave. We shared the same room, but again he didn't touch me. We went for a walk to the seaside. I thought, how nice! While it was still daylight, we drove for half an hour and stopped by a field in the countryside. He told me that I had to go to England in a lorry and that I would be met by a friend. I should stay with Gena (*pronounced Gyanor*) until he joined me in England. There were lots of lorries parked there. My lorry was waiting for me. I don't know what the lorry was carrying because I was preoccupied with other things. I sat in the front next to the driver and his mate, who were talking to each other in English. I didn't speak to them.

I think my visa had run out and I was there illegally, but I'm not sure. Poly may have given my passport to Dmitrov. I think they used a fake passport for me. The driver had everybody's documents and he talked to them at immigration when we stopped at the border. We travelled for a long time. We boarded the ferry in France. The boat journey lasted an hour. We got off at Dover, I think, and then we drove to London. There were no problems with immigration at Dover. We stopped somewhere near London and waited for Gena. He was Albanian but he spoke Russian because his wife, Katya, was Russian. It was dark. We went to his flat. He said he was very glad to see me and that everything was going to be all right. He knew about the incident in the forest. I became friends with Katya almost immediately. She said 'you look like a child'. She cooked for me. She was in her twenties and she didn't have any children. She was working as a prostitute in some parlour. Her husband was her pimp. When I asked how her husband could prostitute her, she said that he loves her anyway and that she wanted to work as a prostitute. She had done it for six years and had no other skills.

Two days later Niki arrived. He took me to a photographic studio. They gave me full make-up before taking pictures. For the first lot of pictures I was not in the nude. He gave me things to wear like a nurse's uniform and sexy underwear. I remember Niki didn't like the way I was posing for the photographs – he said I didn't look sexy, I looked tired. But we went really early in the morning – like 11.00 a.m.! The police have those air-brushed photos in their possession. Niki put them up on a website advertising the 'youngest escort in London'. I only found out about that during the court case. I didn't know what he was going to do with the photos. Gena explained that the photos would be put up on a website and if somebody liked the look of me they would call up the agency. The agency would call Niki, and then Niki would call me if there was a client who wanted to see me. Niki started taking me to a flat in Bayswater to work from 11 a.m. to midnight. All the girls in the flat relied on the website to get business. Clients would also come through newspaper ads and cards in nightclubs and lap-dancing clubs. We stayed with that couple for a few weeks. That was my temporary home flat. I would go back there to sleep every night.

Niki raped me in London. I don't know why he didn't do anything in Brussels. We had a bunk-bed in Gena's flat. The first time it happened was during the day when the couple were in the living-room. I was getting changed in the bedroom. He came in, closed the door behind him, and started making advances. I pushed him away. I don't know where I got the courage. He held me by my throat and nearly suffocated me. I remember that even now. He said, 'you have to do what I tell you or I will kill you'. Do I have to talk about him or can we change the subject? (*We decide to come back to it when she's feeling more able to talk about it.*)

In the flat, I had only two clients every day. I quite liked it. There were two Lithuanian girls who lived and worked there. They said they wanted to do this work – maybe they were told to say that. One girl had worked in the UK before. She went back home, faced some difficulties and decided to return. She had a fake Spanish passport – at that time Lithuania wasn't a part of the EU. We talked about our past and what was happening in our countries, had a laugh and a joke. We would chat and watch the telly. I liked comedies even though I didn't understand them, but I used to try and guess. I watched the music channels mainly. I love music. I spent seven years learning to play the piano as a child. I played Russian pop music and Mozart, but I didn't like the Russian composers. Later on I found out that the girls didn't like me. When Niki was screaming at me one day, he said that they didn't want me to work there. He was probably trying to destroy my confidence.

Niki used to scream all the time because I wasn't getting enough clients. He thought it was my fault. They didn't come back because I wasn't nice to them. I wasn't working well because I didn't like the work. I suppose it would be more fun for the client if the woman was willing. More value for money, isn't it? It would depend from client to client whether I had to be sexually active or passive. If I had to sit on top of the client, then it was difficult, but what choice did I have? I used to work seven nights a week, even through my periods. When I told Niki that I didn't want to do it during my periods, he shouted at me. At least Poly used to give me time off then.

It was a two-bedroom flat. I worked in this flat for three months. We never all had clients at the same time. These girls were controlled by Niki's friends. I think the pimps shared the expenses of the flat. I don't remember how much we were charging. I think it was £120 an hour. It included straight sex and a blow-job. I would take the money and then give it to Niki. I can't remember what the men were like. I had very few clothes. Katya gave me some. She bought me a pair of jeans. Niki didn't worry about clothes because I had to meet the clients in my underwear anyway. He bought me two sets of red underwear. Three of us would sit in the living-room in our fancy underwear. Thankfully, the flat was well-heated! When my client came, I would take him to the bedroom. Sometimes I would get a call from Niki at the same time as the other girls got a call from their pimp. We would all go to the door in our underwear when the bell rang. A couple of times our neighbours walked past at this point and stared. We would have to ask the client who he had come for. My name was Dominique. The client would take a look at all of us and decide who he wanted.

After two weeks with Gena and Katya, Niki and I moved to a flat in Holloway. I was either at work or at home. He would go out and eat. I tried to cook for myself – spaghetti, macaroni and sausages. He would take me shopping for groceries sometimes. But Niki said I wasn't going to work there any more because I wasn't making enough money and there weren't a lot of clients. (*A quick calculation suggests that she was earning him approximately £1,700 per week, if she worked seven days a week and had two clients on average per day.*) But Niki had to pay the agencies, rent on the flat where we lived and where I worked, so I don't think he had much left at the end of the day.

He started looking through ads in the newspapers asking for girls to work in massage parlours. We didn't find anything for a week or so. He told me what to say on the phone. 'Say that you are nineteen (I was seventeen) years old. Just answer the questions that they ask you.' But it was difficult because my English was poor. We were not getting very far. They said they needed girls who can speak English. We went to one massage parlour. A Russian woman interviewed me. It lasted five to ten minutes. She asked about my work experience. I told her about the flat. She said she would call me back but she never did. I didn't have to do a twirl or anything, thank God. Niki was waiting outside for me.

One day he said that he had found something suitable. He knew a Latvian woman who worked as a receptionist in a massage parlour in Hendon called 'Paradise' and she spoke Russian. She understood straight away that I was Russian and started talking to me in Russian. She asked me to come for an interview. I had a twenty-minute interview with the owner the next day. He was an Indian guy, David, a Catholic as well! It was a friendly chat. I remember he didn't believe me when I said that I was nineteen. He thought I looked fifteen.

The girl on reception said that he was going to give me a job because he needed girls. I didn't ask how much I could expect to earn because I didn't care. I think Niki knew how much I would earn because he didn't ask me about money. David told me the pricing structure. There was real massage on the list which I wasn't able to do, of course. There was always massage plus something. The cheapest one was massage plus blow-job, then there was massage plus sex for half an hour, for one hour, for two hours – which was at a discounted rate. If they wanted a massage I would do it. I was getting better and better at it. The lighting was interesting. The place was dark but nice. There was a big bed. We had to change sheets after each client. There were two rooms and a lounge. Each room was about 7 sq ft.

Usually there were four girls working there, but sometimes only two of us. The system was that the client went to the bedroom, the girls went in one after the other to say hello to him in their underwear and very, very high heels. Then the receptionist would go with the price list to see him, she would explain what was what to him and he would say which girl he liked best and then he would pay the receptionist. Then she would give a condom to the chosen girl and off we went. My name there was Natasha. The Indian guy said I was the most popular. I was making him the most money. He said he didn't know what he would do without me. I had a really good figure then, a pretty face and blonde hair. Now I have become fat. I had a minimum of three clients per day, but one time I had eight. It was a bad day. The day started at 11 a.m. and finished at 10 p.m. Most clients came for half an hour, some for an hour, a couple for two hours and one for three hours!

One was an old Englishman who used to come for a chat, but I guess there aren't many places you can go for a chat with a girl sitting in her underwear. Sometimes I would sit there without a bra if he wanted me to. He was fifty years old. I knew enough English by then to be able to understand him. He wanted to find out about my life and tell me about his – I can't remember if he got a discount. The Indian guy took half my money for that client because he said he had found him for me. I don't think Niki was making that much even though I was popular. He said that he had paid £3,000 for me and I had to pay it back. At least he didn't lie to me like Poly who pretended that it was money for expenses. I earned approximately £80 to £160 per day after I paid 30 per cent to the owner of the massage parlour. That was less than I was earning in the Bayswater flat. It didn't make sense. Maybe he had fallen out with the other pimps. Maybe he had fewer expenses this way.

David was nice. I think he suspected something. He wanted to know what I spent my money on. He didn't ask direct questions, but he kind of implied that I was underage. It was a friendly environment there. There were a lot of Russian girls there. All day you could have normal interaction. It was better than sitting at home with that bastard. I don't know whether the other girls were trafficked. Maybe they were there on a student visa! Learning massage! We didn't talk about these things because I didn't trust them. If Niki knew the Latvian girl, he might have known the other girls. The clients were mainly English, some Chinese and some Indians. David's friends would come. They would drink and then want time with me – free! I worked there for four months. No, that doesn't add up. I must have spent less than three months in Bayswater. I started at Hendon in April and we were raided at the beginning of June. So it was five months in total in the UK.

(*I ask if we can talk about Niki now.*) I hate him and I don't like to remember him, but let's go on. He used to treat me worse than a dog. He made me do everything. He made me clean the house and wash his clothes, but he was constantly unhappy. Whatever I was earning, it was never enough. He said that I was very young and very stupid. Once I said to him, 'if I am so young why don't you let me go home?' Oh – that was a big mistake. He made me pay for it! He smashed up my face. He hit me so hard that I saw stars. Luckily I was in the bedroom. I fell on the bed. That's when it became hell. Because I was bruised, I couldn't go to work, and because I couldn't go to work I had to spend time with him and that was awful. It happened when I was at Bayswater and at Hendon. At Hendon it was OK because I could talk to people, not about the violence but things in general. I would be bruised on the back. Once he ripped my ear. He hit me and somehow my stud ear-ring ripped through my ear. At one point my whole face was black and blue. I ran away from one abuser and ended up with another one in another country. I thought this was my fate.

I did everything I could to please him, but whatever I did it made no difference. I thought maybe he was mad and nothing would work. I could not have told him that he was stupid to 'damage' the goods from which he was hoping to make money. If I had, it would have made it worse. If we are not going to count the time he suffocated me, the first time he hit me was when one client complained about me in

Bayswater while we were still staying with Gena and Katya. The client said I behaved strangely. He couldn't get everything he wanted from me. I behaved with him the way I behaved with everyone else. Niki asked Gena to explain things to me as we both spoke the same language. Gena said that I should behave with the client the way they wanted me to. I never took an active role with the clients. I would let them get on with it. Maybe that's why they complained and why Niki got angry. I don't know.

In Brussels they had no one to complain to because our whole system of working was different. Niki said, 'I hate the way you try and defend your mistakes'. He started hitting me. Gena tried to stop him, saying, 'there is no point in beating her like that because she won't be able to work'. He used to beat me constantly but not severely. He beat me severely about four times in that whole period, when I had bruising and when everything was hurting. I'm not counting slaps, which happened every day. Once he didn't like the way I looked at Katya, so Niki slapped me. Then Gena came and slapped me. Niki raped me every day for a long time. He would want me to do a blow-job on him sometimes for an hour. He would be watching TV. My mouth would ache. He was paranoid that I didn't respect him. And yes, I hated him. Initially Niki used to drop me off and pick up me after work, but in the last two weeks of my job I had started using the underground by myself. He knew I couldn't run away because I knew nobody, didn't speak the language and had no money.

The day we got busted, I was at work. It was June 2004. I remember that we didn't have any clients at all. We had lots of enquiries on the phone but nobody came to see us. I was in the Sudbury branch of the massage parlour where the receptionist was an Indian girl. I had moved there at the end of May. Both places belonged to David. He would make sure that the same girls were not working in the same place every day. In total there were about ten girls. The police came at three or four in the afternoon. There were two men and two women without uniform. The receptionist and I were in a room upstairs. They rang the bell and she went down to open the door. There was no intercom system. I couldn't hear what they were saying. Two of them came up to the room where I was and they walked around looking at everything. They asked to see my documents. I had a photocopy of my Lithuanian passport. Niki had the original. He had given me a copy because he knew such an occasion might arise. I think I had a visa in my passport. (*Lithuania joined the EEC on 1 May 2004, so her presence as a 'Lithuanian' made her legal.*)

The police were very nice, not at all threatening. They asked me where the original was. I told them 'it's at home'. According to the passport, I was twenty-three. That's when they became suspicious. They asked me how old I was. Then they made some enquiries and found that it was a stolen passport. They said I wasn't the first person to use a stolen passport. I'm not sure if they really checked it out or whether they were just bluffing. They said, 'tell us the real story'. I didn't know what to do but then I decided to admit that I was seventeen. As soon as I said that, they said we had to go to the station.

I didn't feel relieved. I didn't see this as my chance to escape Niki. I didn't know what they were going to do to me. I was frightened that they might lock me up. And then after that, they might just chuck me on the street. I didn't think at that point that I could be deported. I didn't know the rules. I would rather have been deported than stay with Niki. The police were talking to the receptionist like they were her friends. They were laughing and joking. I wondered whether she had informed the police. Of course, that would mean that she would lose her job, but I think she felt sorry for me. We used to chat. I didn't tell her the full story but I told her bits which might have made her think that my position wasn't good. I told her that I wasn't working for myself. I didn't mention any names. I told her that I was beaten up. Then I thought it might have been David who had blown the whistle. But if I was the girl who was making him the most money, why would he want to get rid of me? He was scared of everything, so I don't think he would have called the police.

The police didn't ask me what I was doing there. I think they knew. No, they couldn't have mistaken me for the cleaner because I don't know any cleaner who goes to work in their underwear and high heels and spends their time watching TV. I went and got dressed, gathered all my belongings and we went to the station in an unmarked police car. The receptionist didn't come with us. They asked me if I was working for myself or for somebody else. In the car I told them that I worked for myself. When we got to the station, they tried to find an interpreter for ages. They decided to interview me in English. I took a risk and decided to tell them everything. Badly, in my English. But they understood me. They took my cell phone away from me almost straight away. Niki called but they didn't answer it. He would usually call me every hour. He called me a few times and then he sent me an SMS saying 'call me when you can, I am worried'. They said they would find an interpreter in the morning. They fed me. Even though they were being nice to me, I didn't relax. I thought, this is just the beginning.

Then they took me to some kind of communal hall of residence or a children's hostel. It looked like a hotel. There were three or four floors with a very big living-room on the ground floor. There were loads of people, including children, there. There was a woman who had been asked to keep an eye on me. I think she was living in the hostel. Actually, if I had wanted to run away from that place, I could have done. But where else could I have run to apart from Niki? I thought that this is one night that I can have a normal sleep without going back to that hell. But, in fact, I didn't sleep that night. I was thinking if this was for better or for worse. In the morning they sent a car for me. I think we were taken to social services. They interviewed me there with an interpreter – not Elena. The police were also present. It lasted about three hours. I told the full story. The social worker said that it was extremely likely that I was going to get deported. I got the feeling that they hated me. There were thousands of people like me and they just couldn't be bothered. The woman said that they have a lot of people and they deport everybody. But the police felt that I might be able to stay. The police and social services had a discussion for two hours. They said, 'we're going to put you on a plane tomorrow'.

There has been a tendency to see victims of trafficking as simply illegal immigrants. This has led to some vulnerable trafficked women being detained and deported. After extensive lobbying by pressure groups, the UK government has recently signed up to the Council of Europe Convention on Action against Trafficking in Human Beings (ECAT), which provides a measure of protection for trafficked women. The convention allows for a reflection period of thirty days, in which survivors of trafficking can get support to aid their recovery, and temporary residence permits in case they face danger from the traffickers in their country of origin and/or to assist with criminal proceedings.

I had very mixed emotions. On the one hand, I was glad that this was all over. I was glad that I was going to see my family. But, on the other hand, I was worried about the gang finding me because they knew where I lived. I was scared to go back home. I think I even cried. I wouldn't have told my mother the truth. I told them that I didn't want to go back. But they were indifferent to what I wanted. Then they had more discussion, more thinking time and decided that they were not going to deport me. They made some calls and discovered that they could not deport me in any case because I did not have a passport. Plus I was a kid.

They told me that I could stay in England for a short period of time. Social services took me to the Home Office the next day. I think there was a woman solicitor there as well. We were at Lunar House (*where the IND was located*) almost the whole day. They took my fingerprints and gave me an ARC card (*issued to all who apply for asylum*).[5] I didn't understand anything, what was happening, the meaning of it. I didn't even understand that I was asking for political asylum in this country. The interpreter didn't explain anything to me. She just interpreted the questions and answers. At some later point I understood what was happening. It was the solicitor who told me. I used to go and see her once a month. She told me that I had asked for asylum, that I can be refused, that I can appeal against my deportation order, that they will let me know in two to three months; but it took one-and-a-half years.

They took me to a house in Seven Sisters where I lived for two or three months. There were two girls there: one from Bangladesh and one from Nigeria or somewhere like that. They were sixteen and seventeen years old. A social worker would visit us every day or every other day to make sure that everything was OK. She was quite nice. I started getting my benefits and I went to college to study English almost straight away in June. I wouldn't have been able to do any of these things without the social worker's help. I asked them to transfer me from Seven Sisters, because I lived in fear of bumping into Niki. He lived in Holloway Road, which was not far. They said there was no other place suitable for me. Social services told me that the police were looking for Niki and that he was going to court. They took me to the police station to give my statement. I must have gone there at least ten times. Each visit lasted about an hour. I gave the police the name and number of the agency in Samara. For some reason I remember that. I don't know if they have closed that office down. When they told me that he had been arrested in July, I relaxed... I need a smoke.

I went to college four days a week from 9 a.m. to 3 p.m. I would come home and watch TV in the evening. I had no friends. Social services bought me a phone. The only people who rang me were the police and social services. But I was so happy that I could do anything I wanted to do and that nobody was going to hit me or do horrible things to me. I was really enjoying sleeping on my own. Nobody was going to rape me. When I slept with Niki, he would sleep kind of touching me and it was revolting. Yeuch!

I didn't tell these girls about my background. I was given a cheque for £80 to buy clothes. The social worker took me to Tesco and bought everything like shampoo and toothpaste, toothbrush, stuff like that. Every time I picked up something, she would say, 'that's too expensive, how about this?' I made friends with one girl in college. She was from Latvia and spoke Russian. I didn't tell her about my past. In the beginning my past did feel like a burden, but now it's better. I prefer to keep quiet about it – to pretend it never happened. So yes, this book project is kind of hard.

Then I found a boyfriend, Thomas, about one month later in July. He was twenty-seven years old. Two weeks after we met it was my eighteenth birthday and he threw a big party for me at his house in Potters Bar to which he invited lots of his friends. I invited one person. I didn't really want to find anyone but that's the way it happened. The girl I met in college introduced me to him. He is a Tamil Christian from Sri Lanka. Life was looking up. I loved him. My English improved. I didn't tell him about my past either. I didn't want to tell other Russians about my story because I thought they would laugh at me. I tell everybody a different story. I told one girl that my parents sent me here to study and, in front of her, I told another girl I had come here with my boyfriend. The first girl said, 'hang on, I thought you came here to study'. I got out of it by saying that at first I didn't want anyone to know that I had come here with my boyfriend. I told my boyfriend that I had come to study here. Ah, no, no, no, I told him something completely different. I told him that I came here on holiday and I liked it so much that I went to the Home Office and asked for asylum.

Elena explains that Russian people do not like to tell each other the real story of how they got here. Some people come illegally and some have reasons that they are embarrassed to disclose. For some Russian women, anything is better than life over there – meeting a man over the internet or a drunk in the pub who has an English or French passport. They get where they want to and then they end the relationship. She regularly comes across women who have married Englishmen who are inferior to them and they sometimes end up facing domestic violence.[6]

Thomas taught me about life in London. He helped me with everything – to register with the GP, for example. I didn't live with him as such. I still had my own accommodation in Seven Sisters but I would stay at his house two or three days at a time. I had my clothes in both places. Neither of us did any cooking. We lived on take-aways. He had an off-licence and owned houses which he rented out. We would wake up at midday. He had a manager and other people to run his business for him. But there was one problem. His parents were quite old and they wanted him to run their business in Sri Lanka. They called him every day asking him to return. We lived together for about a year. At the end of that year he went to Sri Lanka for a month. When he came back he said he didn't want to live here any more. He asked me to marry him and go to Sri Lanka with him. I didn't want to go so we split up.

Ever since social services had given me a phone, I'd been able to call my mum once in a while. I still couldn't tell her about what had happened, but at least we were in touch and she knew I was all right. When I called her on my eighteenth birthday, she told me that she had received a threatening phone call: somebody who was very rude had rung her and had given her a phone number to pass on to me – 'Tell your daughter to ring that number otherwise we will kill you!' She was so shocked by the call that she didn't ask any more questions. When she asked me who these people were and why they were ringing, I said that I had had to borrow money and I hadn't paid it back. She advised me to pay it back as soon as I could. I gave that number to the police. They said it was a Bulgarian number but they didn't tell me whether they had made contact with anyone. I wonder if it was Gena who made that call because he and his wife had been thinking of moving to Bulgaria before I was caught.

The court case happened in November (about five months after I was busted), while I was with my boyfriend. It lasted two days. Not the case, just my evidence. He didn't really ask me where I was going. During that period I went back to my flat so that I didn't have to answer any awkward questions. I was embarrassed that I was lying to him. I wanted to tell him but by then it was too late. He would've asked me why I didn't tell him before. I'm sure he wouldn't have left me if I had told him. He was quite open-minded. I didn't want him to feel sorry for me. It is difficult to understand, I know. As we say in Russian, the less you know the better you sleep.

The police came to get me early in the morning to take me to the court in Southwark. I had changed my mind several times about giving evidence. One day I would think that I must give evidence otherwise Niki is going to walk. The next day I would think, I can't do that, I won't be able to look at him. The police officer said 'don't look at him then'. I asked her how many years they would put him away for. She wasn't sure. Nobody told me what to expect, but I lived through it. Nobody cared.

Elena met Natasha for the first time two days before the case. She had gone to her place with the police just to make sure that she was OK to give evidence, to get to know each other, and to make sure that she was comfortable giving evidence through Elena.

The police did not force me to give evidence. The police have been nice. They said that it was my right not to give evidence, but as I was the only witness it would be better if I went to court. Without my evidence he would get released. I wanted very much for him to go to gaol. After I gave evidence, I felt so much better within myself. I felt relief. I don't think he was a big fish. He was just a particularly nasty and vindictive one. I don't know how many women he was controlling – maybe I was the only one. To tell you the truth, I wasn't thinking about the other girls. There were so many people doing this kind of thing and his contribution to the global situation was very small.

According to Amnesty International, trafficked women are being deported if they refuse to assist with police investigations, in spite of the dangers of returning home, although this appears not to have been the case with Natasha. The POPPY Project which, until recently, was the only safe house for trafficked women, cannot give them refuge unless they are prepared to give evidence to the police. Funded by the Home Office and the Association of Local Government (ALG), the POPPY Project was set up in 2001 by Denise Marshall, Chief Executive of Eaves Housing, who discovered a huge gap in services for women who had been trafficked into prostitution. Demand far outstrips its supply of thirty-five bed spaces. In 2006, the police estimated that 5,000 women had been trafficked into the UK. Carlo Narboni, a police officer with the Metropolitan Police Vice Squad, who gave evidence at Natasha's trial, does not believe there is a need for more supported places, but in a nine-month period, Denise Marshall estimated that they had to turn away thirty women. The police use accommodation provided by social services. However, the range of services provided by POPPY cannot be matched.

Women at the POPPY Project have up to thirty days to consider whether or not they are prepared to give evidence to the police, and/or whether or not they wish to claim asylum, before there is any threat of removal. This time, spent housed in secure accommodation and with access to support workers, medical and counselling staff, and competent female legal advisers, may enable women to prepare their cases and to deal with some of the issues of trauma, late disclosure and lack of evidence that are often used to discredit and dismiss their asylum claims.

According to a report written jointly by POPPY Project and Asylum Aid, 80 per cent of POPPY clients were given asylum or Humanitarian Protection on appeal. This figure is six times higher than the acceptance rates of asylum appeals overall. The police are unable to give advice to women about claims for asylum as it could be interpreted as an incentive and/or perceived to contaminate evidence given in court against traffickers. Similarly, the immigration service cannot provide information on asylum because of the overall focus on removal/deportation. The report has argued for an independent adviser to be present at the early stages so that they receive the right information.[7]

I slept in the witness protection room until 12 noon while I was waiting to be called. I hadn't slept all night because of nerves and I had a terrible headache in the morning. I started giving evidence just one hour before lunch and continued until the end of the next day. I remember I saw the receptionist from the massage parlour at Sudbury Hill. She was again being very familiar with the police. I wasn't allowed to speak to her because I was a witness. I gave evidence about Gena as well. I can't remember very much about the trial. I remember I smoked a lot. I smoked ten cigarettes in three hours in the corridor, which is where I saw the receptionist. What does stand out in my mind is the moment when I heard that Niki had a wife.

Elena adds 'and a child'. Natasha cannot remember that. Elena says Natasha's mouth fell open at the point at which that revelation was made. Although Elena translates for a number of trafficking cases, she appears to remember more than Natasha. Elena says that the Crown Counsel took her through her story in the standard way – where were you born? What did you do? How did you come to be here? The cross-examination was shorter than the main one. The evidence was so strong that they couldn't really trip her up.

I had tried to avoid looking at him, but when I heard about his wife I automatically looked at him. He had a mocking look in his eyes. He seemed so self-satisfied that he had come out with that story about his wife and child. Surely he would have had to provide evidence. His lawyer mentioned the wife because he was trying to prove that Niki wasn't living with me. Maybe he had a wife in Albania. I said that I knew nothing about his wife and that he was with me all the time. His barrister said that there wasn't any women's clothing in his room. Then the police turned up with my clothes and the nurse's uniform. They held this up in court. It was quite funny. His counsel just shut up when the police produced the clothes. The other time I looked at him by mistake was while I was giving evidence. He smiled as if to say, you carry on with whatever you're doing, you won't succeed and when I come out, I'll come and get you. Niki's defence was that I was working of my own free will and he was only helping me. He denied that he raped me or that he was my pimp. He also said that he didn't get any money from me. I also gave evidence about his violence.

His barrister put it to me that I had had plenty of chances to escape. He asked me if I spoke English. I said 'no'. He said, 'you know the word "help", you could just have gone and asked somebody for help'. Who could I have asked? The people in the street, how could they have helped me? He kept pressing this point. He asked if I knew the telephone number of the police in this country. I said 'no'. He showed me a map of Brussels. He told me that I was working five minutes away from the police station. 'Why didn't you go to the police?' I didn't even know there was a police station. I remember being very embarrassed when they showed the photographs from the agency to everybody – there were pictures of me in the nude. Elena said that I looked like a child.

I remember the moment they produced my Russian passport. It had been in Niki's possession. It had travelled to Poly and onwards. It was overwhelming evidence in my favour. What could he say in his defence? The fact that my passport was with him was proof that he had been holding me against his will. That was a crowning moment, I think. They didn't tell me anything about the passport before so that the jury would notice my jaw dropping. The jurors were really sad. I was surprised when one of the ladies on the jury cried as I was talking. Later, when it was all finished, they called me to say that he had been put away for six years.

Operation Pentameter, the anti-trafficking initiative launched by the police in February 2006 and wrapped up, four months later, in May, estimates that 5,000 women and girls are trafficked into the UK every year. Legislation dealing with trafficking for sexual exploitation was introduced for the first time under the Sexual Offences Act 2003. Since then there have been seven cases and fourteen convictions, according to Home Office figures. If the police estimate of 5,000 women is anywhere near accurate, then they are barely denting this juggernaut of an industry.

He will probably come out of jail and continue this thing. He may even come in search of me. I think he may go to my mother's place and do something terrible to them. In four or five years I want to tell my mother to move. I have to give her a reason. I don't know what it will be. Maybe I will tell her the truth. By then I will be twenty-four and I can say that it happened in the past and then it won't matter so much. But of course she will have to convince my father to move as well. That may not be so easy. There are many reasons why I don't want to tell her the truth. She will worry that those men might do something to me. Our relationship might change. Maybe she will have a bad opinion of me. After all, it was my fault that I left home without telling her anything.

Niki was very fiery. He was a bomb waiting to go off at any possible moment. Sometimes if I said one word that he did not like, only one word, he would start screaming and shouting and waving his arms about as if he could hit me at any minute. He wanted to be treated with respect. If any one word implied that I was being disrespectful, that would set him off. And his eyes, his crazy eyes. His face would go all red. His scary look, I used to get really scared by the way he looked at me.

In February 2005, the Immigration tribunal refused my application for asylum. I cried for a long time. I started packing my case and getting ready to go home.

Her application was refused because it was felt that her case was not eligible under the Geneva Convention. There was no danger in returning because she could have been relocated to another part of Russia. The Home Office noted that her mother had received threatening phone calls in July and August 2004, but as no approaches had been made since then they concluded that the traffickers could not find her in Russia and they did not have the capability to harm her family. They also believed that the Russian authorities would be able to provide protection.

Then I remembered that I can appeal and I went to the solicitor. She said she would appeal on human rights grounds. I have a copy of the appeal judge's decision somewhere. It was very interesting what the judge decided. I won the appeal under two separate laws, the refugee law and human rights law.

The adjudicator found Natasha to be an 'entirely credible witness', rejected the idea of relocation by referring to 'the cost of moving, the undeveloped housing market and registration requirements on internal travel', and accepted that the collapse of the Soviet Union had provided 'unprecedented opportunities for flourishing of criminal organizations'. The adjudicator relied on the CIPU report which stated that the police were in cahoots with the criminals. Natasha's appeal was allowed under the Geneva Convention. In a precedent-setting case in 2003, an immigration judge had argued that women who had been trafficked into the UK formed part of a particular social group and therefore the provisions of the Geneva Convention would apply to them. This case has influenced a number of asylum decisions for trafficked women. The adjudicator also ruled that if Natasha were deported, it would amount to a breach of Article 3 of the ECHR, which decrees that no one will be subjected to torture, degrading or inhuman treatment.

I got my ILR in July 2005.[8] The police have my passport but I have a travel document. In my travel document it says that I can travel to any country apart from Russia. Anybody who gets leave to remain is not allowed to go back to their own country. I don't want to live there but I would like to visit my home town for a week or so.

A refugee who gets ILR cannot travel to their own country or use their own country's passport or any consular facilities as that may be deemed to be accepting their protection, even if the case is not about state persecution but about non-state agents, as is the case with Natasha, where the state is unable or unwilling to protect. If she becomes a British citizen she will be able to travel home on her British passport.[9]

I met my mother earlier this year for a week in Barcelona. I told her that I could not go back to Russia. In any case, it was cheaper for her to go to Spain but even then she had to save for a very long time. I used the money paid by the newspapers to pay for my trip.

Natasha's story appeared in the News of the World *and the* Evening Standard. *Reporters from various newspapers were present when the trial was held at the County Court. After the case was reported by* The Independent, *the other papers felt it would be good to carry an interview of the woman whose evidence led to Niki's conviction. They approached the police officer, who asked Natasha via Elena if she was prepared to talk to them. The articles were accompanied by partial photos of her, which protected her anonymity.*

I worked as a cashier in an off-licence/small supermarket in Harrow for a little while last year. I was working approximately six hours a day for six days a week, sometimes more. I was getting paid £4 an hour. I earned £100-something per week, but I wasn't paying any tax. It was all under-the-counter. I wasn't getting any benefits at that point because I had moved in with Thomas and I had just got my stay. I worked there during September/October. Then I got sacked. I don't know why. Maybe they didn't like my work. The management had changed. I haven't worked since.

I went to the Job Centre after that and started claiming benefits – approximately £45 per week, which is what I am living on now. It's very little but I get by. Travel costs me £12.50 per week. I buy two packs of cigarettes per week, which cost me £2.60 each. These are Russian cigarettes which you can buy in Russian shops. They're all over the place, one in Finchley Road, one in Walthamstow. In Russia I would have got the equivalent of £10 to £15 per month jobseekers' allowance, but you need at least £80 to survive and you don't get any housing benefit. There are a lot of homeless people there. I don't cook much. Mostly I eat take-aways. Yes, I do have a little money left over for a drink in the pub, but often my friends buy me a drink. I have forgotten the last time I bought myself clothes. Thomas usually bought my clothes.

I have noticed that I am not the same as before. Last year I was happier. Maybe it's something to do with my splitting up with Thomas. I know I said I wanted to be a lawyer when you first started interviewing me two months ago. But now I want to run a bar for East Europeans. What do you think? Thomas has promised to help me but first I have to do a degree in business management and to finish my ESOL Level 2 in English. He is still here. He keeps saying that he is going to Sri Lanka. I don't know why he hasn't gone. We can't get back together if he is still planning to go away.

Elena feels she is more subdued now compared to last year and asks her if the court case gave her a sense of excitement. Natasha has sad eyes. Elena feels the greyness of everyday life is getting to her.

It is true. Maybe I have grown up a bit and realized that things are not going to be good all the time. Even though things have improved now, life is not as colourful as I had hoped. If I had a little sister growing up in Samara today, I would say to her, 'don't get involved with anything like this'. Nobody ever taught us that we have to be careful in this world, or warned us about girls being lured away from home under false pretences. It doesn't matter how bad things are at home, you are better off with your family.

Natasha is doing an access course in law at the moment. She has to do a lot of reading so she is finding it quite difficult. She has got a conditional (on passing her access course) offer from South Bank University, starting in September 2007. She speaks to her mother every week and sounds quite content.

NAOMI CONTÉ: I said OK

Naomi comes from Sierra Leone – a tragic irony given that it was the hub of the transatlantic slave trade in the eighteenth century. The ease with which I was able to locate African children trafficked or smuggled into Britain as domestic slaves only compounds the irony. One Unaccompanied Minors team in one London Borough alone were able to refer three children from Sierra Leone, all of whose stories could have appeared here.

In 1792 the capital, Freetown, was established as a haven for 1,200 former slaves, known as the Black Loyalists, who had moved from the USA to Nova Scotia when they were given their freedom in exchange for fighting on the British side in the American War of Independence. Those Black Loyalists who had travelled to London and not fared well were also shipped out to Freetown as part of an initiative by the Committee for the Relief of the Black Poor. These settlers, with their western ways, did not mix well with the indigenous tribes, which included the Temne and Mende peoples each accounting for 30 per cent of the population, with the Limba tribe making up part of the remainder. English is the official language, but it is understood by only a minority, as most people speak their own tribal languages. Although some estimates say that Krios, descendants of enslaved Africans, constitute 1 per cent of a popu-lation of 5m, the language Krio, English-based Creole, is widely spoken and shows the disproportionate influence of Krios.

Sierra Leone is probably one of the poorest countries in the world, with the lowest rate of life expectancy – men can expect to live to forty-two and women to forty-eight. It has the highest rate of maternal deaths of any country. According to a report from the World Health Organization (2000), there are 2,000 maternal deaths per 100,000 live births as compared to approximately 5 per 100,000 in the UK. The literacy rate is only 36 per cent. It is 99 per cent here.

The curse of Sierra Leone is that it is rich in diamonds. Since 1991, a war has been fought between a brutal rebel force, the Revolutionary United Front (RUF), and the government for control of the diamond mines. In 2002, the government declared the end of the war and a large UN peacekeeping force of 17,000 troops was brought in to enforce it. Exhaustive research has established that some of the largest diamond companies in the world have fuelled this war through the purchase of 'blood diamonds', no questions asked. Most of the diamonds were smuggled across the border into Liberia. Charles Taylor, President of Liberia until 2003, backed the RUF and facilitated the diamond trade. It was only when the Washington Post ran an article looking at the connection between Sierra Leonean diamonds and Al-Quaeda in the wake of the 9/11 attacks that the world felt the pain of the blood diamonds. Apparently, Osama Bin Laden's terrorist network began buying diamonds from the RUF of Sierra Leone in 1998, the same year Al-Quaeda operatives blew up US embassies in Kenya and Sudan. Two Al-Quaeda men implicated in those attacks were in Sierra Leone in 2001, overseeing RUF diamond production. Months before the 9/11 attacks, Al-Quaeda had laundered millions of dollars by buying untraceable diamonds from Sierra Leone. This probably allowed them continued access to money even when $100m worth of their assets world-wide were frozen by the United States and its allies post-11 September. The diamonds brought only bloodshed and anguish to the people of Sierra Leone. As Naomi's story shows, the grinding poverty of the country was not ameliorated by its natural wealth. Rampant smuggling across the border into Liberia has meant that revenue from taxes on exports is very low.

*

I speak to Naomi on the phone at first. Her voice is slow, halting, broken, her story heart-breaking. When I meet her for the first time, I expect to see someone small, diminished by her life experiences. Instead she is defiantly tall, a beautiful, black woman, graceful despite her pregnant bump and looking older than her sixteen years.

She speaks a mixture of Krio and English but is in a transitional stage – some of her sentences are perfectly formed while others slide back into their habitual shape. When I ask her for her address, all she can say is that she lives in Bermondsey – she doesn't know the name of her street. I am half-way to telling her that when she goes home tonight she will see at the beginning of her road a signboard with the name of her road written on it. But it suddenly occurs to me that perhaps she cannot read or write. I stop myself.

Naomi shares her flat with two other young women. When the mail arrives and she's waiting for an important letter, she cannot work out which of the letters are for her; and when one of the other women hands her the mail, she opens it but cannot work out who it's from and what it's about until her social worker comes. As the other girls don't know her business, she can't entrust them with the letters. I wonder how she files her papers so she knows what has come from whom. She has recently learned her alphabet so I ask her the names of her flatmates. One of them shares the same first letter but not the second letter of her name, so I explain how to look for the second letter, and if it says 'a' then the letter is for her. She is delighted at this discovery and the fact that it will enable her to sort out her own mail. These little achievements are huge milestones for Naomi as she struggles to take control of her life.

This is one life which I cannot run past its owner for comment. Naomi, to whom this story belongs, does not have that most basic of resources – written language – which so many of us take for granted in this part of the world. Of course, I could read it to her, but she has no way of verifying it for herself. Nor does she appear to care. After all, they are only words and words in print don't exist in her world as yet. I ask her if she wants to appear under her own name in the book. She says 'no', uttering her assumed name without a moment's hesitation.

Renaming herself becomes wish-fulfilment, as if another name would magically whisk her to another life. When she finishes telling me her story and I discover how utterly alone she is in this world, I ask her why she wants to be anonymous.

I don't know. I have no idea about that. I just say that I don't want my name in the book. It might be if I give you my name, I get my problems again. What if I go ahead with my life and one day my baby buys the book? It might be that when I have the baby, I won't tell him how he came. Maybe I'll get married to somebody and I don't tell him my past. If somebody find out about my life later, it will bring shame onto my baby. That's the way I come up. My baby will come on 2 October. I will call him Roy or Emmanuel – which was Jesus Christ's name.

When I went for the scan, the baby was moving and I asked her, 'is that the baby in my tummy?' and she said 'yes', and tears was coming down my eyes. I didn't watch the scan because it was hard for me to watch the baby. I cried because I didn't want the baby. I had decided that I would take the baby out. I asked how long the baby had been inside and the lady told me twenty-two weeks. Then I asked, 'can I pull the baby out now?' and she said, 'no, the baby is too far now. You got to have the baby now.' Then I started to cry. I asked, 'what is the baby?' They said, 'it's a boy'. Then I said 'OK'. She said the doctor was going to check me. I said, 'no, I don't want nobody to check me again'. Then they took blood from my hand... And the midwife said they will let me know at the end of the month. As long as they don't contact me up to now, it's good news. (*For Aids?*) Yeah.

The lady, Maria, who was in charge of me, she told me that in this country if you don't want baby, you can get rid of it. 'It was not right what they did to you, sleeping with you.' I said, 'OK'. Then I said, 'my religion says it's not right to kill somebody'. She said to me if I don't know the baby's father, it's my own decision, I have to make that decision, no one can make it for me. I said, 'it's not right, but what am I going to tell the baby when he grow up? About his father.' At least I knew my father. I won't see him again, but I knew him.

I'm trying not to think about the past. If I think about the past, I will hate the baby. I am trying to get love for him. If I give the baby away, I have to sign a paper and I can never have the baby back again. Then I said, 'OK'. My mum didn't give me away. Claudette, my social worker, said the baby don't deserve that. She will come with me to the hospital when I have the baby. If I give the baby away, they are going to treat the baby the same like they did to me and I don't want that. I'm going to be there, swallow the pain and say the baby will be my baby. I wish good for him. When he grow up, I will be there strong to tell him the history of what happened. I don't think about the baby any more because it's mine. I'll take it home. I won't give the baby away.

The social worker said to me the last time, one day I am going to be on my own. She said she won't always be with me. She ask me, 'when the baby cry what are you doing with the baby?' I say, 'I tell the baby not to cry'. She said, 'no way. You have to raise the baby up, give the baby food, pat the baby to sleep, check the baby nappy'. I ask, 'why the baby going to cry without me doing nothing?' She says, 'if you don't be careful, if you don't look after the baby, in this country they take the baby from you'. I say, 'I'll try.'

When I was in Maria's house, I found out that I was pregnant. She asked how many month? I said, 'I don't know, I was having my period but then it got cut off'. I first saw Maria when I was on the street and I said to her, 'give me money'. And she said, 'what are you doing here?' I said nothing. She said, 'you are so young, what are you doing on the street?' I told her, 'nothing, I just need money.' She asked me where I was from. 'Africa'. 'Where in Africa?' 'Sierra Leone.' Then I started to move because she started to ask me a lot of things. She said, 'follow me'. I asked, 'where we going?' If I stand there, she stand there, if I move, she move. I said, 'what do you want?' She said, 'you are not allowed to beg in the street'. She said I should live in a house and go to school. I said, 'I don't go to school and I don't read, I don't write. People come and pretend to me, but everybody is bad.' She said, 'what are you talking about?' I said, 'I don't want tell nobody my things. I just want to be left alone.' She said, 'you know, I have got children like you'. I said, 'are you a mother?' She said 'yes'. Then I started to come closer again. Maybe it be OK this time. She said, 'I got three girls. Come with me.' I said, 'no way, I'm not going nobody's house because when you're going their house, they're going to change.' It was Friday. She said, 'this is the weekend, I can't do nothing. On Monday I'll take you somewhere. It's my job to find children in the street. I'm not going to keep you in my house.' I take a chance and I follow her.

Then I come in her house. She give me clothes. She show me the bathroom. She told me to go and have a shower. She give me food. Then she ask me again, 'how did you come into this country?' I said, 'somebody brought me here'. She asked me about my passport. I said, 'what's that?' I don't go to school so I know nothing about that stuff, just that the lady, Farah, took me to get my picture. Maria took me to the Refugee Council on Monday, where I go now. On Saturday and Sunday, I stay in her house. I meet her children. One is tall like me. They were nice. The mum said, 'this is Naomi, she don't have nobody in this country, so she is with us'. At the Refugee Council, they ask me, how did I get here, where's my passport? I said, 'the lady who brought me from Africa just give me luggage in my hand, she don't give me nothing. I think the lady have two book in her hand. I don't know. Is that what you call passport?' After these questions, the next day Maria take me to the office where the social worker was working.

Mohammed Sesay, the manager of the Unaccompanied Minors team where Naomi ended up, tells me that he happened to be in the reception area that morning and he remembers Naomi telling him that Maria from Peckham had driven her there. But Maria had disappeared by the time he popped out to look for her. When he checked the video cameras to see if they had got a record of her car and number plate, he was told that as it was early in the morning they had not yet put a tape in. The manager was puzzled. He had never come across anyone called Maria whose 'job' it was to pick up homeless children and he feels he would have as they are both working in the same field. And if Maria was legit., why did she drive away? This is usually the modus operandi of people-

smugglers, where a smuggler has been paid to bring someone into the country illegally for a sum of money and the person is then abandoned at a place where they are likely to find help. However the manager feels that Naomi does not have the guile to lie. Perhaps Maria is simply a good soul who feels the urge to help but does not want to be caught up in the inevitable bureaucracy and questioning that would take place if she had waited with Naomi.

Unaccompanied Minors teams were set up in social service departments of local authorities, especially those that are near ports of entry, as a result of the Children Act (1989). The Southwark team, who are looking after Naomi, was set up in 1999/2000 as part of a second wave, in recognition of the fact that local authorities, such as Hillingdon, Croydon, Kent and Liverpool, were unable to cope with disproportionate numbers of unaccompanied children. There is now a rota system in place and the Home Office refers children by turn to authorities across London and the south-east. There are two types of support which these teams are empowered, by the Children Act, to give children under their care. Section 17 provides subsistence and accommodation assistance, while Section 20 provides, in addition to this, an allocated social worker, regular reviews to ensure other needs are being met, and support, such as health and education. Southwark has 105 unaccompanied minors in its care and all of them receive Section 20 support, which is not always the case with other local authorities.

Then I had a scan and it show me how many weeks I was pregnant. (*I ask her why the scan took place in August when she knew she was pregnant in April.*) The social worker told me it had to be step by step. I have to finish with the Home Office first. I cannot go to hospital until then. I ask them, 'what is Home Office?' They said, 'it's a big office, they have to know that you are in this country and how you got here because you are not allowed to be here. So you have to go there and then they will make their decision.' My social worker was trying to take details from me to take to the Home Office. She told me when you come to this country you have to have asylum. Some people come

113 | I SAID OK

and study, some people come and work, they were naming things what people came here for.

One week before I go to Home Office, they told me the social worker is going to do an assessment. I don't know what it is so I go and do an assessment. The social worker assess me for a week. They write my answers on a piece of paper and I have to take that paper to the Home Office. A lady from the Refugee Council was taking me everywhere. She would give me map and bus number and write something on the paper and then I would stop someone and ask for help and they would tell me get off here. Sometimes I take the train from the wrong side. I show people the paper. I count the stops on my fingers. I ask people how many stops. I just got lost. Then they asked me same questions at the Home Office – how did you get here?

I told them. A Lebanese lady, Missus Farah, bring me here. There was a war in my country. It was in the night in my village called Makeni (*the capital of Northern Province*). I was sleeping. I heard people screaming and guns and like something's falling, they're shooting and shouting. Oh my baby, oh my daughter... people are saying different, different things. They're banging on the tin door. My daddy told me something's going on. They're fighting. Little children like me was crying. I opened the door. And I watch. Then my neighbour come to the door. She said they're coming. The noise and gunshot were getting closer. So I have to run. But my dad couldn't make it. My dad was sick. He could not stand up. I don't know what was wrong with him. We didn't have money for the hospital. Maybe they could've made him better. I think I was seven or eight. I asked him what I should do. 'You just go, I'll come.' He said I should go with the neighbour. I called her aunty. She had four children.

We left with nothing. We reached another village. I remember thinking that I had to be strong because I had nobody. I sleep in the grass. Short, short grass. The grass was scratching my body. I sleep easily but if I hear any sound, I wake up. I remember the rain was coming. All my clothes were wet but we still had to sit there. I would cover my face with leaf, leaf, leaf, so if somebody's coming, they can see nothing. Just have to be quiet. It might have been two weeks, I don't know, I don't count days. You get monkeys and birds in the bush. The adults would go and dig, like, cassava, for us. I didn't know how to cook it but some people were very nice. If they saw that you had nobody they would feed you. We would eat anything that we could find.

Then I go back with the neighbours who want to go and check if it was safe to return to the village. I went to look for my daddy but I couldn't find the house anywhere. Still there's shooting going on. People were saying that they were catching people and putting them in their house and burning them in it. My father was burned inside the house. When I lost him, I feel like I lost everything. My neighbours had nowhere to go so they asked me to go with them to Freetown. It was very far.

I remember a very, very hard walk. My feet were swelling and I got a cut in my leg, a thorn tore my flesh when I put my foot in somewhere deep like peat while we were running. I couldn't stop. So I just found a piece of cloth and tied the sore. I don't know what cut it because it is like bush. Thank God I got healed. I just left it like that because there was no way of getting medicine. Then some people put us in a truck. When we reached Freetown, it was dark. The neighbour said to me, 'there is no more help, everybody has to go on his own'. Sometimes I think it was not the neighbour. They would not leave me on the street like this. I don't know. I can't remember. I sleep on the street. I had to find a place, anywhere, and lie down. I was wearing a top and a skirt but I had nothing on my feet, I had been walking with no shoes.

Then I watch – there's nobody again, only me. (*She closes her eyes and big tear drops streak down her cheeks. She weeps silently.*) I was living in the street, begging people for money, begging for food. Lots of people would be in the street in the evening. I would say *kushe*, hello, please can I have some money? Some people said, 'what do you want?', (*she raises her voice*) 'move from here, go to your parents'. I tell them, 'please I'm hungry'. Some people buy you food. Give you bread. I keep some in my hand, and eat it later. Some people will give you money. Then I'd go and buy rice. If I can, I eat rice with some fish in sauce. If I want to beg from you, I will come up behind you. I will tap you on the arm. I'll be crying. If you don't give me money, I will tell you, you're wicked. Then I will change place where I am begging because there will be somebody who doesn't want to give me money who will see me again and they'll say 'you always beg'.

I don't know how much I earned. If I had some coins, I would go and buy something to eat. When I had money I don't buy nothing, just food. I didn't understand money. If I want to buy something, the man will tell me, 'no it's not enough'. If I have more, I will give him more, maybe he will sell me what I want. I don't know how much I need to give him. I used to go to a shop where they used to cook and sell the food. Maybe somebody will leave food on their plate. I will take it and eat. (*She says the word 'eat' with real passion.*)

There were a lot of children in the street like me. Some of them had parents. I made friends with younger children. We just roamed about. We didn't beg all day – when my stomach was full, I'd stop begging because I'd eaten. Some people would give us each some food or coins, one by one, but others would say you must share, then there would be a fight. Sometimes older children would take my money. They said they would beat me up if I didn't give them the money, so I just gave it to them. Even though I was tall, it didn't stop the other children fighting me. They would say, 'she just tall, she just a big fool. I'm not scared of you.' They hit me. They would say 'fuck off'. It's better to go on your own.

When I finished for the day, I would look for a place to sleep. Sometimes I would sleep in the market on the tables. Before going to bed, we played in the streets at night. Sometimes I wished the other kids were my sisters and brothers, then they would care about me and look out for me. I would say to God, please help me, save my life. I am going to bed now, please show me the way to live. My dad told me to pray. He says to me you are a Christian from the Limba tribe. And when I woke up in the morning, I would give thanks for letting me see another day. That's what my father say to me – when you wake up you have to say thanks. My language is the language of the Limba people, but I was young when we left Makeni and I've forgotten it. Everybody speaks Krio. But if somebody speaks my language I can hear it, and some words of Arabic too.

I never washed, I was just dirty on the street with one set of clothes. There was a tap, but that was for drinking. We would do toilet where there was not many people. It was very hard. I remember it was raining a lot and we would have to find cover. Once I was laying down on the ground, people were running up and down trying to find somewhere to stay. Then I heard shooting. There were men with guns, they didn't have uniforms like soldiers, they catch somebody and burned him. They put a tyre round him and set it on fire. I ran. I wanted to move on, away from this place.

It's hard to establish how long Naomi was on the streets. I ask her if she remembers an annual event like the Christmas holidays? Would Freetown look different at that time? She nods. She says the people tie coloured ribbons to the tree branches at Christmas, but she can't remember precisely how many times she has seen this. She is struggling to remember, then she decides she only saw this once when she was on the streets. I ask her if she remembers a lot of fighting in the streets in Freetown one month after her tenth birthday in January 1999. She can't remember. I checked out various news items about the outbreak of war in Makeni but there were too many to be able to pinpoint the one that would have affected Naomi. According to news reports, however, there appears to have been a particularly brutal period in February 1998, when she would have been nine, when all the people from Makeni appear to have fled into the bush as a result of the rebels going on the rampage.[1] It is possible that Naomi only spent a few months on the streets.

One day when I was begging from the cars in Freetown, one car stopped in the traffic and there was a white lady inside. She was sitting in the back. She had a black driver. It was better to go to white people.

Black people won't give you money. She said, 'oh, you look pretty, what are you doing on the street?' I asked her, 'can you give me money?' She said, 'to do what?' I said, 'to go and buy food.' 'Where do you live?' she asked. I said 'I live on the street'. She said, 'why?' I told her 'my mum dead, my dad dead'. She said, 'come'. I was scared. She said, 'I won't hurt you'. I can't remember how long I'd been on the streets – many months. I don't know how old I was. Maybe eight or ten. She said, 'come to my house. I will put you in my car'. I had never gone in a car before. I said, 'yeah, I'll come with you'. I'm going in somebody's house from the streets. I was very, very happy with that. She was white, pretty, she had nice clothes. I was thinking, maybe she will make me dress like her. She will take care of me. She will be my parent. She will make me like her. Her name was Farah.

She took me to have a shower. She gave me clothes. She gave me soap. There was a tap in the compound. I had a shower there. Then she showed me round: 'this is the house'. It was a nice house. I never saw a house like that in my whole life. So clean. She had mirrors. When I have my shower, I go in front of the mirror and see myself – 'you look nice', I say. In the village we didn't have a mirror. I never seen my face. Sometimes when you go in fresh water, you can see your face there. When I was on the streets, I was wearing a small *lappa*, not the big one. You tie a cloth around your waist with a blouse on top. I did not have breasts so I didn't cover. When I was with my father, I wear only underwear. When I come to these people's house, they told me, no, I am not allowed to dress like this. I had only one set of clothes, but they throw them, I didn't find the clothes again. They bring a boy to cut my hair. My hair was knot, knot, knot.

The house was big. They had two bedrooms, a sitting-room, a dining-room, kitchen and bathroom. They had somebody to sweep the compound and somebody to drive the car. They were all black. They had a soldier with a gun to look after the door. (*It sounded like they paid rebel soldiers to guard the flat.*) Soldiers want money, they want food. They cooked for themselves. I didn't have to cook for them. From the window, I saw soldiers on the street with guns. They were wearing green clothes, their faces were painted black, they were shouting in Krio. I could hear the sound of shooting – po, po. People were carrying their things on their head and running. People are scared because the soldiers are violent – they cut off your hands or your legs. Sometimes there was shooting in the night, soldiers would come into the house and tell us to lie down on the floor. Men with guns would come and the Lebanese family would give them money to make them go, but they would still come back and steal the car.

Missus Farah said, 'I'll teach you how to do things – how to tidy up, work. You live here.' I told her 'OK'. I was sleeping on a cloth in the same room as the baby, Rachelle. I don't know how old she was – she could sit and crawl, but she couldn't walk. She teach me to look after the little girl. If the baby wake up at night, Missus Farah come and wake me to give the baby food or, if it was wet, to change the clothes, or to try and put her back to sleep. Every night the baby would wake up, sometimes once, sometimes it would cry all the time. I didn't know what it wanted, but the mum would come and tell me to give her food. I would be tired. I don't know what time I started working in the morning. I would be sleeping. It would be dark. She would come and wake me to do some work. But it was better than being on the street. In the morning, I would tidy the house, sweep, clean the house, the kitchen, wash the dishes, wash the clothes, all by hand. Work, work, work all day.

In the beginning she was nice to me. But later, no way. She didn't give me any money. I was not allowed to go out and she never took me out. When she went out, she would bring other black people like me who were working in other people's houses to sit with me. I learned things from them – these were Lebanese people and their language is called Arab. I used to call her 'missus' and I called her husband 'master'. She would raise her hand and hit me if I broke something. She'd slap me or cuss me – 'that's why you ended up on the street' – she regretted the day she bring me from the streets. She said I was no good, that's why my parents died. '*Basta pikin we no yeri in mam in wod, na trit go men am*', she would shout, a bastard child who doesn't listen to its mother will be brought up by the street. She would call me bastard, *pikin*. For no reason. I would just sit, crying every day. When her husband come back, it's the same. They treated me like I was different from them.

She teach me to cook. The way the Lebanese people cook their lamb with garlic, they call it *kuzbara*, that's the way they teach me. It was hard for me to eat because I don't know the food. But when you are starving, you just give it a try. They don't eat pepper. But I like pepper in my food. When they had eaten, they would give me what was left – bread, or rice, maybe a little sauce with it. In the morning, I would be working before they let me eat. Sometimes they would give me food two times a day. Just depends. I couldn't take anything. You had to wait till they give you it. If I was hungry and if I asked her for food, she would say, 'you're just sitting here to eat, go and work first'. So if the baby left her food, I would take that and eat it. Sometimes they would leave food on the plate and when I took it to wash, I would eat what was on the plate. I was hungry. I still preferred being in her house than on the streets.

The Lebanese community is 4,000 strong and dominates the diamond industry in Sierra Leone.[2] Siaka Stevens, who became Prime Minister (later President) in 1967, emerged out of a corrupt elite, which included the Lebanese merchant community, who became his partners in criminalizing the diamond industry. There is evidence to suggest that the Lebanese have helped to finance the activities of Hezbollah back home.

Sometimes I would talk to the baby. But when the mother got annoyed and shouted at me, I would make an angry face at the baby and be horrible to her. If she smacked me for no reason, I would shout at the baby and say 'your mummy is being horrible to me. Don't watch me!' But the baby would just smile and come closer. The baby didn't know – it wasn't her fault, so then I would forget my anger and I'd play with her again. In the evening, if the baby was there with missus, then I was allowed in the living-room to watch TV. If not, they would say, 'go to your room or go sit in the kitchen'. When the baby went to sleep, they would tell me to iron the baby things. Then I could go to bed. I was always thinking about running away, but somebody was always at the gate with a gun. I was not allowed to go to the gate anyway.

One day, she told me that she will take me to get my picture – now they tell me this was for passport, but I didn't know then. She took me in the car. It was only the second time I went in that car after she brought me home in it. I was very happy. That was my first picture. Where she took me was run by black people and they showed my picture to me. I thought I looked nice. 'Is that me?' I asked. The lady said, 'yeah'. I said 'OK then'. She said to me, 'we're going somewhere on a trip'. I didn't ask where. I had been at her house for a long time by now, and never stepped outside. I was growing up, I had even started to get breasts. I was surprised. Wow! I am getting like other people. When I was little I was stuffing other clothes in my top to see how it look.

We try and work out exactly how long Naomi had been living with this Lebanese family; the age of the baby makes a good benchmark. By the time she left, the baby was talking in full sentences but still not toilet-trained and not going to school or nursery. Making allowances for different cultural practices in child-rearing, the child was probably no older than four. Did they have birthday parties for the baby? Did she count the candles on the cake? She doesn't know. She had to sit in the kitchen when anybody came to visit. Naomi came to this country in January 2005 just after she had turned fifteen. We agree that she must have worked for them for a maximum of three-and-a-half years, which means she must have been eleven when she came off the streets.

You know you cannot ask people too many questions. Any time they tell me to do something, I just follow them and go. She said to pack three sets of clothes, put them in plastic and put them in her bag. She made me a new dress for the journey. Somebody fix my hair for me. That was the first time a person came in her house to do my plaits. My hair was growing. When she wanted to cut my hair again, I didn't agree. When the other girls came to be with me when the lady went out, they told me I have to be strong and say no. When Missus Farah asked me who filled your head with ideas, I told her nobody. She hit me. I was scared. Then she go and get me cream, you have to put it in the hair to make it soft. My hair was hard. Sometimes if I begged those girls who came to the lady's house, they would oil my hair.

She gave me all the bags to carry. And we got on this thing, she said it was called a plane. I said wow. I was happy sitting in the plane. I was thinking, where am I going, but I was scared when it took off. She said, 'don't be scared, there's all the people around you'. I fell asleep and I woke up and it was moving. I didn't go to the toilet. I didn't dare go anywhere. They gave me food. Somebody came and served me. I didn't know how to use knife and fork so I use my hands like normal. Then it come down. She said we have reached where we are going. I said, 'where we are going?' She said, 'this is another country'. She gave me thick clothes and said put this on. It was cold. She said, 'this country is like that, take this bag, let's go'. I still didn't ask her anything. I saw people moving on stairs but they weren't walking. I said wow. I gripped on so that I didn't fall. It just moved with you. I never see that in Africa.

A lot of people got off the plane. I don't know the name of the airport. Nobody came to pick us up at the airport. It was morning. We travelled far from the airport. A man took us in his car, took our things out of the car and dropped us outside a house and went away – she told me this was a taxi. I don't know which town we went to. The house had a kitchen, sitting-room downstairs and a lot of rooms upstairs. They had four rooms to sleep in. The people in the house told me to *gwan*, eat, and 'go to bed, you must be tired'. Then, when I woke up, the new lady sent me in the kitchen and started to show me her house. My Lebanese lady stayed for maybe three days. I thought we had just come for a visit, but she told me that Lubna was her sister and I must work for her. I don't know if she was. She said, 'she's a nice lady, she will look after you and buy you things'. I said 'OK'. 'She is going to pay you but she will save the money for you', she told me. 'You have no parents so you can live in this country.' I told her 'OK'. She had three boys in the house. They were taller than me except for the baby, Karim. I don't know how old they were. They didn't talk to me except when they wanted something like a glass of water or they said 'iron this for me'. I didn't sit with them. I sat in the kitchen.

It seems likely that the Lebanese woman was not a trafficker, in that it was not a regular business, but was bringing Naomi over on a one-off basis. Debbie Ariyo, Founder and Executive Director of Africans Unite Against Child Abuse (AFRUCA), says that the use of child labour in Africa is extensive. Middle-class African families in the UK might bring a child from their extended kinship or friendship networks to provide childcare and do domestic work. The fact that the children do not go to school and work from morning to night is not even seen as abuse. A large part of AFRUCA's work concentrates on raising awareness among African communities in the UK of what constitutes abuse and in Africa against the notion of a 'better life', which often convinces parents to let their children go to the UK. According to the 2001 census, there are over 587,000 Africans in the UK, with 78 per cent living in London. They are the fastest-growing ethnic group and that is reflected in the increase in numbers of trafficked children. Children are trafficked from Africa predominantly for domestic labour and sometimes for sexual slavery or benefit fraud.[3]

At first, things were fine. They would wake me up very, very early in the morning to start work. They had two sitting-rooms. I had to tidy up the whole house – so much work again and only me. They showed me how to use hoover because in Africa we sweep. I would put clothes for washing in the machine. That is the only difference – I didn't have to wash by hand. Everywhere you go, they make you work, work, work. There were a lot of clothes, and it was very tiring. They gave me a foam mat to sleep on, to put on the floor in the same room as the baby. I had to look after the baby again in the night. Sometimes it would sleep. If he woke up, I would try very hard to make him go to sleep because I was so tired from standing up in the kitchen, washing dishes and tidying up all day. I did the same job. I had to put food on the table before they woke up. I didn't have problem with the children and the man, they were OK. The children would leave after they had eaten, maybe to go to school, I don't know. I was too scared to ask questions. It was very lonely in the house.

If somebody came and knocked at the door, they'd say to me, 'go, go quick. Hide! Run!' Making me like a thief. 'Don't come down', they'd say. They wouldn't call me to come down until the visitor had left. If there were people coming around, they would make me work very fast, wake me up early to tidy up before they came. If I was in the kitchen, Lubna pulled the blinds down so I couldn't be seen. They locked me in when they went out – I wasn't allowed out of the house. When I was with Missus Farah in Africa, she don't do that to me. She'd close the door, she'd tell me not to go out but be in the compound. But here there's no compound. I was thinking in my head, why are they doing this? One day she told me that in this country you are not allowed to be in the street, the police will catch you. I thought in Africa the police will only catch you if you are a thief. Why is she telling me this? I said, 'OK, I am not going out'. 'If somebody knocks, you're not allowed to open the door.' I said 'OK'. 'If the phone rings, you're not allowed to answer.' I said 'OK'. If I broke something, she would hit me, tell me I am a fool, using bad words. If I'm scared of people, I shake, and sometimes, something would just fall from my hand. She would come, 'breaking things in this house? What happened to you?' I would say 'sorry'. 'Is that all you can say?' She didn't leave any bruises. I was scared of her. She say to me, 'that's why you have no parents, the way you behave'. I thought why do these people go on about my parents?

One day I saw the key in the door. They don't leave the key in there. I was thinking, if I open the door and they see me there will be big trouble. Or if I go outside and the police catch me, what am I going to say to them? I didn't steal anything. I will tell them what they're doing to me in the house. I turned the key, I opened the door quietly (*her voice becomes conspiratorial*). I don't think I even shut the door properly. The lady and her husband were sleeping in the sitting-room after a party had finished. Maybe they had too much to drink. I know nothing about what they're doing. It was not very dark outside, but it was cold. In the house, she used to give me something thick to wear because I was cold. I had my slippers on, but no socks. It was before Christmas. I ran. I cannot remember the area. I didn't know where I was going, I was just going. It was a big road, lots of cars, moving up and down. I stopped. I had gone about five to ten minutes down the street. I was crying. I tried to find a place to hide where no one could see me. In the corner.

Then I saw somebody come up to me. This one guy asked me, 'what are you doing there, why are you crying?' He's a black man. Tall. Dressed up. He speak English first, 'what happened to you?' I didn't respond. 'What happened to you?' I said nothing. Then he said to me, 'are you from Sierra Leone?' I say, 'yes', then he start speaking to me in Krio, saying 'you're from the same country like me'. I say 'OK'. I got a smiling face now. I speak Krio, even to the Lebanese. 'How your body?' he ask. I tell him I fine. *Weytin na yu neym?* What's your name? He said, 'what did you cry for?' I said, 'I don't want no talk'. He said, 'why, tell me'. I said 'somebody bring me to this country. I know nothing about this country. I know nobody.' He tell me, 'OK, come with me, I'm gonna take care of you.' I remembered that this lady said she will take care of me, now this man says he will take care of me. Then I got confused. I don't know where to go.

Naomi goes into a long and deep silence.

He was a grown man, not a boy. His name was Alesine. He took me to his house. I didn't have anything with me, just what I was wearing. We got in a train to Bermiya*. He took me shopping. For the first time somebody bought me clothes. I chose trousers and shoes. He was

* Birmingham

living in the city centre in a flat with one room, a kitchen and toilet. He used to take me shopping to the Bull Ring. They have lots of different, different things. It's a very big building and there was a market where we used to go and buy fish, meat. Things were fine. He told me, 'don't go out, stay in the house. There's food here, everything you want.' He was nice, and sometimes we laughed too or went out walking in the streets. I cooked – I know how to cook now. I used to clean the house and do all the work just like for the other family. I don't know if he had a job. He would just come and go, but it wasn't the same every day. Sometimes he'd be in the house. I don't ask questions because people don't like it. That is my big problem.

Naomi has developed a habit of not asking questions because she feels, as a result of her experiences, that it is not her place to do so. In the most simple ways, this impacts on her life and her ability to take control of it. I ask her if she remembers my name. She doesn't. I say 'what will you do if you tell someone that your story is going to appear in a book and they ask you for the name of the writer?' She says she was going to ask me to write my name down on a piece of paper at the end of the interviews. I say 'that's good, just to know gives you power. You can take control of your life.' She didn't in the end ask for my name.

Where she lives in Bermondsey, she only ever turns left when she comes out of the house. When we turn right in search of a restaurant and walk towards the station, a ten-minute walk from her house, she is filled with wonder. She didn't know she lived so close to the trains. She only ever takes the bus. She tells her flat-mate about her discovery and is somewhat miffed when the flat-mate says she knows.

It's always the same when I go out. I go the way I know, I don't want to get lost or end up somewhere dangerous or difficult. I am trying to be more normal now, asking if I don't know. Before, when somebody said something to me, I'd cry. I let it go. I close my eyes and let the tears fall and I say, OK, they've done this to me, OK, I'll go. I'll have courage, I'll be strong. Alesine knew that I couldn't read or write. I told him I never went to school. I didn't speak any English and he would tell me what to say. He used to tell me how to say hello to people, what do you want? Sometimes when we would sit quiet, he would teach me how to write because I couldn't hold the pen. He was holding the pen with me and he'd write with me. I can copy the letter but my handwriting doesn't look like this (*pointing to a printed sheet*). Every day I would copy out letters. When we finished eating, we would switch off the TV. I was happy that I found someone who showed me how to write. I can pick things up from people. I'm quick, I don't struggle to learn things from people. I wanted to be with him, but when he went out I was happy. I can live better with nobody.

Then he just changed. People are always nice at the beginning, then later… they're horrible to me. He don't go to Church, he don't take me to Church. We had one bed, I was sleeping on one bed with a man, but at first he don't do nothing to me. I was fifteen, but he never asked me my age. Then one night he said 'you have to sleep with me'. I said 'what do you mean?' I had been there for one month by then.

I didn't know anything about that. Nothing. I had nobody to ask. Yeah, the street children talked. But they didn't know anything because they didn't do it. I saw things on TV but I didn't really think about it. When I lived with the Lebanese people in Freetown, they say that only when you are married you can have a husband and you can sleep in one room. Then I say 'OK'. I never forgot that. There was a black woman coming to their house who told me about periods. One day I was just sitting down and my tummy was paining me. The lady said, 'I will bring somebody in the house and you can tell her what is going on with you.' She is the one who told me they call it a period. I ask 'what is that?' She teach me how to use cotton cloth. To put it in your underwear so you rub on to it and when I finish I wash it and dry it and pack it to use again. She told me that it will come every month and that if I sleep with any man, I will get like baby in my tummy. 'How come?' I said. 'That's what happen when you sleep with a man.' I got scared. She told me that before you get a baby you have to marry. I said 'yeah?' She said, 'yeah'. She said 'because you're

Christian, it's not right'. I said, 'I don't want baby.' I learned something from her.

*Today Naomi speaks even more haltingly than usual. She lays her head
on the table and says that her stomach is hurting. I ask if she needs to go
to the hospital and if she would like to cut short the interview but
she says no to both. We continue but she speaks in a hardly audible
monotone.*

But in Alesine's house there was some cassette he was showing me.
Men and women doing things. He told me that's what we have to do.
How to be with men, I learned from him. He put the cassette on. I
saw what they're doing. He said 'watch, you can see they're playing
with each other'. Then he would sit beside me and start to play with
me. I told him it was not right. I said, 'I will have baby in my tummy'.
He say, 'it's not true. Look at those women on the film, they don't
have a baby.' I say 'it's true' but I still say no. Then he said, 'OK, you
will go and live outside on the street. I will drive you back.' Then
later… I sleep with him. It was painful. I bleed. Because I was crying,
he told me 'don't cry. It's going to be OK'. He sleep with me two times
before he brought the men to the house. He don't use a condom. I
don't know what condom is. When they took me to hospital, they ask
me about it and I said 'what is that?' They show us in a group how to
use it. I remember I saw it in the street in Freetown. I used to pick it
up and blow it like a balloon. He started to bring men in the house.
I don't know if they were his friends. They don't use condoms. He
told me, this country is not easy. If I sleep with men, they will give me
money.

The first one, he started to touch my body. I said to him, 'don't do
that, it's not right'. Then he spoke to Alesine who told me that I have
to sleep with the man. I don't know how much money they give me.
I can't count. They give it all to him. Because I'm living in his house.
I'm not working and I'm bringing no money. He has to buy food.
I don't know where the men were from. You don't talk with them.

Alesine would be there in the house, outside the room. Sometimes one man would come, sometimes two – not together inside the room, one would wait outside. It would not take long but I didn't watch the clock.

I ask her if she had to do a blow-job. She doesn't know the word. I realize how embarrassing it is when you can't use the usual euphemisms. Just as I am about to say never mind, she latches on.

Yeah. They were doing this same thing in the cassette. Go down and take the thing from the man and put it in your mouth. He told me to do it to the others because they're paying me money. I don't like to talk about that. I can't remember how many men I had to sleep with. There were a lot of them. Sometimes the same ones would come again, sometimes there were different people. After that he didn't sleep with me again. He didn't take me out again. He didn't teach me to write again. I asked him 'why you are doing this to me?' He said, oh, this is the only way he can help me.

She squeezes her eyes shut and weeps her large, silent tears.

I was thinking where will I live if I don't do this. I was thinking about living on the street, but here not everybody is black. OK, then I better do it. But this happened over and over. It's not right. I was using my body for money. I told him that if I went in the street like I used to do in my country and begged from people, if I did it here, I'm just going to be dead. He said, 'where you going to live?' I said, 'anywhere, in the street'. He said, 'this is not Africa'. I said, 'I don't know what is Africa and what is Europe, so I'm going.' He said to me, 'fine. You will never be able to come back to me again if you go. But if you want to go, go.'

The ease with which he let her go seems strange considering that he was making money from her. Perhaps he thought an unco-operative girl was bad for business and there were plenty of other fish in the sea.

*

I told him, 'if the men come, I'm not going to do it'. He was shouting 'if you don't do it, you're not going to stay in the house'. I said 'OK then, I'm going'. The last time he brought a man, I started to scream, 'lef me, leave me alone'. Then Alesine started to fight me. That man said 'leave her, leave her, she's screaming'. I said, 'it's not right. You have to be married'. I was banging, banging in the house and breaking everything. I don't care what I'm doing. Anything can happen now. It's better if I'm dead. I screamed, then he got scared. When I have been so soft, saying 'no, no, no', that's when people do things to me. That made me learn things. He said, 'you did not talk before'. I said, 'you showed me how to be strong'. When I vexed, I come in my room and close the door. I'll just be on my own. After a few days I'll be OK. But this time I screamed.

Then I don't cook for him, I don't talk to him, I don't sleep with him in his bed, I put cloth on the ground and I lie down. If he gives me something, I don't want it. I stopped eating. I said it was much better for me to be dead, not to be in this world. This went on for two days. Then he said 'if you want to go, you can go'. I said, 'my life will be better without people. I'll be strong.' He said nothing. He just watched me.

I didn't go to police. In my country, if you go to the police and they hold you, they treat you bad, they beat you up, kick you, do bad, bad things. I was scared that they would do the same to me here. I didn't know the address where Alesine was living. But now I know my rights, nobody will do that to me again. He give me money to buy my ticket for the bus, and I had some change from it, some coins. He said I can't take anything with me. I told him I think people are all the same. Everybody's bad. They say 'Naomi, come I will help you' but they're wicked to me.

The journey took a long time. I sleep. I wake. This was in February, so I had been about three months in Bermiya. He dropped me off in the morning and when I got to London, it was still light. I didn't know where I was. I asked the driver and he told me this was the last station. I followed the people when I got down from the coach. I asked where there were a lot of buses and they showed me where the bus garage was. I didn't have enough money so I begged the people to give me coins. I took a bus, but I didn't know where it was going. I could read the numbers 1, 2 and 3 by then, but I don't remember which ones were on the bus. I give money. I tell them that I want to go out of the main town. They give me a ticket. The plan I had was to go to the people I was living with. I preferred slavery to those men treating me like that. I knew they lived very far so I was thinking if I sit in the bus and go very, very far, I might find their house. I stayed on the street for three days and started begging money. I would find a hiding-place and sleep there. It might be some corner. I was not feeling that cold because my clothes were thick, I was wearing something double. I beg money and go and buy food. The same as I used to do in Freetown. Some people give you money.

This was when I saw Maria. I came to her house. I told her I haven't had my period. She told me to bring my pee, I gave her my pee and she told me I was pregnant. She ask me about father. I say 'I don't know who the baby's father is'. When I have my baby, what I am thinking is that I would like to introduce baby, this is your... but I don't have no family. I can find out more about that. I have just real-ized that. I know my dad's name, Joseph, and I know my second name and my mum's name is Mariamma. Maybe I have grandparents or uncles and aunties, but I don't know because I never met them. I could try to find them. There were a lot of people in Makeni but it was not a very big place. I don't know because I was only allowed to play with the neighbour's children. As I don't walk around, I couldn't tell how big the village was. My dad didn't have money to send me to school. I am the first-born of my mother. What happened was that my mum was pregnant with her second child. When she was having the baby, she died. I don't know how old I was. I don't remember much about my mum, only what my dad told me. I don't think she went to hospital, otherwise she wouldn't have died. I don't think she had the money for that. Someone would have come to the hut to help her have the baby.

I lived with my dad and the neighbours looked after me. I would do work for them and they would give me food. Everybody went in the bush to find sticks of wood for cooking. I'd follow them. When I was with the neighbours, I went with their children. I'd bring fresh water and help them cook. We had to go very, very far to bring water. Sometimes the water in the well would not be clean so you had to go to another place. There were many wells. Or you had to sit down and wait for the water to come. Sometimes it would be packed because you have to make a line to get water, you put your pots in line, then you walk, walk, walk to another place. We used to play, we were running as we went along so I don't know how far we walked. People would tell you to go to another well where it was not busy. Sometimes you go in the morning and, if you're not careful, you might come home in the afternoon or late in the night because it's not easy to get water. I would carry a plastic bucket full of water. For me and my dad, maybe I go two times a day. You need water to drink and you have to give the neighbour some to cook. To wash our clothes we would go to this big river. We wash our body, we wash our things. Washed clothes would be heavy. You have to struggle with them but you have to do them.

We eat in my neighbour's house, in the hut next to us. We used the same kitchen because we cook outside. We would eat rice. Sometimes we would eat fish, sometimes there was no money so we would just boil things together. When we had fish, it was only one small fish each about the size of my finger. We didn't live by the sea. The fish came mostly from the city and we would buy it in the market. I will eat chicken sometimes when it's a holiday. Or when a chicken is sick, and is going to die, then we kill it and eat it. We cook it with cassava leaves. Sometimes we would climb a mango tree and get mangoes or papaw and other fruits.

I ask Naomi to draw her house for me because she cannot describe it. She says she can't draw and recoils from the pen and paper as if they will turn on her. I draw a house and a car to encourage her but to no avail.

There were no walls. The door was made out of tin. Everything was made out of tin, the top was made with grass. The ground was just ground. I slept on a piece of cloth. There was no running water, no electricity. We had no lamp. We wake up when the sun come up and we sleep when it's dark. When we have no money to buy candles, we just sleep like that.

We used to play hide-and-seek. And the six cup game, I love that game. You put six stones in a pile and knock it down with a ball. We use an orange for the ball, then run and hide. The other team have to catch the orange and throw it at me. If it touches me, then they have to play. If it didn't touch me, then I will try and come back and pack the cup the way it was. If I pack it, then I can play again. We used to play another game. We stand opposite each other, whatever I do you have to do it. If you do the same like me, then you can play. I keep changing my leg so you have to get it right. The neighbours would plait my hair. I can't remember them very much. It was a big family. I used to play with a little girl. She must have grown up by now. She might not even be alive. I was OK that time.

My dad was tall. When I became tall and big and strong, I knew that I looked like him. I don't have any pictures. I have nothing. My dad told me 'you look like your mum'. He would tell me stories about how my mum died when she was going to have a second baby. My dad was strict with me but he didn't want me to feel like I don't have a mum. He used to work on a farm planting rice sometimes, groundnuts sometimes, depending on the weather. I don't know if it was his land. I don't have any idea about land and things like that.

There is one fruit we were eating in Africa. We call it *kushu* (*probably another name for cashew*), a fruit on the top and a seed at the bottom, it grows on a tree. Sometimes it's sweet and sometimes sour – we'd use it to draw on our bodies. One time, nobody was around. This girl put the seed in the fire. Not me. A girl who could read and write, older than me. The seed roasted. Then you take a stick, put it in the seed and mark the skin. It makes a wound on your skin – not a cut but a sore. I have these marks on my body, and I found out later it is the letters of my name. (*Like a fading black tattoo, her initials have been inscribed into her upper arm. It reminds her of the shape of the letters when she has to sign something.*) She told me that you are not allowed to scratch it even though it was itching. I had to keep it from my dad, not to say. If he found out, he'd be angry and beat me up for that. My dad had cut, cut, cut on his face from his tribe. But he didn't do it to me. 'Why I do this', my dad say.

I feel so shy wherever I go because I can't even write my name. When you ask people something, they will give you paper, with letters on it, to look at. I will look at the letters but what do they stand for, I don't know. When I sign a paper, I don't know why I am signing it. I want to go to school. I want to learn. For a long time that has been the dream I was crying for. Some people, they can use a pen. For me, I can't. I wish everyone could have the opportunity to go to school. When you go to school, you learn to ask questions. Before I do something, I want to know why and what is that? I'll never do something again just like that.

I go for classes now. In my first lesson the lady asked me if I know how many months make a year, how many days make a week. I said 'no'. So she told me from Monday to Sunday, from January to December. I go over and over in my head before I go to bed. Sometimes I will come and sit at this table and copy them. This girl who lives here, sometimes at night, she comes and sits with me and I ask her for help. Be honest with you, sometimes I'm too shy.

I ask her to trace everything she has learned as far back as she can remember. For example how did she know how old she was?

When I lived with my parent, every time my birthday used to come, my father used to tell me: December is your birthday. That's always in my head. 17 December. He said, 'you can help yourself, anywhere you go, you can tell people'. Then he told me the year was one, nine, eight, nine, in my Limba language. Sometimes I will ask people, which month are we? I can hear people say, 'this is December'. I will try and keep it in my head.

Every Tuesday I go to a foster family. My social worker says to me, 'don't stay alone in the house'. When I'm alone, I find myself crying. The last few days, I am happier to be on my own. But I'm trying to go out and make friends and come out from the life that I have been living. They do games. All of us wrote our names and put them in a box. Each name was pulled out and the person got a present. I got a book. I want to read the book. That's my dream. I don't know anything about the book, but I play with the book. It is in my room as decoration.

When I got papers from Home Office, I didn't know what they were. They gave me lots of papers. Keep them, you have to appeal. It has my photograph. I put it separate in a different envelope. Before I turn eighteen I have to take them back to my lawyer. The social worker will take it if it's an important letter, or if it has an appointment she'll write the date down and count the days and say it will be the week after this week. When I go shopping, I sometimes take the girl in my house with me and she will help me to find the things I want. Sometimes I can tell from the picture or the colours on the packet. I'll pick what I want and go to the girls at the till and give them the money. Now I go to buy water alone. I will give £10 paper and they will give me coins. I will try and check that.

Sometimes I am thinking, maybe my dad escaped from the house. I can't sleep. Like when I moved to this house, I was in this room and I couldn't sleep. I was scared. I was thinking, thinking. Sometimes I can hear people talking, people walking. I'm scared that somebody will snatch me from the room. I just think bad things, that people are after me. My baby is going to be in this room. One thing I've learned – my social worker told me I'm a Christian, I have to pray. I don't have to be scared of anything. She's Christian. She's told God to watch me, nothing will happen to me. My social worker says 'you cannot fight for yourself. You need God to fight for you.' I have a cassette where they are saying prayers and I put it in the tape machine and say it with them. When I finish, I'll sleep. Last night I felt somebody was holding onto me and going to kill me. When I come in this house, this girl was going to Church. I follow her. I feel happy when I've been to Church, I go every Sunday. Lot of black people singing and dancing. I didn't think there was no God. I thought if there's God somewhere, then one day he will save me.

I'm trying not to think of the baby. He's gonna be with me all the time. And I want to learn, go to school. Baby will want me to talk to him. Hope he's not crying, crying. I want quiet. Wish I can have power to help little children like me in the street in Africa so they won't go through what I went through, won't see what I have seen. Thank God for where I am living. I have life. Before I was thinking that there is no hope for me but now I know there is God. And now I know not every-body is wicked.

Her baby was born on 27 September 2006. When I rang to congratulate her, she said, laughing delightedly, 'he's lovely, he hardly cries', but she is finding the responsibility difficult. I had not heard her laugh before. I went to visit her at Christmas with a gift for her son. I think these are the only new clothes he has received. Often during my visits, I would find her hand-washing and drying second-hand baby clothes that she had been given. The room where I had interviewed her before has been converted into their bedroom. It is wide enough to take a single bed and a cot. To lift him out of his cot, she has to clamber onto the foot of her bed, crawl to the front end and kneel on her bed in order to reach him. But her face is etched with the joy of having someone to call her own at last.

Naomi has few friends and fewer resources. When she turns eighteen, in December 2007, her social worker, who is her lifeline, will have no duty of care towards her. Naomi's social worker said she often loses touch with her young charges once they have reached eighteen. However, Mohammed Sesay, the manager of the Southwark Unaccompanied Minors team, says that under the Children (Leaving Care) Act (2000) they are obliged to provide care until she is twenty-one, or twenty-four should she want to go to university. A personal adviser (an unqualified social worker) will be allocated to look after Naomi even if she does not succeed in her asylum claim. The personal adviser will help with all the same issues that may have come up earlier with the social worker – health, housing, money, education, childcare – except that the onus is on Naomi to ask, whereas before the social worker involvement was mandatory. Southwark will assist her with her application to the Home Office for leave to remain. There are no guarantees that she will succeed.

In 2005, 25 unaccompanied children from Sierra Leone applied for asylum. In the same year the highest number of children to apply from any single country was 530 from Afghanistan. The numbers are miniscule. Despite that, there are worrying rumours that the Home Office is planning to send 500 children, failed asylum seekers without families in the UK, back to their countries of origin even if it is not in their best interest.[4] This means that they will not even be eligible for Discretionary Leave to remain until eighteen, as Naomi was. Immigration legislation and duties under the Children Acts 1989 and 2004 are not easily reconciled, since immigration controls take precedence over welfare considerations. Even at the age of eighteen, Naomi will be deeply vulnerable. If Naomi were sent back, she would not be able to look after herself or her son. It is possible that they would end up on the streets of Freetown in that vicious noose of history which dangles over those who have few options.

LIU BAO REN: Journey's End

*Liu Bao Ren is slim and wiry; much younger-looking than his
forty-two years. As he greets us with broad smiles, I notice his glossy
hair, cut into a pudding-bowl shape and the crows' feet around his eyes.
We are an hour late for the first interview. His house lies just outside the
London A-Z and we ended up getting quite lost. Even though he lives in
Britain, the house is furnished in the functional style of rural areas in
the developing world, like Fujian province in south-western China
where Liu comes from. In the vast expanse of the through lounge, where
even the corridor walls have been knocked out to make an open-plan
staircase, there are only two single sofas, a TV, and a small dining-table
with four miscellaneous chairs. The walls are virtually bare, with only a
string of Christmas lights, a map of the world in English, a rail map for
people with reduced mobility, a Chinese calendar with a picture of an
artificially-blue lake and a cherry blossom tree, and a Chinese charm of
four little drums connected with red thread.*

*Liu's wife, Wang Li, is just recovering from an eye operation, but
nonetheless she is animated and bustles around us happily, chattering
and laughing. She has two red spots of colour on her cheeks, which make
her look like a Russian doll. There are two children at home, a girl of
about fifteen and a boy of about eight. The little boy reappears from
time to time during the day, darting noisily across the living-room in the*

happy knowledge that he is breaking the rules. On another occasion we discover that Liu also has an older son of eighteen. During our first interview, we talk mostly to Liu about his childhood and growing up. Wang Li sits down by his side, filling in the missing bits in his memory and laughing delightedly at his stories. Sometimes her laughter and chatter continue over the translation so what was missing in his memory remains missing in my story. Interestingly though, after that first meeting Wang Li busied herself with the housework despite the fact that she had never heard the details of Liu's tortuous journey to the UK. Perhaps she felt she was better off not knowing what he went through.

According to the 2001 census, the Chinese population in the UK is approximately quarter of a million strong, representing a miniscule 0.4 per cent of the total. Obviously, there is no way of knowing the number of underground Chinese. Some estimates suggest that there are 70,000 unauthorized Chinese workers in food-processing chains, agriculture, catering and construction.[1] The pattern of emigration from China is too complex and diverse to do adequate justice to it in a summary. According to Bobby Chen, who has worked at the Central London Law Centre since 1982 as an advocate for and adviser to the Chinese immigrant community, a large number of Chinese applied for asylum after the Tiananmen Square massacre in 1989. They were mostly from cities such as Beijing, Shanghai, Guangzhou. The British government had a China policy which said that any student who arrived before 4 June 1989 would be allowed to stay in this country. However, fewer people than expected claimed asylum.

After 1995, the picture changed. Emigration took place mainly from rural areas in coastal provinces like Fujian and Guangdong. Fujian province is right opposite Taiwan. It is not the poorest province in China, but it does not have much manufacturing or production because it is on a permanent war-footing with Taiwan. Hundreds of ballistic missiles pointing towards Taiwan are based in Fujian province. Taiwan has always been a thorn in the side of China. When Chiang Kai-shek and his Nationalist party lost the power struggle with Mao and the Communists in 1949, they fled to Taiwan, an island which is 125 miles off the coast of China. They set up their Kuomintang (KMT) government-in-exile and hoped to overthrow the Communist regime and return to power in Beijing one day, supported by the Americans as part of their policy to contain and isolate China. When the KMT rule ended in 2000, the party of the ethnic Taiwanese, who had been repressed by the KMT, came to power and started pushing for independence from China as opposed to the 'one-China' policy of their predecessors. Any talk of independence is met by China with threats of military intervention.

The Fujianese have a long tradition of emigration. Their exodus first started in the nineteenth century when Britain was looking for cheap labour for its colonies after the international slave trade had been abolished.[2] During the Cultural Revolution of 1966–76 and, in fact, from the time of the Communist takeover in 1949, having relatives abroad was frowned upon and could lead to charges of spying and political harassment. Today, however, it is common for many Fujianese to have relatives living abroad and the provincial economy has been transformed by the money they send home. The conspicuous consumption of overseas Chinese on holiday tempts even more Fujianese peasants to emigrate.

Common destinations for Fujianese immigrants are Japan, Taiwan, the United States and Australia. Japan is popular because it is cheaper to go there and the wages are higher. But the Japanese government routinely deports those arrested back to China, informing the Fujian provincial authorities as they do so.[3] Many Fujianese believe that immigration officials in the United States are much more lenient than those in Japan and Taiwan. Only 1 per cent of Fujianese migrants leave for political reasons and Liu Bao Ren belongs to that category.

As the demand for people-smuggling services is high in Fujian province, the snakeheads are correspondingly very active there, to the extent that they advertise publicly for workers required for overseas factories. They smuggle people to the West through the use of fake passports, visas, bribes or by transporting their human cargo in lorries and ships. The Fujianese gangs co-operate with Taiwanese gangs in taking stowaways in boats from the coastal ports to Japan and North America. Although the Western media tends to make a distinction between triads and snakeheads, it would seem that they are quite closely linked. According to Liu, snakeheads could be seen as one department in the criminal corporation of triads, who are involved in drug smuggling, money-laundering, loan-sharking and extortion, illegal gambling, DVD piracy, tax evasion and VAT fraud, among other activities. The snakeheads who brought Liu over were not triads, although they had informal links with them. Bobby Chen describes how fast boats used for illegal running of cigarettes come in handy for people-running. The people-smuggling industry is as lucrative as the drug trade – across Europe the business is supposed to be worth £8bn.

The triads were established to form a resistance to the Manchu Qing (pronounced Ching) Dynasty in the 1760s. Over the centuries they lost their original purpose. Unable to reintegrate into civilian life, they turned into criminal organizations. In 1949 when the Communists took over and introduced strict law and order, organized crime migrated southwards to Hong Kong, then a British colony. There were eight main triad groups and they carved Hong Kong up into geographical areas which were controlled by different ethnic groups. Nowadays, there are approximately fifty-seven triad societies in Hong Kong. The scale of triad membership is difficult even for leaders to ascertain. Although some triads have only fifty members, larger ones have over thirty thousand members. It is alleged that public figures like Chiang Kai-shek were members, and the latter apparently instructed triad members to torture Communists. Triads, such as the 14K group, first appeared in cities like London, Birmingham, Manchester and Liverpool as early as 1952. The Wo Shing Wo, considered to be the largest, and the Sun Yee On are two of the other major triad groups.[4] In the high streets of London I have seen many Chinese women standing on a mat of DVD covers stuck together with tape. They wear jackets with large pockets from which they remove pirated DVDs for sale. These women are probably the visible end of a chain that leads back to a triad boss at the end. Liu mentions other gangs such as Vietnam Pai, Changle Pai and Fuqing Pai but he is understandably reluctant to divulge which, if any, of these groups he became involved with.

Liu Bao Ren is a real storyteller. Once he gets into his flow, it can be difficult to stop him, especially for a gentle soul like Xiao Xing (pronounced Shiao Sing), the Chinese translator I have found for the job. As a result, this ended up being the longest interview I conducted. Using a translator makes it easier for me to ask hard questions because I don't have to make eye contact with Liu. And I can repeat a question without embarrassment. And repeat I certainly have to. Although Liu can talk you into the ground, the nuggets that we are interested in have to be extracted slowly through constant persuasion, and reassurance that I will do nothing to endanger his safety. He is the most frightened of all the interviewees. He appears to be caught in a web of intrigue, triad gangs and snakeheads. Very few people have been brave enough to speak out against them.

I came to Britain by mistake. I wouldn't have been here to tell my story if there hadn't been a cock-up. Even people-smugglers make mistakes and send consignments to the wrong place – but in this game there are no refunds and the consequences are literally life-changing. I wanted to go to Italy to join a friend in the leather business and when I started my journey that's where I thought I was going, but I ended up in the UK. It took me four months to get here. But that's nothing. One of my closest friends borrowed £30,000 for the journey and it took him four years. He ended up in France twice and spent one year begging on the streets in Africa. He was abducted by one set of snakeheads trying to pinch customers off another group, jumped ship and ran straight into the arms of the police. It's a complicated story.

The amount you pay decides how comfortable your journey is – tell that to my friend! I paid a decent amount so my journey was not as bad as some, but I didn't have much time to plan it. I was on the run. I'd been arrested in September 1997 in the middle of a meditation meeting of my Buddhist group, the Quan Yin Method, which is banned in China. The head of this group, Supreme Master Ching Hai, lives in Taiwan. Ching Hai's teachings, in fluent English, are to be found on a website called, without any sense of irony, godsdirectcontact.com. The Chinese authorities were always jumpy about anyone from Taiwan having any kind of influence, even spiritual influence, especially in Fujian province which was right across the water from Taiwan. The year before I was arrested, there was a lot of tension between Taiwan and China. They thought that I was a Taiwanese spy. On one occasion, I had hired a speedboat and strayed into international waters in the narrow straits between China and Taiwan. Suddenly, in one second, there were Chinese Navy speedboats coming towards me from every direction.

According to the government's CIPU country report on China of October 2003,[5] this 'meditation practice' claimed to have half a million followers in seven provinces. When they discovered a bona fide list of several thousand members the authorities labelled it a 'reactionary religious organisation' at first and then redefined it as an 'evil cult' after the Falun Gong ban of July 1999, when 10,000 followers staged a mass sit-in in front of the walled leadership compound in Beijing. The Chinese government had become particularly sensitive to any mass mobilization of people, as became evident in the infamous Tiananmen Square massacre of pro-democracy activists in 1989–90. These 'religions' were seen to be providing a focal point for anti-regime views. During the crackdown, the offices, schools and other facilities of the Quan Yin Method were forced to close down, their assets confiscated and their key personnel detained or arrested.[6]

As a member of this group, I became vegetarian and followed all the other dos and don'ts, like not killing living things, not lying, not drinking alcohol, taking drugs or having sex outside marriage. It isn't a religion as such, more just a way of life. I suppose I joined this group when I felt that science wasn't providing explanations for some of the things that had happened to me. For example, I can't swim. I fell into a river once and lost consciousness. I woke up and found myself on the other bank. There was no obvious explanation for this except that it was a miracle. Another time, when I was doing construction work, I fell from the third floor and I didn't get hurt.

Every evening at 7 p.m., about a hundred people would meet in my brick factory for a meditation conducted by one of the masters. They came from all over the place, not just those who worked there. One of my not-so-happy employees must have informed the authorities. You expected this sort of thing to happen in the 1970s, but not in the 1990s. Back then, people used to settle personal scores by reporting others to government officials. It created mistrust among people. But China is getting better now. You still have to be careful about what you say: if they find out that you have been criticizing them, you could be beaten badly or taken to the police station and made to sit on broken glass. That evening I was arrested for membership of a counter-revolutionary religious group. I didn't dare ask which religious group, according to the authorities, could be called revolutionary.

After the arrest at the brick factory I was taken to a remand prison, where you can stay for a maximum of one year. It's the same as a proper prison, the only difference being that here you can bribe the officials because there hasn't been a trial. In each cell there were five to six people. The good thing about being a political prisoner was that you got a cell all to yourself. They wouldn't let you mix with the others – normally, you're allowed to socialize once a day. The walls, floor and ceiling were painted black. There were no windows. There was no mattress on the bed, just some dry grass and a thin, poor-quality blanket. There was a metal door with a small opening with bars across it. In the morning, you got a little bit of rice in water. This would cost RMB1 outside, but here it cost RMB3. They brought the food and showed it to you. If you didn't pay, they threw the food away in front of you. There was no toilet. They gave you a bucket.

It isn't legal to torture people in China but the warders kick you, shake you and beat you up in a way that leaves no marks. The other forms of torture, which they put me through, are known as 'Beauty, look in the mirror' and 'Beauty, wash your face'. In the first one, they hold your face millimetres above a bucket full of urine for half an hour at a time so that you never know when they are going to dunk your face into it. In the second one they soak a towel in the urine and rub your face with it. It isn't always pure urine. It is sometimes mixed with shit and it isn't yours either. I don't think there was any shit that day. I didn't breathe while they were doing it, I scrunched my eyes and sort of shut my brain down. I sealed my lips so firmly that when they took the towel away, my lips had gone numb and I almost passed out with not having breathed for so long. Until the urine dries, you can smell it every time you take a breath. It makes you sick. But I wasn't going to give them the satisfaction of retching out loud. They kept asking me about the Quan Yin Method, how many times I had visited Taiwan and so forth. I told them everything. The Chinese authorities knew all of it anyway.

I didn't want to go through all that again, so I got a message to my brother, asking him to bribe the governors and prison warders with RMB20,000 (*approximately £1,400*) to allow me to escape. One day they asked me to slop out. You have to go to the toilet to do that. There is only one door from the toilet to the road. Everybody knows you can escape from the toilet. I just walked out of that door. As I had already given them enough money they didn't stop me. I was in prison for two weeks. It wasn't safe for me to continue living in Fujian province anymore. I would have been picked up and constantly harassed by the police. I couldn't afford to keep on paying bribes. I asked my cousin and brother to return the land that I had rented for the factory to the farmers, to stop the government taking it all, and to sell the machinery and use some of the money to pay salaries to my sixty employees. I went home to say goodbye to my family before leaving for Beijing. I was really sad about the factory. I had put all my money (*his savings amounted to nearly half a million RMB (renmimbi), or £35,000*), energy, my whole life into the factory. After I left, I heard the government demolished the factory.

It took two days and three nights to get to Beijing. It cost RMB100 which would have been about half a week's average salary in those days. Today, that journey costs RMB500. I knew that I would be safe there for a little while before the authorities caught up with me. We need permission to travel from city to city, a temporary ID card which you apply for through the police. If I tried to get work in any other part of China, I'd need an ID card, which I'd never get now that I'd been blacklisted. I didn't know what I was going to do. One day, a friend of a friend said that there were opportunities to work abroad. I decided to go. If I had the money, he said he would help me. He was probably a snakehead. It cost RMB100,000 (*approximately £7,000*) to go to Hungary. We agreed on RMB80,000 as I was a friend. He arranged a fake passport for me, in the name of a friend of mine, which cost another RMB10,000. A legal passport costs RMB200 or RMB300 (*£13–£20*). I had to sort out my own visa. Otherwise I would've had to pay another RMB10,000. It's a pity I didn't ask this guy about the cost of going all the way to Italy. It would have been cheaper if I had organized it in China. But I didn't know where I wanted to go. That's why I only paid to get to Hungary. The flight to Hungary on its own would have cost no more than RMB7,000, RMB3,000 for the Beijing hotel where we stayed while waiting for our flight, and RMB70,000 for all the paperwork. It's not that expensive. In China you have to do a health check, police check, give proof of employment and a family check. To get false papers, you have to bribe people along the way, which is why the snakeheads need such a wide network of contacts in the government.

Xiao Xing used to work for a government-approved agency which recruited Chinese people legally to work abroad, charging RMB20,000 for the service. But Liu could not go down this route because, being blacklisted, his paperwork would never be passed by the authorities.

I went to the Hungarian embassy twice before I got an interview for my business visa. I waited for two days. The weather was really cold and my toes got frozen waiting all day on the street. At night I went to my friend's place. On the second day, I got lucky. I was the last person to be seen. The snakehead had organized an invitation letter from an 'uncle' in Hungary. At the embassy, they asked how much money I was intending to invest in my business venture. I said I could only answer that after I had done my research. I think I got through because my answers were realistic – they gave me a three-month visa. Although my passport was fake, I felt I would be entering Hungary legally. I didn't want to do it the cheap way and be illegal from the beginning.

I stayed in Beijing in a five-storey hotel which was reserved by the snakeheads for their clients. On the ground floor there were shops, and on the fifth floor there was a karaoke bar. The 100 people who were going abroad stayed on the floors in between. Four people, including me, were from Fujian. Two of our group left to go to Italy two weeks before us. I was travelling with a friend, Zhang Qi Ming. His reasons for leaving China were very complicated. You don't know how corrupt the Chinese government is and how the bureaucrats shield each other. Ming was a senior law officer in Fujian. When he discovered criminal activity and brought it to the attention of his boss, he was sacked and blacklisted. His boss was probably in the pay of the criminals.

According to Bobby Chen, the local government is very powerful. China is a centralized state but it has difficulties controlling the outlying states. Even in Communist times in the 50s, the important thing was 'who's your general?' That's why the Chinese government constantly moved the general from province to province just to be sure that they weren't building their private armies. There have been cases where central government officers have come down to investigate cases of corruption and have mysteriously been burned to death. There's a joke that it's better to be a local officer than be a general in Beijing because there's too many generals anyway.

We each paid a deposit of RMB50,000 (£3,300) in the hope that we would get to the front of the queue (*usually you only pay RMB20,000, approximately £1,400*). Even so, we still had to wait for a month. I did as much sightseeing as I could take. When I got bored, I visited various friends and their businesses. Although I called my family a few times, I didn't tell them where I was going. They knew that I had to go abroad for a little while and they didn't expect to know the details of my plans; they didn't care which country as long as I was safe. I usually make the decisions, but I do discuss things with my wife. She listens to me.

My wife was seventeen when we got married in 1987. She used her sister's birth certificate because you are not allowed to marry before the age of twenty. As I was doing well in my business, lots of people introduced girls to me. My wife is from the same village as me. Usually girls get married to someone from another village. We didn't know each other though. I had seen her ride a bike past me one day, but that was it. Nor were we related to each other. As there were 200 families living in the village there was no fear of inbreeding. But I was actually supposed to marry her older sister. Her sister had another suitor, a military man, whom she preferred. Before we got engaged, I had to give the girl's side RMB1,000 and then I had to spend RMB3,000 for the cost of the wedding and gifts. In the old days both the girl's side and the boy's side had to spend money, but that has changed recently and the girl's side has to spend more. Nowadays, in a rich family the girl's side might spend RMB50-60,000. Even an average family will spend about 10,000. (*The average rural wage is RMB400 per month.*) My wife's side bought the furniture and TV and paid for her clothes and jewellery.

My family was quite poor. My grandfather had gone to Singapore to do business and sent his earnings to my grandmother, who brought up all her children on her own. She was only thirty years old when he died in Singapore and she never remarried. They had invested all the money in land. When Mao began his collectivization programme and took all the private land back from the people, we lost everything overnight. My sisters didn't go to school because my parents couldn't afford to send all six of us. In those days families only sent one or two children to school. We had to pay for books – about RMB1.6 per term, and there were two terms. Today it translates as 10p, but that doesn't even begin to take account of how much it really meant to us. We didn't have uniforms. Me and my brother, who was three years older than me, went to school. We had no cycles in those days. I walked to school. Every village had its own school. So I only had to walk for five minutes. There was no electricity and no transport. We couldn't afford to feed my youngest sister so she was sent to live with an aunt. I only found out about her when I met her at a family wedding when I was thirty-three. My older sister would go to the forest to cut wood and sell it to earn some extra money for my education. She started working when she was seven years old. She sacrificed her schooling for me.

By the end of the summer of 1956 nearly 90 ninety per cent of China's farmers had joined a collective farm. The average collective consisted of around 170 families. The family unit remained, each family eating and living together under the same roof. And each family was allowed its own small plot of land and to sell the produce from these private plots as they pleased. Free enterprise continued, but in a much diminished form.[7]

Officially, you can start working for the government when you turn fourteen. When I came home from school, I sometimes helped my parents on the farm or helped my sister to cut wood and sell it. The woods were connected to the farmland, so only the farmers had access to it. We would sell it in town. Wood was used for cooking and heating the house. The government used to give us a ticket for everything: a ticket to buy 5 m of fabric for your whole family, for example. We lived in a small, two-roomed, two-storey mud house with a wooden roof. After my brothers and sisters were born, (my grandmother helped to deliver them at home) we built another two rooms. Thirty families (fifty to sixty workers, including some of the women) worked together on our farm and had to share the harvest equally according to the number of people who worked. Women's labour only counted as half a share. My mother worked side by side with my father and we got 1.5 shares of the harvest, but it wasn't enough for our large family. There were six children and my grandmother who lived with us. We grew rice, wheat and sweet potato. The village itself had about two hundred families living in it, all in separate 'production groups'. From 1979 onwards, the government changed its policy and started giving land to the peasants for their own use. But the quality of the land wasn't good. Even grass didn't grow on it.

Where was I? Yes, the journey. We were to fly to Hungary via Moscow. Those of us who'd paid a lot of money were not accompanied by snakeheads – they felt they could trust us. Although I had no plans to stay in Moscow, I was told that there was a snakehead outside each airport to catch any absconders. People who had taken the cheaper route by train would have someone with them. At check-in at Beijing airport the Chinese authorities took away my passport and ticket. They always double-check Fujianese passports. When I got my passport back, the ticket was missing. Then I had to run all over the place to find it. It was also compulsory for all travellers to buy a small pack of basic medicines to help you if you fall ill abroad. They don't enforce this, but when they found out that I didn't have one they made me go and buy it. By now, I was sweating with anxiety. When I finally got on the plane, the fans weren't working, so I was really hot although it was December.

The Interpol website describes how people-smuggling networks change constantly in response to legal changes and law enforcement activities. Flexibility is key to their survival. The routes used by people-smugglers may sometimes be simple and direct, at other times circuitous. The time between departure and arrival may vary from some days to several months or even years. Smuggling is carried out by land, air or sea.

Migrants from the Asian region mainly use the route via Kazakhstan, Kyrgyzstan, Uzbekistan, Tajikistan and Turkmenistan to Russia, and from there, via Ukraine, Slovakia and the Czech Republic, to western European countries or even further to the United States and Canada.

Migrants to the United States, using false passports, are often smuggled by air. Ships bound for the west coast was a popular route, but use of this route has dropped considerably.[8]

We arrived in Moscow at 4 p.m. and were due to catch our connecting flight the next day. We decided to sleep at the airport because it was cheaper than booking into a hotel, which would cost $50 for one night. And because we didn't know the language we were worried that we might not find our way back. I was carrying a small rucksack with a few clothes and sunflower seeds, a popular snack in China. A bottle of water cost $5 whereas in China it cost only a few cents. Luckily, there was a Chinese lady with us who knew some Russian. She told us that we were eligible for free food. We presented our vouchers at the airport restaurant and got an egg, a sausage and a glass of juice. Without her we would have missed our flights. There were a lot of people from my home town going to Hungary probably being taken by other snakehead gangs.

For the next leg of our journey we took a small aeroplane carrying about fifteen people. Despite it being a rough flight to Budapest, I fell asleep. In Hungary we were met by four huge Chinese guys who were part of the snakehead gang – rather unexpectedly, they asked us if we'd had a good journey! I had come armed with lots of telephone numbers of Chinese people in Hungary, Italy, Germany and other European countries in case I needed help. These guys said, 'don't worry we'll help you find your friends'. We drove through the city centre until we came to the suburbs. It was a really run-down area with very poor housing and one tall building that stuck out like a sore thumb. The snakeheads had a whole floor of this building, which is where they took us. Straight away they took our passports, saying they needed them to book us into a hotel, but then they told us that the hotels were fully booked. For one night they said we had no option but to stay in the flat. They took us to one small room where eight people were sleeping. Everyone slept on one big bed. When I objected that there were too many people, one of the snakeheads said 'you can sleep in our room'. There were only six people in that room and each person had a single bed to themselves.

At the beginning I was very scared. I was in a new country and I didn't know how to communicate with people, but, more importantly, none of us knew what lay ahead. Ming was even more scared than I was. On the second day, the snakehead told us that he had sent people to book a hotel but they hadn't got back so we had to stay there another day. Some of the people in the flat, who'd already been there for some time, told us that our passports wouldn't be returned until we had decided where we wanted to go. If we decided to stay on in Hungary, they would want the rest of the money. If we wanted to go elsewhere, we would have to pay extra. We were locked in the flat. It was a four-bedroom flat with one living-room where two women slept. The two guys who worked for the snakeheads, who were called *mazhai*, bought all the provisions. One person from each room was sent to cook for everyone in his room, in rotation. You cook whatever is available in the fridge. In the other rooms, people had made up their minds about their final destination in China, but even so they had been waiting one month, sometimes two, depending on the route they'd chosen. Some routes become dangerous when the government clamps down on them, and they had to wait for a safer route to be found.

I tried to get my passport back from the *mazhai*, but they kept making excuses. In fact, I never got my passport back from them. I am sure they would have recycled it. After one week, when Ming and I had decided that we would go to Italy, they put me in touch with the snakehead A. Jian, in China. Usually you cannot transfer to another group, but sometimes they do deals among themselves. If one group is better organized on certain routes, they will swap customers. If you run away from one gang and you are found by another, they will return you to your original snakehead. But they are also in competition. If your snakehead isn't powerful, then other snakeheads will kidnap his customers. If that happens, you might end up paying money twice.

To go to Italy, we were asked to pay another RMB40,000 (£2,600). We waited in Hungary for two weeks. At the end of the second week the *mazhai* asked if he could borrow $300 from each of us, saying that he would be able to arrange the trip quicker. This was in addition to what they would charge to take us to Italy. I said my friend didn't have enough money, so would $500 be acceptable from both of us? He agreed to arrange our departure that very night. A whole group of eighteen people were leaving that night anyway. I think the man pretended he was speeding it up in order to get more money from us.

From then on the journey just got worse and worse. We were packed about seven people to a small car and driven to some woods in three cars. We were in the second car. The journey took forty minutes. Each car was parked at some distance from the other. They thought it would be unsafe to have a large group of people travel together. We walked in our separate groups through the woods to the base of this mountain where we would join up again and make our way up a steep and dangerous road. It was about 4 p.m. and not that dark, but it was raining and the road was wet. Then it dawned on me that we were expected to climb this mountain. I was absolutely furious. I hadn't paid all that money to walk to Italy, but we'd been lumped together with people who were paying less and travelling cheaply. There was nothing we could do even when they didn't keep their part of the bargain. If you didn't pay, they could beat up your family.

When we got to the base of the mountain, we were told to wait for another *mazhai* who would take us across. He arrived after an hour. He was carrying a gun. He spoke English and appeared to be a local. We had to wait till it got really dark before we started. My rucksack was already feeling quite heavy. Half-way up the mountain people started throwing things out to lighten their luggage. Some people were reluctant to let things go. Others advised them it was better to throw things out than die. There is a Chinese saying: What is the point of hoarding seeds? When you die, there will be no one to grow them. Then one guy fell and rolled all the way to the bottom. Fortunately, he was travelling with three friends who went back and helped him up. He was hurt, but not badly enough not to be able to walk. The path was narrow and the idea was to walk close to the mountainside so you could clutch the long grass and save yourself from falling. The guy who fell was walking in the middle of the path and couldn't reach the grass.

Matters were made worse by the fact that none of us was wearing the right clothes for these conditions. We hadn't been told that we were going to be climbing a mountain. Ming used to be in the army so he found the climb quite easy – even without the gear. I was wearing a leather jacket and leather shoes. I didn't get very wet but as it was January we were quite cold. My gloves were in the bag. I couldn't get them out in the middle of the mountain because it was hard to see and I would have got left behind, so my hands got frozen. It was so dark that Ming thought that the *mazhai* was carrying a stick, not a gun. The *mazhai* obviously knew the road well. He was always 5 m ahead of us. He was walking fast and didn't bother to help us or warn us to take care. Half-way up, the path got even harder. There was a 2 m deep ditch in the middle. One guy fell into it. There was no time to change out of his wet clothes, so he just kept walking. He became really cold. From then on, we made sure to look out for pitfalls and warn each other. We were particularly worried about the two women. When we got to the top, we could see another big mountain in front of us. There was a searchlight. We were at the border of northern Hungary with Slovakia, I think. I have never looked at an atlas to check my route out. It's too painful to relive it.

It had taken us two hours to get to this point. We were told to hide when the searchlight came towards us. There was a lake between us and the mountain that we were going to climb next. We had to get round the lake very carefully because the path was steep. This took about three hours. The grass was too short to grab onto, so the only way to stop ourselves from falling off the path was to walk on all fours, plunging our hands into the soft clay for stability. As it had been raining, the ground was all squelchy. For a long time we had to walk doubled over – and I can tell you, that really takes it out of you. This time the *mazhai* actually warned us that the path was dangerous. It was a moonless night, but each time the searchlight swept around we got an idea of the lay of the land. Two people nearly fell into the lake. The first guy grabbed the trouser belt of the guy closest to him. That guy clung on to my rucksack and, if I hadn't grabbed a slender tree trunk, all of us would have landed in the lake. After this corner, the road became easier, less steep.

We kept walking and left the lake behind us. Then we heard dogs barking. There were some soldiers patrolling the border. The *mazhai* asked us to hide in the ditch, which was 2 m deep and half full of water. He said the water would put the dogs off our scent. There were many ditches along the road and the tall grass camouflaged us. The *mazhai* was still standing on the road with his gun, looking as if he was getting ready for a hunt. The soldiers thought that the dogs were barking at him.

As the soldiers walked past, the *mazhai* asked us to get out of the ditches quickly and cross the road to the other side. That was the border. There was no barbed wire. There was a truck, big enough for eighteen people or so, with two tables in the back, waiting for us. The driver was sitting in the cab and another man was standing by the truck. All of us were very wet and dog-tired. We wanted to change inside the truck but they told us to wait till we got to our destination. The driver's companion, a Vietnamese guy, came to the back and counted all of us. We set off and after five minutes we crossed a bridge and we saw a lot of lights. We hadn't seen any lights for five hours. We felt safe. It might seem strange, but I was more excited by the lights than by the fact that we were sitting in a truck and no longer walking through the wet and cold.

We stopped at a house in the suburbs. It had an unusual layout because the front door was at the side and it was slightly raised. The truck pulled up close to the front door, they pulled the curtains aside and we jumped from the back of the lorry straight into the house without being seen by the neighbours. The room that we went into was divided by a curtain. It was about 12 sq ft in size. In one part there was a sink only, no toilets. That was where we could change our clothes. In the other section there was a wooden platform built into the wall for people to sleep on. The rest of us had to sleep on the ground. There were no mattresses and no carpet on the wooden floor. It was freezing cold. We weren't given anything to cover ourselves so we had to use what few clothes we were carrying to keep us warm. To stop shivering we wrapped our arms around our bodies tightly. We were given a small piece of baguette and an egg to eat. Somehow I fell asleep like this.

Some people got up in the night to use the toilet. The *mazhai*, who was sitting by the door, didn't understand English or Chinese; he just looked at us dumbly and we had to hold it in all night. Another *mazhai* arrived only at 11 a.m. the next day and let us use the toilet, which was in the back garden. There were two wooden huts. The toilets were filthy. There was no water. There was no toilet paper. You had to squat on a wooden platform above a pot. You had to use your own tissues – that is, if you had any. We washed our hands at the sink inside the room.

Once we were back in the house, the snakehead locked us in. There was a boarded-up window so we couldn't see out and no light came in. Because of the cold weather and lack of warm clothes many of us fell sick. Fortunately I didn't. The two women had a high fever and the four men in their group looked after them. They took double the recommended dose of Chinese herbal medicine so that they could get better quickly. We asked for food. They asked us what we had done with the bread that we were given the previous night. At 4 p.m., another guy came and brought some bread. There was enough for only two people not eighteen. People shared the bread out thinking that there would be more, but no more came. Those of us who were standing near the door managed to get some bread. The others had to go hungry. Ming, who was near the door, shared his little piece with me. I was too hungry to worry about the others. We were told that we weren't being given more food because we were leaving soon. This early on in our journey people were still prepared to share what little we were given. It was later, in Holland, that people started fighting over food. I think they kept us hungry so that we would feel too weak to run away.

That evening, at about 5 p.m., when it was still light, we continued on our journey. We were put into three separate cars again. After an hour's journey we arrived at what looked like a car repair garage. I think this was in Austria. The roads were mostly deserted, so the fact that so many Chinese people were travelling together in the Slovakian countryside wouldn't have been noticed. A few cars drove past at such speed that I don't think the drivers would have seen us. Of the three cars, only two turned up at the garage. When I returned from the toilet, I noticed that our group of twelve had further reduced to six. Apparently, the other group had come to the wrong place, so they got back into the car and were driven somewhere else.

We were asked to go down to the basement of this house where there were at least eight or nine rooms. There were people from all over the world. There was an African woman with small children, including a baby, who were very hungry. There were people from India, Iraq, Iran and Afghanistan. Most were from the Middle East. They were tall and fearsome-looking. Some people were sick. All the rooms were interconnected. There was no corridor. We were each given a small rug to sit or sleep on. Apart from that our room had no furniture. There were two toilets, which could be reached via a small room which had an old table where you could sit and drink water. There were about two hundred people there, although it was hard to tell because they kept coming and going. There was always a queue to go to the toilet! Forty customers belonged to my snakehead but they were all going in different directions.

As there was no kitchen, we had to buy food. We gave some money to the *mazhai*. We were worried that they would see that we had all this money with us and they might try and steal it. But we were desperate and hungry; we were prepared to take chances. Going by my experience at Moscow airport, I expected everything to be quite expensive, so I gave them a $10 bill for bread and water. I thought I would get a small bottle of water and a little bread. When he came back, he brought three bags of bread and a big bottle for each person. I gave a bag of bread and a bottle of water to the African woman whose children were so skinny. The guys from the Middle East saw this and tried to steal our money and our food. They thought they could bully us because we were small. All the six Chinese people were put into one room. I had gone to the toilet and three other guys were walking around. Only two guys were left to look after the luggage. The Middle Eastern group were eight in number. A fight broke out. Two Indians and some Africans came to help the Chinese to fight back. All our stuff was thrown everywhere. The Chinese guys' faces were swollen and bleeding. The fight lasted only three minutes. The *mazhai* heard what was going on and dashed to the spot to break up the fighting. The *mazhai* were more efficient than policemen! We almost felt safe with them.

The Arabs were taken into a small room and beaten up. After that they became very quiet. The *mazhai* would kill people if necessary. Some people die on the journey through fatigue. If people fall behind from fatigue, the *mazhai* would tell us to leave them and continue on our journey. They might take care if you're related or a friend of the snakehead. Mercifully, there were no deaths on our journey.

You have to pay them the money in stages and God help you if you don't have it. The snakeheads will tell them how much to collect from each person. They don't usually break your legs. They will try and hurt you 'inside' so that you might survive the journey but you will die quickly on arrival at your final destination. They pin you against the wall, one person holds each arm, as if you are Christ on the cross, and one person punches you in your chest and abdomen area. If you double up in pain and they let go of your arms, someone will use a stick to hit you on the back. They will call your family on the phone as they are beating you up so that they can hear you screaming in agony. In Holland, the *mazhai* did this to one guy who didn't have enough money. No parent or sibling can bear to hear their loved one being tortured – so, the money would be transferred by the family to the designated account. If they didn't have the money, they would borrow it at very high rates of interest.

All your brothers and sisters have to sign an agreement to return the money within three years. If you don't have close relatives, some rich person with the same surname may step in to lend your family the money. Some snakeheads may allow you to pay after you get to your destination and start earning if you are really poor. Very few people are in that situation though, maybe no more than one in a thousand. Often they are women who have to go into prostitution to repay the money to the snakeheads – you have to pay up within three days of reaching your destination. It's very difficult for women. They get raped by the *mazhai* on the journey even if they are travelling with parents or relatives. They have no power if the *mazhai* come and ask the girl to go into another room with them. They might get to their destination and give birth to a child and not know who the father is. I know a few women in this situation. I saw these things after Slovakia.

Snakeheads don't find work for their customers. They are not gang-masters. The triads, the Chinese mafia, will find you work at a price. The *mazhai* refer to their snakehead as 'Boss'. There are various bosses: Nan Ba Tian means 'king of all snakeheads'; Guang Tou means 'bald one'; Ping Tou means 'one with a little hair'; American Mei Guo Gou means 'hawk-like nose'; and when you don't know which nationality they are you call them Gui Lau – *gui* means devil and is also a derogatory term for foreigners. Triad bosses are known as 'Big Boss', *Lao Da* in Mandarin, *Dai Lao* in Cantonese. (*This translates literally as 'Big Brother'.*)

We stayed in this place for two days. Every two to three hours, a group would be brought to that garage and people would leave in groups of fifty or sixty. Even though I was really tired, I couldn't fall asleep because I was so frightened. I just shut my eyes from time to time. The following night, just as I was falling asleep, someone told us to pack our stuff because we were leaving. It was probably 3 a.m. In the basement, we couldn't tell day from night, but by now I reckoned that, including the month in Beijing, I had been on the road for nearly seven weeks. We were transported in a 40 ft container that was so crowded that there was standing room only. There were already at least forty people in it who had been picked up from some other place and perhaps thirty to forty had joined from our basement. I tried to stand at one end of the container by the corner so that if I needed to pee I could do it through a crack. Also, I would get fresh air and light when it was daytime.

I had started my journey with $1,800. They wouldn't have let me into Hungary unless I was carrying enough money. I had bought the dollars on the black market. It cost me $40 over the exchange rate. I had used up a few hundred so far. In China we have a secret pocket stitched into our underwear or collar. I hid some of my money in my underwear and kept some in a secret section of my big leather jacket. At the end, when I had only a few hundred dollars, I kept them in the toothpaste tube. Some people carry money in their shoes, but if you fall asleep you can be robbed by the people you're travelling with. The *mazhai* don't steal money like that. They ask to borrow money which they never return. If you say you don't have any money left, then they might search your luggage or your clothes when you are asleep. Or they will take you to another room under some excuse, make you strip, and tell you to pay for things that were already included in the price. These are the *mazhai*'s perks when the boss isn't around. You can't complain to the snakehead because the *mazhai* manage you on a day-to-day basis and they will beat you if you do.

My snakehead would ring the *mazhai* in whichever country I reached and ask them to treat me well, saying 'he is my valued customer'. I wasn't treated badly because the snakehead knew that I used to have a factory and so I had some standing. I also had a rich businessman friend, Shiyou En in Beijing, who had acted as my guarantor, which reassured them. If I needed any money, I could always ring him and ask him to transfer money. He and I hadn't come to any agreement about when I should return the money – just that I should pay it as and when I could. My family paid him back from the money they raised from the sale of the factory.

We were told as we got into the container that we had to be very quiet. After a few minutes I heard shouting from the people in the front. People were asking them to hush. I recognized the dialect. It was from my province. They were shouting '*Gui Lau*' (*evil foreigners*) and I wondered what was going on. There were five Fujian people in my group so we fought our way to the front to help them. Someone was trying to steal money from one of the Fujianese. They got scared when they saw us coming and realized that they had support. There were no *mazhai* to keep discipline. They would never put one *mazhai* in with so many people because feelings run so high they might gang up on him and beat him up. Ratios were carefully managed. All the people from China got very close, even those from different provinces. Once we got off the container we started talking to each other about our different routes. Some who came via Ukraine had travelled in a very small wooden box.

It was good having a friend on the journey. In practical terms, it meant that we could take turns sleeping while the other looked after our belongings. It gave me a lot of strength. We had a very long journey in the container. When the fight started, I think we were climbing a mountain. People were urinating along the back of the container – who cares when you are in that situation especially in the dark? The place stank of piss. We reached the border at daybreak after travelling for two or three hours. Although there were no windows in the container and it was very dark, light would seep through the odd crack and I could see that it was dawn. I heard people say that we had stopped at a Customs checkpoint – we were lucky that the African woman's children didn't cry when we stopped. The youngest was only a year or two old. We would all have been discovered. We waited inside the container while the driver jumped out and handled the paperwork. If the Customs officials had checked the container, that would have been it; we weren't hidden. So many lorries travelled through the checkpoint that they couldn't possibly check them all – they might check one in a thousand. We had entered the Czech Republic, and after a few hours we reached our destination. It was a house on a hill by a lake. There wasn't a soul to be seen.

We got out of the container and lay down in the grass and stretched. It was January and very cold, but it was such a relief to be out of the container we didn't care. It felt like we were on a day trip to the countryside. We did not have to hide away, it was like we were meant to be there, not that we were illegal. Suddenly, out of the blue, white cars came towards us from different directions. I wondered if they were police cars that had been lying in wait for us. Some people ran and hid in the long grass. But then we noticed that people were getting into these cars. They belonged to the snakeheads and had come to pick us up! Some of the vehicles were twenty-seater coaches. We had a password by which we identified which gang of snakeheads we belonged to. Our answer had to match their question. If they said 'the weather looks good today', you may have to say 'no, it's windy and it is going to rain'. On top of that, we had to know the name of the head of our gang. The *mazhai* would shout for Boss Lau's customers. They would all group together. The word *lau* translates as 'number five'. So in response to the question, 'where do you live?', you might say 'we live at the bottom of Number Five Mountain and our house number is 7683'. As there were four in that group, one of those four numbers would be allocated to each of them. If you gave them the right answer, you jumped into their car. This was particularly important when we were transferring from country to country. You could end up in the wrong place. And that is exactly what happened on this occasion.

Our guys didn't turn up for some reason. No one called out our snakehead's name. I can't tell you what our password was because I am scared of being identified. I can't even tell you the name of my boss, because he has a reputation for having killed many people. Even if they change passwords, they keep a record of which ones they used in a particular year and that might identify me. Even though it was a deserted place, we had to transfer quickly. Finally we went with a group of four people who were still on the container. They asked the *mazhai* the question 'where do you live?' The *mazhai* did not recognize the password. He said, 'it is none of your business' and drove away because he didn't want to be beaten up by them for refusing to take them. The *mazhai* rang his boss to find out why he hadn't been given the right password. Then he came back for them and gave the right answer. We asked the *mazhai* whether he would take us as well. By chance, my boss lived in the same building as his own boss back in China. His boss agreed to our request.

We squeezed into a car with the four of them and the *mazhai* and, as far as we were concerned, we were on our way to Italy. Three of the others were going to Germany; the fourth hadn't made up his mind as yet. When we got to our destination forty minutes later there were a lot of people who recognized me. They said, 'we used to buy bricks from your factory'. Although I couldn't remember them, I said I knew them. We were taken to a very nice house. It looked like a holiday home that belonged to a rich person who lived in the city. It had a big garden in front. The house was very clean and in a good condition. I heard from the others that this boss was a very kind person. He gives you whatever food you want to eat. A woman who looked as if she was in her twenties took us around and showed us the house: the living-room where we could watch TV and read, the bathroom, and our bedroom. We were two to a room. She said we could cook whatever we liked but we shouldn't make too much noise and we weren't allowed to go out. The curtains had to remain drawn day and night for our own security. Nor could we use the telephone. I didn't care, it felt like I was on holiday.

I spoke to this boss in China and asked if we could switch to him. We had to pay $50 for a two-minute call on a mobile. He said he would speak to my boss. Unfortunately my boss didn't agree and we were only in that house for a few hours – much to my disappointment. The *mazhai* were very strict about phone calls – if we asked to call anyone, relations or friends, they would stand over you to make sure you didn't criticize them. A car came to fetch us. It took us about thirty minutes to drive to an eight-storey building, like a council block, in Prague. There were about fifteen of us there, all from Fujian province, in a three-bedroom flat with a tiny living-room. It felt like being back with family. Remember the two people who left before us in Beijing to go to Italy? I met one of them here. (*We all laugh.*) He warned us that if we talked too loudly we would be taken to the next room, which was called 'the killer room', a small room which no one could describe when they came out because they were so badly beaten up in there. I never saw the inside of that room. That left only two bedrooms and the living-room for fifteen people. The dining-table had to be big enough for so many people. It dwarfed the living-room. Four people were sleeping under the dining-table because there wasn't enough room.

There was a small kitchen off the living-room. During the month we stayed here, there were a lot of petty tensions around cooking and eating. We were cooking in groups, so those who went first took the best things out of the fridge and left very little for the others. Or it took so long for everyone to finish that the group who made their breakfast first were already in the queue for cooking their lunch when some people hadn't even started their breakfast. The *mazhai* would beat us up if we fought in the queue. One guy from my village had his money taken by the *mazhai*. He complained to the snakehead and after a couple of days got badly beaten. When the snakehead came to visit, my friend told him he was beaten for having snitched on him. The *mazhai* said he was actually beating him up because he had cooked in the morning and wanted to cook again when other people were still waiting in the queue. On another occasion, one guy went to the toilet and flushed it loudly. He was hauled into a room by the *mazhai* who asked him why he made so much noise when flushing the toilet and gave him two slaps. Another guy saw this, got scared, and didn't flush the toilet. He was hauled up by the *mazhai* and slapped for not flushing the toilet. This was their petty dictatorship.

Just before we got to this flat, we heard that a big fight had taken place there. A group of people had tried to cross the German border, failed, and returned to the flat. They were hungry and wanted to cook noodles. The three *mazhai* told them that they weren't allowed to eat, saying, 'we'll give you a beating in proportion to the amount of food you eat'. The *mazhai* were eating chicken and drinking beer. Their guns were out of reach on another table. A *mazhai*'s wife was in the kitchen. She suddenly started screaming. The hungry men had picked up a knife and threatened to kill her unless they were allowed to eat. The *mazhai* didn't go for their guns when they saw that the woman was being held at knife-point. Then three men pinned them down and grabbed the guns. The men took the woman to the street. She was in her night-clothes with her hair all messed up and screaming with fear. The police thought that she had mental problems and laughed at her instead of coming to her rescue. The men snatched a phone from one of the snakeheads and rang the boss in China saying they wanted to be transferred to a new group. Within minutes, two other *mazhai* turned up and took the ten men to another flat. This shows you how sophisticated the snakehead network is.

The worst part of my entire journey was from the Czech Republic to Germany. Although Germany was in the opposite direction to Italy, we didn't suspect anything. The routes they choose are not necessarily the shortest, but the easiest. Having said that, it had become really hard to get into Germany. The group before us had tried to get in more than ten times. The last time, they managed to get past the Czech border but were stopped by a policeman at the German end. It didn't bode well for us. Six of us left Prague by car in the afternoon. It was snowing heavily. The guy driving the car was going really fast and I had a nagging feeling in the pit of my stomach. I started to get a head-ache and the car-sickness I sometimes suffer from got really bad. I felt dizzy and numb. I hadn't eaten much so I felt weak. After about three hours we were dropped off by some woods. It was very cold. I was wearing all my clothes because the *mazhai* had said that we wouldn't be able to carry any luggage. I had on two sets of underwear. (*Xiao Xing and Liu laugh in mutual recognition.*) The Chinese have a habit of wearing many pairs of underwear – I also had on a jumper, a suit and a leather jacket. I wore one pair of shoes and my spare pair was tied by shoelaces to my belt. Even the climb up the mountain wasn't as bad as walking in this heavy snow. With every step my foot sank into snow right up to my knees. A Vietnamese *mazhai* who spoke a little Chinese accompanied us. He had fought in the Vietnamese war so he was able to do this walk, no problem.

I had been told that the border crossing between the Czech Republic and Germany was quite short. I expected to be walking for maybe an hour. But after two hours we were still in the middle of nowhere. When we asked the *mazhai* how long it would take, all he said was 'keep walking'. Again we had to keep ducking to avoid the searchlights, so we must have been quite close to the border. We had started in the afternoon and we walked through the night and the following day and didn't reach our destination until it was almost nightfall. There was no food to keep us going. There was a woman with us who we had literally to drag along the ground. Snow got into our shoes. Our feet got frozen and swollen as we squelched along with melted snow filling our shoes. I felt terrible – weak and tired. The *mazhai* was wearing waterproof, fur-lined boots up to his thighs. The guy kept telling us to walk quickly. When we wanted to have a rest, he said 'no, it is dangerous, there are wild wolves here'. At the beginning we said 'OK, OK, let's keep moving'. But after some time we didn't care if we were eaten alive. We just lay on the ground. When we had to hide, we could hardly find the strength to jump across the ditches on either side of the narrow road on which we were walking.

Our hands were bleeding and cut. We couldn't even hold onto anything to help us to walk. Our hands were numb. For the final stretch I just crawled into Germany. I couldn't keep up with the rest of the group. I was so tired, I didn't care if I got lost, all I wanted was to have a rest. But then, somewhere in my subconscious mind something must've told me to catch up with the rest of the group. The border was marked by a wire fence and we had to crawl alongside it. It was very narrow. I guess it took us so long to cross this border because they had to invent a really long, windy route because so many of the previous attempts had failed.

Once we got into Germany, the *mazhai* told us to wait where we were and left. We crouched in the grass and snow waiting for a car to pick us up. I don't know how the system worked. Maybe he phoned someone to tell them where we were. After an hour a minibus came and parked in the road. We waited for a few minutes trying to work out whether it was for us. Just as well that we didn't show ourselves, because it drove off after a little while. Many hours later a truck pulled up. It must have been around 4 p.m. The driver got out of the truck and blew a whistle. Ming said, 'I don't care if it is the police. I'm too cold and tired.' We walked over. Then the others felt it was safe to join us.

We were so tired we just crawled into the truck. I can't remember how long the journey took. It was the worst twenty-four hours of my whole life. There were no seats, so we just slumped on the floor – 'one breath short of death', as the Chinese saying goes. We looked like pigs slumped in a sty. At the next stop, we shuffled off the truck. When the truck had gone, one of the *mazhai* noticed that we were two people, a man and a woman, short. Had we left someone behind in the grass still waiting for the truck? They rang the truck driver, who checked the back of his truck and discovered them sleeping there. When the truck came back, the *mazhai* jumped into the back and asked them to get off. But they were so tired, they kept sleeping. Eventually, they were dragged off the truck.

All I remember of the place that we were taken to is a long corridor. When we finally got into the warmth, our hands started hurting like mad. One *mazhai* wasn't prepared to give us any food. The other *mazhai* persuaded him, saying, 'look they nearly died, they need to eat'. They gave us Pot Noodles and cans of Coke. We were so tired that we couldn't even get up to boil the water for Pot Noodles so we just ate it dry out of the packet. After we had eaten half the Pot Noodles and felt a little bit of energy flow back, we went into the kitchen and poured hot water into the other half. As our hands warmed up, we realized that they were full of tiny splinters – it really hurt to pull them out. We were filthy and wet but there were no showers. Usually we wore our clothes for two or three days and if we couldn't wash them, or the clothes were too dirty, we just threw them away.

Everywhere we went we would find bags of clothes which people had left behind. We used these clothes to keep us warm when the room was really cold. That night we went to sleep as we were, in our wet clothes. We just couldn't care less.

Sleeping conditions were bad. There were fifteen to sixteen people in one room, no bed, no blankets. The room was freezing. It was originally two rooms but they had knocked down the dividing wall. One half was carpeted and the other half wasn't. I was in the carpeted section. This place is hard to describe. From the main road you turned into a narrow road through an iron gate. At the end of this road there was another iron gate which led to a long alleyway. It was like a warehouse. I think it was built specially for transporting people. We were supposed to stay in that place for two days. But they got worried that the two who got left on the truck were going to die, so we were sent off the following day. The van came to collect us from the second iron gate. The back opened into the alleyway so we could get in without being noticed. The journey probably took about five to six hours but it felt longer because I was feeling sick. This bout of car-sickness was worse than before. I wanted to be sick but my stomach was empty. It was very uncomfortable. I got pins and needles in my hands and feet. I felt like I had lost my mind. I wasn't asleep, but I didn't know what was going on around me. This was the first time I felt that I shouldn't have left China. Surely I could have found some small corner where I would have been safe? I felt I was going to die. My whole body was in pain. I had turned blue-green in colour. Ming and other people sitting next to me tried to warm me up and to keep me alert. I didn't feel like this even when crossing into Germany.

I'm not sure whether we went to Amsterdam or Rotterdam. All these places that we went to, we didn't know exactly where we were. We would overhear others saying 'this is Czech Republic' or 'Germany'. I think it was Amsterdam because there was an underground train. (*Both cities have the Metro*). We drove into a big square and were split up into small groups and made to wait in different parts of the square so we wouldn't attract attention. It was a crowded square but people weren't really interested in us. After about ten minutes or so, I started feeling better. A *mazhai* came to pick us up. We travelled by train for forty minutes to where we were staying, which was like being in the countryside. It only took a few minutes to walk to the place, which was some kind of warehouse. The big front door was locked. We went through a small door next to it. Inside there was a window in the wall through which we could see a big hall. We climbed up a narrow and scary staircase to a small room under the roof. Two other people from the van joined us shortly but not the rest of them. The biggest snakehead gang in the world operates in the Netherlands. They have many houses. There may be four to five hundred people in the Netherlands at any one time.

By now Liu has been on the road for three months and has crossed seven borders. In the Netherlands, the Chinese population is 80,000 strong, a quarter of the size of that in the UK.[9] Liu tells his story haltingly today. He is not well. He's drinking some special Chinese herbal tea and burping a lot. He explains that his stomach is often upset these days, blaming it on the prolonged periods of severe hunger he suffered. He says that when he feels hungry now, his body starts shaking. Despite feeling unwell, he doesn't cry off – he has a huge capacity to keep going.

There were two floors in the building. We weren't allowed to mix with people on the first floor. On my floor there were two rooms, with about fifteen people in each room. The *mazhai* bought all the food, like in the other places, and kept it in the kitchen which was downstairs. There were similar problems about who cooked first and got the best food. Here things were even worse because there was no queuing system. Ping Jie, the snakehead boss, would tell the *mazhai* to buy nice food for us but most of the time they would keep the extra money. That's why there was never enough nice food to go around. Throughout the journey the powerful people ate better. The weaker people would wake up early to cook but would get into trouble for making noise and waking the others. The best food was chicken legs and eggs. When the chicken legs were finished, all that would be left was the very tip of the chicken wing. As I am a vegetarian, it didn't bother me. I preferred boiled rice with soya sauce and a small portion of vegetables anyway.

The rooms were small. People came and went all the time. When four of us turned up there wasn't enough room to sleep, so I moved to another room where there were four single beds, each to be shared by two people. The *mazhai* didn't mind because I had given them enough money, plus I didn't get aggressive with them. I made sure they knew that I had learned *kung fu* in China. The truth is that we weren't eating well so we were quite weak and I probably wouldn't have been able to protect myself if I had been put to the test. I also showed them magic tricks, did *zaji* (*acrobatics*) and acted the clown to please them.

I shared a bed with Ping Jie's ex-brother-in-law. He was the only one who agreed to share his bed. It was difficult to sleep on such a narrow bed. You have to hold the edge of the bed to make sure that you don't fall down, and on the other side you have to make sure that you don't squash the other person. The floor would have been better but it was full of people already. I couldn't sleep well. The guys in this room all had a criminal background in China. They had killed people. We had never come across such nasty types before. The *mazhai* couldn't control them. They got into a lot of fights with the others because they would use up all the best food. I always cooked with Ming and two other guys from our village, who were in a different room, and kept a distance from these guys.

I did, however, get quite friendly with the guy I shared the bed with. He was the younger brother of the Governor of Fujian province. The Governor had taken a younger mistress so his first wife, Ping Jie, had to find a means of living. She became a powerful snakehead and was protected by her connections. This is the problem with catching snakeheads in China: many people in government are implicated. When these people lose power, then their network of snakeheads gets smashed. This guy didn't get on well with his brother, so he asked his ex-sister-in-law to help him get out of China by an illegal route. He told me a lot about Ping Jie. That's how I know so much about the snakeheads. Ping Jie controls the largest gang in the Netherlands. I wasn't her customer, but the way it worked was that all those who came to the Netherlands became her customer. I met Ping Jie (*'Jie' means sister*) a few times when she came to see her brother-in-law, accompanied by her American boyfriend. She is a tall, good-looking woman who has had a few husbands in her time.

It hadn't occurred to me that there might be women in charge of triads or snakeheads. However, the only reference I could find to this was a website which stated blandly that triads are becoming more businesslike and, like all modern corporations, are taking on women. Liu says that he came across only five women at the higher levels during his journey but this seems to be quite a high number.

There were reports in 2003 of a snakehead Boss, Sister Ping, who was imprisoned for her people-smuggling activities. Ping is believed to have smuggled more than 200,000 men and women into the EU and her organization has been linked to the Dover tragedy.[10] 'Using a combination of violence and intimidation, Sister Ping swept all her rivals aside and cornered the people-smuggling market between Holland and Britain soon after arriving in Rotterdam in 1997. Through her connections to the triads – her boyfriend is the head of the triad gang 14K in Rotterdam – she was able to hire muscle to do her dirty work whenever necessary.'[11] Liu cannot believe that she has been arrested. He asks if this woman was tall. I say that the news report didn't mention that.

Yet another case of a Sister Ping, this time based in the US, was reported in 2006. She was a 56-year-old grandmother who was responsible for the Golden Venture ship, packed with 300 immigrants, of whom 10 died, which ran aground on the shores of New York city. At her trial, she was described by the authorities as 'the mother of all snakeheads', and charged with operating what prosecutors called 'a conglomerate built upon misery and greed'.[12]

*

I asked Ping Jie whether I was going to Italy. She called China and spoke to my snakehead. She said, 'no you are going to Britain'. But I was supposed to go to Italy! This is the trick that the snakeheads play on you. Italy wasn't a popular destination. It becomes very expensive to send just two people so they try and send you as a group to one place. When you get to a place that you didn't want to go to, they ask for more money to go to your original destination. Normally, I would have paid RMB20–30,000 from the Netherlands to the UK. But I had to pay RMB50,000 because I wasn't Ping Jie's customer. The snakeheads then sort it out between them. From China to Italy it only costs RMB130,000 in total. I paid a total of RMB180,000 to come to the UK (*over £12,000*). I called En in Beijing and asked him to transfer the money into the boss's bank account. Once the mistake has happened, it has happened. The snakehead in China knew that we weren't going to Italy when we were sent from Germany to the Netherlands. Only we weren't told. At the beginning I was quite upset that they had cheated me. Later I thought, I don't really mind where I am going because in Italy I only have the one friend. Even when you have a friend, you have to depend on yourself. I thought about staying in the Netherlands, but they said that if I did I would have to pay RMB20,000 extra because the Netherlands wasn't my destination. At that point I suppose I could have tried to run away, but I remembered that one of my friends who ran away was caught and beaten and then made to pay double the price.

We stayed in the Netherlands for three to four weeks. At the beginning we used to ask the *mazhai* how long we were going to stay. They would say that they were awaiting instructions from head office, and eventually we realized that there was no point asking. We didn't have much to do with our time while we were waiting. We would fight or talk and tell each other stories. There were no books to read, no TV and we couldn't go out. We used to do arm-wrestling. The strongest guy in the room, who had become number one in the house, couldn't be challenged by anyone, not even the *mazhai*. One day this baldy challenged me to arm-wrestling. We went downstairs in search of a quiet area. We weren't allowed to go to another floor normally, but the *mazhai* wasn't there.

He was quite strong but every game was a draw. So he suggested another form of arm-wrestling. (*At this point Liu gets up and demonstrates with a mop handle and asks Xiao Xing to stand up and hold one end of it.*) Basically, each person, facing opposite directions, holds one end of a wooden plank behind their back with one hand. With their free hands they do arm-wrestling in mid-air, but in the process the stronger man can force the other to bend backwards over the plank, which is quite painful to the spine and quickly brings an end to the game. When we played this, I was in a difficult position. I could have won – our arm strength was about the same, but my legs and waist were stronger than his – but I didn't want him to be toppled from his number one position in case his people beat me up later. I couldn't take his place because the people from my village were fewer than the people from his village. I knew we couldn't win as a group. We held this stalemate position for a little while. But he got tired and said 'you win'. His guys did try to beat me up for defeating him, and Ming, who tried to protect me, got hurt. I crouched down and protected my head with my arms and ducked out of the way as often as I could, even though they tried to pin me down. I got hit on my arms and legs but it wasn't serious.

The criminals left after a week. They were replaced by new people who respected those who were there before them, so we only had two or three *mazhai* looking after us and the atmosphere was less tense. One day Ming and I were told to get ready to leave. A group of six was leaving that day to go to Britain. We weren't supposed to be travelling with them but for some reason they took two people off that group and sent us instead. We walked a short distance to a shabby-looking house where a small lorry was waiting. It was dark but we could see the house because there was a small light. We got into the lorry. After driving for twenty minutes we stopped on a road which had trees on both sides, like woods. We were asked to transfer to a waiting container full of cartons and people. This container wasn't made from steel but hard-wearing, waterproof fabric. We had to climb on top of the cartons and crawl to the far end in the dark where there was a gap between the cartons and the wall dividing us from the driver's cab. There was a 2 ft gap between the top of the boxes and the roof of the lorry. We guessed that there were washing-machines in the boxes. There was a wooden shelf half-way down this narrow space. People could stand below the shelf and others could stand or sit on the shelf.

When my eyes got used to the dark, I could see that we were all tightly packed together. There were sixteen of us in all. It was really cold. To avoid being squashed, I stood neither on nor below the shelf. Instead, I wedged my feet between the two layers of cardboard boxes and held onto the metal framework which surrounded them. Whenever I got tired, I would crawl over the top of the cartons and lie down. They told us not to stay there because we might be seen if somebody asked them to open up. It was a twenty-hour journey and no toilet stops. There was such a dank and mouldy smell in the container already that even if people pissed inside the truck I wouldn't have been able to smell it. Usually it doesn't take that long, but they had a flat tyre – we could hear them changing it from inside. The container was opened three times during the journey. We would tell each other to be quiet and if we were at the top we would go to our hiding places.

When I arrived in the UK, I didn't pay attention to where they took us. I think we docked at Dover, but because we were hiding inside the container we were never sure where we had stopped and why. I didn't even realize we had gone through Customs. It had taken four months to get here. We were taken by car to a small, dark house somewhere in London, where we stayed for two days. Ming was still with me. They asked me where I would like to go. I was confused and worried. I didn't know what I was going to do next, I didn't know anybody here, and I didn't know what was going to happen to me. I asked them to send us to Chinatown, where we could find some work. My friend, En, in Beijing paid all the money that was owed to the snakehead. Two of the guys didn't have the rest of the money so they were beaten up in that house. I don't know where they are and what happened to them. I got quite close to some people I met on the journey and they still keep in touch although they are not exactly friends. People would come to me for stories and I liked that. I would tell them Kung Fu stories and military stories from the Mao Zedong period. After the fight in the Netherlands I think people started to respect me.

We were walking around Chinatown when we were approached by some Chinese guys who asked us if we wanted a place to stay. I don't know how they could tell we were new to the UK. They seemed to be working in pairs for different companies, and their job was to pick up new immigrants. They offered to help us apply for refugee status. A third pair of guys offered us the same thing. Then one of them said, 'I know you, I know your friend in Beijing. Your friend told me to look after you.' I thought the snakeheads must have told En that we were going to Chinatown and he must have rung some people and told them to look out for us. We went with them. En is very well-connected, especially with members of the government. But when I called En, he said he hadn't told anyone to look out for us in Chinatown. It's possible that our lorry driver told these guys about us. Their boss was the biggest in London. It is still the most powerful group. The UK is divided up into regions in which different triad gangs are powerful. They said, 'we will help you but don't play games with us'. We went on bus 238 on a one-hour journey to the place where we would stay. (*Liu wouldn't tell us the name of the area where he and Ming were taken for fear of reprisals.*) The building was on three floors. We had to pay RMB10,000 (£680) for one month's rent. The rent money included protection money and help with applying for refugee status, but not food. If we had any problems, we could go to them for help. We were dealing in RMB for the first few months because we didn't have any English money. The $500 that I had left from the journey wasn't enough. On our floor there were many apartments on both sides of a long corridor, but they were all closed. It was very quiet. The building belonged to some Vietnamese. We had a furnished two-bedroom flat; one bedroom was like a box-room.

Although I had entered without a passport and was technically illegal, I wasn't scared because we went to the Home Office the very next day to apply for refugee status. I thought how well everything had been arranged by the snakeheads. How good the British system was! One of the triad guys took me to the Home Office to fill out a form so that I could apply for refugee status. At that point, they don't ask you many questions, just your name and how you came to this country, the travel route, how many members in your family, what language you speak; and after that they tell you to wait. I said I flew to Budapest via Moscow, went by car to the Czech Republic and then by lorry to Britain. At the interview six months later, they asked me why I didn't apply for asylum in the first safe country I arrived in. I said we were more or less prisoners of the snakeheads and couldn't have gone anywhere without them noticing. The triad guys didn't come with us to this interview. There were interpreters at the Home Office. The triad guys had sold us an expensive package of accommodation and refugee status as if they were going to do the whole thing for us.

It was only three years later that the Home Office asked about my reasons for leaving China. The lawyer who had been introduced to me by the triad guys helped me to write my story. However, my application for asylum was turned down. If you are deported to Fujian province – Beijing is different – the police will catch you and make you pay a penalty of RMB20-30,000. If you can't pay it, they will beat you up. This isn't official policy. As a deportee, you are expected to pay RMB2,000, but in places like Fujian you are made to pay ten times more.

We stayed in that flat for about twenty days. When we first moved in there it was empty. Then lots of people moved in, about eight in total. I ended up without a bed or a blanket and had to use my jacket to keep warm. Sometimes after a gang fight the triad henchmen would also come to sleep there. Once in a while we were asked to fight on behalf of the Big Boss – you didn't have any choice. Basically, we had to become his thugs and we'd be sent out to fight other gangs for more business, customers like me, drugs and guns. I was told to make

12 inch iron coshes out of an iron bed we'd found in a skip. We cut the metal and used a special machine to smooth off the edges so you didn't injure yourself when you were carrying one. They were tied close to your body so that they couldn't be seen when you were walking on the street. Once when I was sent to fight, the man I was supposed to beat up turned out to be from the village next to mine. My Big Boss had bought a house in Colindale next to the police station. They would fight on the streets and the police wouldn't pay any attention to them. Another time I was sent to fight I got there just as it was finishing. One man had broken his ankle. I guess that's what you call good luck.

The Big Boss's henchmen would find us small jobs to keep us going, working for shopkeepers who needed porters, for example. I would get paid £20–30 for two to three hours each time, which wasn't bad. It wasn't worked out on an hourly basis. We would have to work quickly to unload a big lorry carrying vegetables and meat for take-away shops. In twenty days I did this on only five or six occasions, so I wasn't earning nearly enough. As the weather was really cold, we used to go to second-hand shops and buy trousers or jumpers for £1. We needed more work to pay for all our expenses. They would give us directions on how to get to places. I knew the alphabet so I would try and match the letters on the signs and my map. When I asked strangers for directions, I would point to the map. They would often misdirect me. After that, I only asked the transport staff. They were very polite. They would walk me to the right platform sometimes.

One lorry driver told us that he could find us work with a construction company and a cheaper place to live. I had worked for two years in a government construction company in Fuqing city after leaving school as an apprentice so I knew the trade. Although we had paid for the whole month, we moved anyway when we got the job offer because people are scared to hire you when you're in the control of a triad gang. Of course, we couldn't have asked for our money back. The job was in Holloway Road, knocking down chimney breasts in a three-storey house in very poor condition. The boss was Chinese and was paying £25 per day for work that started at 9 a.m. and finished at 8 p.m. The first week I worked seven days. This was in the spring of 1998. We had moved to Catford where the rent was £20 per week. It cost us £20 per week to travel to work, so you can see I didn't have much money left over. I remember buying a blanket for £14 – more than half a day's pay! This job only lasted three weeks. Plus, I had to pay £200 to the lorry driver because he had found me the job. I borrowed the money from a guy from my village. We shared the place with two other people who we hadn't known before, but we then became friends with them. It was a council house being rented out by Vietnamese. Four of us were in the living-room on two double beds. There were four people in another bedroom. And two people each in the other three bedrooms. Ming couldn't bring himself to do labouring jobs after working as a professional in China. So instead of working he was using the dollars that were left over from the journey.

They didn't give us masks to protect our lungs against all that dust. I got so choked up with it that I couldn't speak. When we asked the boss to buy masks he said that we should have brought towels with us. I got sick after seven days. I couldn't eat. Ming gave me Chinese medicine to make me better. When we didn't go to work, the employer called us. We said we were too sick to work. We rested for four or five days. He called us again and we went back to finish off the work. This was the first job I got in Britain and it was the worst one. It was very dangerous work. On the first day of that job we had to remove tiles from the roof. While I was doing this I fell to the floor below and, because the wood was damaged, I went through it but got stuck. My legs were dangling through the ceiling of the second floor. A fellow worker gave me some Chinese herbal cream to put on all my cuts and I rested for an hour. The supervisor said it was OK to rest because the employer had gone out to buy some materials. He returned just as we were picking up all the tiles that had fallen off the roof when I fell. He started swearing and shouting at us, 'I was going to re-use those tiles, now you have gone and broken them all, you fuckers.' One of my fellow workers was still bleeding from the cuts and the guy said he would prefer him to die than waste all his tiles. Later we discovered that he had been imprisoned in China many times. Last year I found out that he was in prison here for beating one of his workers so badly that he ended up in hospital for a few months.

The building was weak. We had bricks and tiles falling on us. The boss then sent us to another building to do an emergency job. The smoke-stack had come away from its moorings and was hanging precariously. I had to climb a ladder to fix it.

This is the beginning of one of many long and complicated stories about the minutiae of building work. Liu is busily drawing a picture, talking louder and louder and getting more and more agitated as he remembers how close he came to having a serious accident. I'm trying to understand the drawing.

The ladder wasn't long enough to reach the smoke-stack. Standing on the very last rung of the ladder, I bent backwards to reach the smoke-stack, when the ladder moved and I was left hanging in the air. I was holding the smoke-stack with one hand and the wall bracket with the other as the wind blew the smoke-stack further and further away from the building. The guy holding the ladder at the bottom had disappeared. The bracket was slowly working loose with my weight. I was getting really tired hanging on. I wanted to change hands but I couldn't. The guy came back and saw my predicament. He knew he couldn't reach me with the ladder. Cleverly, he used the ladder to pin the smoke-stack against the wall so that it was no longer swinging. I then slid down the smoke-stack to try and reach the ladder. Because I was moving so fast and the angle was wrong, I missed my footing and fell backwards onto the sloping outhouse roof. The edge of the roof, which was slightly raised, broke my fall... My fellow worker came to help me get off the roof, which was about 4 m off the ground. I somersaulted onto the ground. I was trying to avoid the blackberry bushes on one side. My hands were numb, bleeding and covered in blisters because of the chafing caused by the bracket and the rough metal of the smoke-stack. I had a lucky escape. I could have been killed that day.

All my energy drained out of me when I reached the ground. Just then the boss returned, saw me 'relaxing' and started abusing us. He wanted me to go back up and finish the smoke-stack. Three of us tried to extend the ladder but we couldn't. We finally tied the smoke-stack at a lower point. In the afternoon, three more people were sent to help us. We got two ladders and approached the smoke-stack from both sides. Between us we managed to get it done. After that we went home. We didn't get any more work from this guy. If it had been a proper company they would have used scaffolding. My body still feels the impact of that fortnight's work. My back hurts. I was damaged 'inside'.

Chinese Medicine divides into two branches – 'internal' and 'external' medicine – and anything to do with organ damage falls into the 'internal' branch.

In traditional Chinese medicine there are eight guiding principles to analyse and differentiate the imbalances in the body, which consist of four polar opposites: yin/yang, cold/heat, deficiency (xu)/excess (shi), and interior/exterior. Exterior conditions are those caused by the invasion of the body by pathogens, and are usually acute and superficially located with a short duration. Exterior symptoms are those that affect the hair, skin, muscles, joints, peripheral nerves and blood vessels. Interior conditions result from pathogens that enter the interior of the body. Interior symptoms affect the organs, deep vessels and nerves, brain, spinal cord, and bones.[13]

I was surprised that health and safety conditions were worse here than in China. The difference was as great as heaven and earth, as we say in China. There they give you warnings about dangerous parts of the building. If you work for the government you do the work step by step. But here we were working for private contractors who were pushing us to finish the work quickly. They cared only about profit.

After that, I didn't have another job for four or five months. To save rent, we moved to Burnt Oak, where we were only paying £10. This was like a place for homeless people, except it was run by private people for profit. The place was really bad. There were no beds. We slept on the floor. You couldn't even go to the toilet at night. I went once and came back to find that my place had been taken by somebody else. I don't know how many people were living there. People came and went. I think there were about ten people on average. I had my blanket and rucksack to sleep on. I was there for one week. Since arriving in England, I have moved house more than twenty times. Two friends who were also living there worked in a restaurant in Chinatown and brought back leftover food. When we moved, they said that we could carry on eating with them.

In the first year, I got only three months' work. I borrowed £3,000 from loan sharks which became £6,000 the following year. Then I moved to a place where I paid £7 rent per week. I couldn't even afford that. I worked in a Chinese restaurant for a couple of months. The boss was Malaysian. The chefs treated me badly. They would shout and scream at you if they weren't happy with your work. You couldn't argue with the chef. One day he asked me to carry a big pot of Jing soup to the stove. His junior chef thought it would be very funny to trip me up – the soup went all over the place and the chef blamed me. I was so angry. We had to buy cigarettes for the chef to keep him happy. Work started at 4 a.m. and finished at 11 p.m. We would go home by bus, get two or three hours sleep, then it started all over again. I got Sundays off. The chef would rest from 1 to 4 in the afternoons, but if you were new you weren't allowed to rest. Our wages were handed out by the senior chef who was given all the money by the owner. The owner had promised me £180 per week, but usually I got only £140 or £130. This was in 1998.

The Labour government introduced a minimum wage of £3.60 per hour in the UK in 1999. Liu's wage works out to £1.58 per hour, if the chef didn't cheat him, and £1.22 per hour if he did. Bobby Chen says that before the influx of the new immigrants in 1989, the older generation of

Chinese restaurateurs had difficulties finding new blood because their own children didn't want to work in a take-away for twelve hours a day. Businesses nowadays are sustained through paying staff well below minimum wages. Workers are exploited because of their lack of skills and because of their immigration status. The Fujianese are at the bottom of the rung, below the Hong Kong Chinese and the Chinese from Beijing and Guangdong who have been here for more than ten years and are in positions like deep frying chef, second chef and head chef, but when they buy their own take-away the Fujianese will move into their jobs. Bobby says that all his clients from 1989/90 are now self-employed with their own take-aways. 'I make a joke sometimes that I am going to draw a map of England to chart where all my clients have set up restaurants and then I can go out and get free dinners.'

Their shop is their only pension. The Chinese don't usually go to the Department of Health and Social Security (DHSS). Newly-arrived workers allow the owners to work on after fifty-five when they can no longer do such hard work, plus they can sell the shop onto them when they are ready to retire. Although the top end of the pay scale may be no more than £300 per week, a poverty wage for their long hours, they manage to pay back their debts and even buy a restaurant by living cheaply. 'They live the life of a sewer rat.' says Bobby. 'They come out, go on the underground, go to work, go home and straight to bed. In the winter they never see the sunlight. There might be four to six people sleeping in a 6 ft by 8 ft room.'

Then we moved to a place that was free. My friends thought they had seen ghosts there. I don't believe in ghosts as such, but I do blame ghosts for not having gone to university. I failed my final school exams despite being in the top five in a class of sixty. The night before the exam, one of the students woke up, saying that he had seen blood dripping from the ceilings. I couldn't sleep. That school was based in buildings where Chinese students had been tortured and killed during the China-Japan war in the 1940s. Later on, I heard that that student had mental health problems.

There were only three of us living in this haunted house with five to six bedrooms. It used to be rented out before, but the tenants didn't have enough money to pay rent. The landlord wasn't in the country so no one looked after it. It was very dirty. Even the front door was broken and it had no proper lock. There was no working kitchen, no electricity or gas. But we had water. We used to steal toilet-paper from restaurants. We slept on dirty, broken mattresses. We ended up staying there for one month – we were so poor that we couldn't even afford 9p to buy bread. We never stole food from a supermarket but we did steal apples from a tree in the garden of a house near the station when it was quiet. We finished all the apples. They were really sour, maybe they were cooking apples. In the garden of the haunted house there was a tree with fruits like the kind I had seen in the supermarket. The tree was very big, the fruit was brown, had a hard shell and was the size of a table tennis ball. I cracked it open and ate the white part on the inside, although it was quite hard. I became sick and Ming got a terrible headache. (*It can only have been conkers, which are easily mistaken for chestnuts.*)

That was one of my lowest points. I thought about going back to China. I wondered whether it would be better in Canada, but I would have needed RMB10-20,000 to get there. It was difficult to earn money in the first two years because I didn't know many people. But, by a stroke of luck, I bumped into this rich guy in Chinatown, who I had known in China. He asked me to work for him and provided me with free accommodation. All I had to do was sit with him when he did business with other people. Sometimes he might ask me to get papers signed by other people. It was like a miracle – he was against the triad, and didn't even ask me to beat people up on his behalf. One of the Big Bosses wanted to join his business but he didn't let him. I don't know what kind of business he was doing. Last year, however, he opened many big restaurants in the UK. But he had a problem with his visa so the Home Office sent him back to China.

This time I didn't have to pay an introduction fee. At first, I wasn't getting paid a salary but I could borrow as much money as I liked. I didn't borrow money from him in case he asked me to do things which I didn't want to do. But my other friends used my connection to borrow money from him. Then he started paying me £125 per week and my 'free' room had a notional rent of £25 per week, so it was £150 in kind and cash. A few months after the Chinese New Year in 1999, he introduced me to one of his friends to redecorate his house. This friend ran a redecorating business and said I could join him at any time. I started working for him because he offered me more money. The work was harder, but it was £30 per day for painting, £40 for woodwork, £50 for electrical work and plumbing. In the second year of working with him, I was able to clear all my debts.

When he went back to China for a couple of months, I worked for another man doing the same kind of thing. He gave us free accommodation and free food. He kept saying he would pay us next week, next week. This went on for more than two months. In the end, he gave us only £100 each. We worked very long days, from very early in the morning till midnight. On one occasion we cemented floors continuously for forty-eight hours without sleep. There were five of us in this situation. One man wanted to stop work earlier than the rest of us, so he went to the boss to ask for money. The boss slapped him, saying, 'how dare you come and ask for money when you haven't finished the work?' We were watching from upstairs. The man had blood coming from his mouth. Two days later, when the job was finished, five of us went to the guy and asked for our money. He said 'you have to wait'. We knew then that we wouldn't get our money so we left.

Then Liu's voice dips and I hear an almost imperceptible tremor in it.

My lowest point in Britain was in 2000 when my older brother was killed on his way here. He was one of the Dover 58 – that woke the British people up to the Chinese presence here.

He goes silent, a silence that feels heavy, following as it does on the heels of his voluble chatter.

Fifty-eight Chinese people, four of whom were women, suffocated to death in the back of a lorry entering Dover on a hot summer day. The driver of the Dutch-registered lorry had just made the crossing from Zeebrugge, Belgium, when his vehicle was pulled over for inspection by a Customs official. According to reports, when the container doors were opened a scene 'out of a nightmare' confronted the officer. Warm and putrid-smelling air rushed out. Two men lay by the doors, gasping for breath. Behind them were fifty-six corpses lying sprawled between crates of tomatoes. Officials who entered the container needed counselling.

It is likely that they died of asphyxiation, although there is a possibility of carbon monoxide poisoning. It is believed that they had been trapped inside the container for more than eighteen hours. Electricity to the refrigeration unit had been turned off throughout the journey. The two survivors were taken to hospital suffering from extreme dehydration.[14]

The survivors were given police protection and granted special leave to remain in the UK to assist police with their investigation. It took the police more than three months to identify the bodies. Families of the dead were denied entry to the UK to arrange their loved ones' funerals. The bodies were eventually sent back to China in January 2001. Seven people were convicted in May 2001 in a court in the Netherlands. They were found guilty of gross negligence over the deaths, but were cleared of manslaughter. Among nine defendants, two Turkish ringleaders – Gursel Ozcan and Haci Demir – were sentenced to ten-and-a-half and five years in gaol.[15]

We wait for the right moment to continue.

Workwise, it was my lowest point as well. For various reasons, it was difficult to find work in London, so I started working in Manchester.

Liu's story begins to fall apart. It seems to be connected with his brother's death. I am not sure whether it is too painful to talk about it or whether

there is another reason. He ducks and dives and does not answer our
questions. I ask him if he is afraid to talk.

I am not afraid of anything. The work became more difficult.
Sometimes we only worked two days a week, sometimes no work. I
did cleaning at restaurants when there was nothing else. It's very complicated. A family friend had arranged my brother's trip abroad. He
borrowed RMB200,000 (*approximately £13,000*). I am now paying it
back. His journey took four to five months. He did contact me occasionally. In between he disappeared for a little while. We didn't know
where he was. His journey wasn't as bad as mine. He flew from
country to country. He didn't have to climb mountains. But he did get
arrested in Hungary and was due to be sent back to China. I spoke to
the snakeheads and asked them to help him escape. They did, but it
was like he was destined to die. When I heard about the Dover 58 on
the news I went to the Central London Law Centre to ask for help to
find out if my brother was on that lorry. I had read about Bobby and
his partner Mr Li in the Chinese newspapers and magazines. Bobby is
a wonderful person. If he can help a perfect stranger, he will. He is not
calculating. I wish there more Chinese people like him. When it was
confirmed that my brother was one of them, I felt very emotional and
spoke to newspapers and TV to expose the Chinese government's
connection to the snakeheads – the deputy mayor of Fujian receives
bribes from snakeheads.

*Such large numbers of people cannot be smuggled out of China without
the co-operation of various government officials and departments. The
speed with which passports are churned out without all the relevant
documentation is possible only because officials in the Public Security
Bureau are bribed by the snakeheads. When groups of up to two
hundred migrants are found aboard ships without the correct paperwork the police turn a blind eye because their palms have been greased.
Apparently, some police officers accept bribes so regularly that they find
it hard to extricate themselves and become de facto members of the*

triad. Although the central government tries to clamp down on it, it is not very successful because provincial government officials are making a lot of money. From time to time central government will take action, like the sacking of the Mayor of Shanghai in 2006, the highest-ranking official to be removed for corruption in a decade. Allegations against him, according to a disciplinary report cited by the state Xinhua news agency, include assisting 'illegal business people', covering up for corrupt staff, and 'furthering the interests of family members'.[16]

A lot of TV companies asked for an interview. But the Fujian provincial government warned me not to help foreign propaganda against the Chinese government. As my mother and family are still living in Fujian I have to be careful. I am only co-operating with your project because you are more interested in my life here. The government sent police to my house in China on more than ten occasions. My brother-in-law was sent to prison for five years – he's just come out – and I felt very guilty. My brother and I were very close when we were young. My brother helped me out a lot with my factory and, after I left China, he spent a lot of time winding down the business. I feel very emotional when I think about that. My brother's case against the snakeheads isn't finished as yet. I can't say more that that.

Chinese civil rights activist, Jabez Lam, fills in the background that the Dover 58's claim for compensation to the Criminal Injuries Board failed. The Board argued that the victims were party to the crime. The lawyers for the campaign argued that the victims were not willing partners, they did not choose their mode of travel and they were not told about the conditions of travel. They sued P&O for compensation, but it denied all responsibility on the grounds that the Dover 58 did not have tickets and that they were not, therefore, passengers. There was a protracted debate in which the campaign argued that they were passengers by virtue of their presence on the boat. P&O did not accept liability but paid compensation known in insurance terms as a 'nuisance payment', which is made to avoid bad publicity and to minimize waste of time and

money. They paid out €500,000 in total to the fifty-eight families. Mr
Liu's family received a payment of €4,000.

I also offended the Big Boss. That's why I couldn't stay in London. The
Big Boss asked the police to arrest me. The house was crawling with
police, but luckily I didn't go home that day. This happened in
July/August. I can't tell you where I was living then because I don't
want to be identified. The landlord asked the police why they had
come but didn't get a proper answer. He got scared and asked me to
leave. I even went to the police station to ask. Later I asked my lawyer
to find out and we were told that it was a misunderstanding. I received
some threatening phone calls, telling me that my life wouldn't be
worth living unless I shut my mouth. I went to Bobby for advice,
whether I should ask the police for protection. In the end I decided
against it because it might make things worse for my family in China
    No company in London wanted to employ me once I had incurred
the wrath of the triads, so I worked in Manchester and other towns in
the north, but also in seaside towns all along the south-eastern coast
for one year. I went up to Manchester because I had a friend who lived
there and worked as a lorry driver. I thought it was far enough to get
me out of the triad's clutches. I stayed there for two months, sleeping
in a garden shed, full of tools, that belonged to a friend of a friend. I
was too scared to go out. I used to do small construction jobs secretly.
In the south-east I would be sent with a team of workers by car to a
house which needed redecorating. That's why I don't know the names
of the places I went to. That employer said, 'you can't tell people that
you are working for me and I won't tell people about you either'.
I didn't really mind how much I was earning as long as I had a place to
stay. I couldn't go back to London. In fact we used to go cockle-
picking by the seaside, but only for ourselves. The boss would only
provide rice, so the other workers and I would go to get seaweed for
myself and fish for them. Difficult to say how much I earned – about
£30 per day. It usually only covered my food and accommodation.
I suppose my days of slavery when I went hungry lasted three years

until the end of 2000. By 2002, I was earning £60 per day for a nine-hour day. The reason why I live in north London now is because the triad is more active in south London. They try and get protection money from people. Last year my friend's window was broken by them. They commit a lot of atrocities.

Bobby helped to sort out my immigration status too. Later, when Bobby tried to get hold of a copy of my previous statement, the Home Office couldn't find it. When he asked the previous lawyers for a copy, they sent only half the information. Then the Home Office called me for the second interview in Liverpool. My appeal was heard four times before I succeeded.

Liu's account of his application for asylum becomes very muddled. Bobby says that the case was adjourned four times. They lost the first appeal, which was heard by the adjudicator, because the Home Office argued that the group to which Liu claimed he belonged did not exist and that Liu had a criminal record. When Liu was doing one of his jobs in a restaurant in Chinatown he had gone to a room above the restaurant to sleep. Early in the morning someone else who lived there was fiddling with the front door key. As he couldn't open the door, a passing policeman got suspicious, thinking he was a thief, arrested him, entered the premises with him and found Liu sleeping. He arrested Liu and took him to the police station but let him go. They won at the tribunal, a higher court, when they explained the circumstances of his ' arrest' and provided evidence of the existence of the Quan Yin Method.

I got my status in November 2003. Once I had my National Insurance number, my wages didn't improve much, but it did allow me to go for the safer jobs. Only the illegal workers would take such risks with their life. My family joined me in September 2004. It cost me less to bring them all here than it did for me to come here. Without Bobby, I would never have got my stay here, and nor would I have been able to bring my family across so quickly. Of course it was difficult for my children to settle in at first. For the first year they couldn't attend school because they couldn't speak English and the authorities were trying to find someone who could help. My daughter particularly has been bullied, cheated out of money and laughed at in school because she couldn't speak English properly. But children are like that all over the world: sometimes they can be nice and sometimes really cruel.

Ming never got his right to stay. He is very disappointed. The lawyers didn't handle his case well. He never received the letter informing him of his interview with the Home Office. He should have had a second chance, but when he asked his lawyer, he said you can either go to an interview or we can write a letter outlining your case. He agreed to a letter being sent, but we found out later that a letter has a 100 per cent failure rate. The Home Office refused his application on the basis that his story wasn't true.

The interview is not optional. However, if someone misses their interview the Home Office may proceed to determine the case without one, and indeed use the failure to attend as a ground of refusal. There will usually also be substantive grounds for refusal, unless there is no information at all before the Home Office. If a client wants an interview, and he did not miss an interview appointment on his own account, he should be able to persuade the Home Office to give him another one, but if they do not accept that it is their fault then he may not get one.

Assessment of credibility of their account and the opportunity for the applicant to be tested at interview by the Home Office are key to asylum claims unless there are clear corroborative documents which support the account (which is rare). This is usually also the key factor in any appeal. In fact, most cases go to appeal and those that succeed, succeed at that stage. Under the Home Office's New Asylum Model procedure, which is currently being rolled out, the intention is for more cases to be granted at the decision-making stage by the Home Office so that the appeal success rate goes down but the overall number of grants remain the same.[17]

Ming went underground. He paid the lawyer £600 to sort out his case, but he did nothing. Bobby says too much time has elapsed now for him to be able to do anything. Ming is an honourable guy, the sort who won't try to get round the regulations by lying. He hasn't seen his family since 1997. He earns £240 per week as a chef. He is in a bad way. There have been many problems in his family so most of his money goes to them and he has huge debts to repay. He wants to return to China but because of his history he is stuck here. Normally, Chinese people who are here illegally can ask their families in China to send their ID card. When they present this at the Chinese embassy here they are given temporary travel papers. But because he is blacklisted his family can't even get hold of an ID card. For the same reason, his family can't get tourist visas to visit him here, even though China has relaxed its policy on foreign travel. The Chinese government doesn't allow foreign travel for the families of those who have been blacklisted. He's still trying to find a way to go back.

I used to be ambitious when I was younger. I feel I am not as successful as I could have been. My English is not good. I feel like a deaf and dumb person in this country. That's why I can only work for Chinese people. Physics used to be my favourite subject in school and I dreamt of becoming like Newton. I dreamt of going to Australia to study. I would've liked to do research. To this day I can remember the weight of the earth and the distance between the earth and the sun. I can sort out electrical problems. I found a broken microwave on the pavement once, brought it home and fixed it – it's still working. When I'm doing construction work and they have an electrical problem, I can usually sort it out, although I don't have a licence to do this. I didn't go to university, mainly because my family couldn't afford for me to continue studying. When you miss an opportunity in life, it never comes back.

I keep changing my dream. That's why I have never been successful. When I was about seven years old, all I dreamt about was 'the iron bowl', a guaranteed job in government from the time you start work till you die, a meal ticket for life. Then, in middle school, I wanted to become a doctor so that my family wouldn't have to pay to see a doctor. When my sister was sick we couldn't find a proper doctor only those 'without shoes' because those were the only ones we could afford. I studied various books of medicine so I know a lot about Chinese herbs. I can heal skin problems, treat blisters and I know the antidote for snakebite.

In 1965, with the launch of the Cultural Revolution, Mao decided to tackle the shortage of doctors in China's rural areas, where 80 per cent of the population lived. Thousands of peasants – men and women who were mostly in their twenties and already had some general education – were selected for an intensive three- to six-month course in basic medical care. The barefoot doctors, as they came to be known, continued farming in the commune fields alongside their comrades. This enabled them to be easily accessible to those in need. They provided basic health care: first aid; immunizations; health education and hygiene; maternal and infant care. Ten years after the Cultural Revolution, there were an estimated one million barefoot doctors in China.[18]

Now I earn £100–200 per day but I still don't have regular work. That's why it's difficult for me to tell you how much I earn. Sometimes I don't have work for a few months at a time. My wife can't work because she has to take our youngest to school and back, and then she has all the cooking and housework to do. Although he has been going to school for over a year, he still doesn't speak much English. My daughter is in year ten and hopes to become a fashion designer. She is very artistic. My older son finished middle school in China and goes to college to study Level 2 English. He is not sure what he wants to do. He thought about becoming a doctor, then getting a job in IT, but feels that his English isn't good enough for either profession.

I hope to buy a house and get my three children educated. I want to buy houses in poor condition, do them up and resell them. Construction materials are cheaper in China, and I'm thinking of importing them and selling them at a higher price or using them in my refurbishment business. The Chinese government encourages its citizens to stay here because the money they send home helps the economy.

Bobby Chen recounts a story, 'Just before Christmas 2004, the Home Office undertook an operation to nick every Chinese person who was here illegally, unauthorised or pending removal and was signing on every month. After they got arrested, they were put into detention centres like Harmondsworth. They had Chinese government officers interviewing them to ascertain whether they were Chinese nationals or not. And if they were removable they would be sent back to China. The local Public Security official told my client that the central government wanted him to take some people back but as a Fujianese, he knew that their remittances were important to the economy. 'Do you want to go back,' he asked. 'No,' said my client. 'Ok,' said the official, 'We'll look into it.' I had three clients in there, two of them are out now because the Chinese government wouldn't accept them.

One of my ambitions is to help build a school or a road in my village back home, to do good works and get a good name for myself. I haven't seen anyone from my family since I left in 1997. I used to speak to them on the phone quite regularly, but now I only phone occasionally, although my wife talks to her parents every week. I feel I am stuck in a rut. Everything has become a hope. I haven't got very far with my English and I have no computer skills. I have tried to watch DVDs of English films to improve my English, but I usually give up and watch Chinese films instead. So much more enjoyable! My health was so damaged by the hard physical labour that I have done in dangerous conditions that I cannot see myself being able to continue with this kind of work. What will I do as I get older and I don't have any other skills? If I hadn't been pushed out of China, I would never have come here. (*Liu sighs deeply.*) Life was better there. When I get old, maybe in ten or twenty years, I'd like to go back to China. I have a feeling that my children won't want to return, but that's up to them. If I can get back safely, then that's what I want more than anything else in the world.

AMBER LOBEPREET: I had Nowhere to Go

Many of the women who come to SBS for help, women from the Asian subcontinent who have married British men and whose marriages have broken down, live lives of sexual and domestic servitude, and are tortured by demands for dowry – a form of buying and selling women – outlawed in India but still an extensive practice. Amber was the first of a number of women I met who found themselves in similar circumstances. I remember she cried all the way through our meeting. Her married life in Britain had all the hallmarks of slavery, but it appeared that at the point of marriage she had acceded willingly, surrendered herself to the romantic myths perpetuated so extensively in the subcontinent by Bollywood. She did not have to be dragged kicking and screaming to her wedding rituals. The kind of forced marriage scenario I had imagined seemed to be more of a feature in the lives of young Asian women brought up in Britain, where parental conditioning was mediated by other values and cultures at school and society at large. British-raised women had other options and the only way they would submit to tradition was through force or parental deception. This brought me to the notion of choice, a theme that has been running just below the surface in every example of slavery I have examined. The notion of choice throws into relief the fine dividing line between arranged and forced marriage and the fact that the underlying logic of the first opens the door into the second.

Even where an arranged marriage goes seriously wrong, many women claim to be in love with their abusive husband. But when you examine this idea of 'love' you discover fear of independence, of censure, of exclusion, of poverty and homelessness, and deeply-embedded ideas of shame and honour. Here are women who have been brought up in rural, isolated societies, steeped in the traditions passed onto them by their parents, without the knowledge or possibility of leading any other kind of life as adults other than as wives.

I returned to Amber six months after our first meeting and found a remarkable transformation. She had acquired a measure of quiet self-confidence. Her wounds were no longer so raw after the benefit of sustained counselling provided by SBS. She did not weep once during the entire interview, although her voice shook occasionally.

I was born in the village of Dhadakhurd, Punjab, India in 1983. My mother fell very ill as a result of my birth. I don't know exactly what happened. I think I was born at home, but I'm not sure. I can't check this information because I am no longer talking to my parents. Generally, babies were born at home with the help of a midwife. My mother had a difficult delivery. I was a big baby and remained quite chubby throughout my childhood. I don't have any photos of myself as a baby. My first photo dates from the age of three, I think. When I grew up I asked my parents why they didn't take photos of me when I was a baby and they said that they never had the time. On top of that, my mother was ill. My mother saved some of my baby clothes and you can see how big I was from that. My God!

My mother was bedridden for about two years. So daddyji[1] looked after me. He used to tie me to his back when he went to work in the fields. He would lie me down on the ground on a piece of cloth while he cut hay for our buffalos. I loved my father a lot. He said it was probably because he had been the number one carer in my early life. I had two older brothers. There is a gap of two years between each of us. My father owned what was known as five fields, two and a half of which were owned by his younger brother. It wasn't considered much.

He would have to work for other landowners to make ends meet. We used to grow wheat, corn, sunflowers and peas. The land was not fertile and there was a big shortage of water. We kept buffalos and cows in a small hut near our house.

I used to sleep with daddyji. We all slept in one big room and stacked up our *charpais*[2] against the wall in the daytime to free up living space. There was a storeroom at the back, a small courtyard which separated the kitchen from our room, and another small room where my paternal grandparents slept. It was a brick-built house. We had running water in our toilet and bathroom because my father had installed a pump and a tank. We even had an English toilet because my grandmother found it hard to squat on the ground.

When I was still young, my father went to work in Dubai for a couple of years as an electrician. He had received some training in that field. He brought back a colour TV and a VCR with him so we gave our old black-and-white TV away. We used to eat quite simply. We were vegetarians anyway. Daddyji would milk the buffalos and my mother would make butter. Every morning we would have *parathas*[3] with a lump of butter and mango pickle. It was heaven. And *saag* with *makai ki roti*.[4]

My brothers and I all went to the same school in another village. I was there from the age of three to eighteen, except for a few months when I went to England. The school was far away and my brother would take me there on his cycle. I studied arts subjects at school. These included English, Punjabi, history, political science, Hindi and maths. I used to get the most marks in politics and Punjabi. I would usually come second or third in school, and won some prizes. My brothers would pass their exams but they didn't get any prizes. My parents would say to my brothers, 'look how intelligent she is, and look at the marks she gets'.

When I was eight, the opportunity arose for us to come to England. My father had made friends with this man in Dubai. His son was going to Britain to study, but as he didn't have enough money my father helped him to get the money together. They became good friends in the process. The son then got married in Delhi and took his wife back to Birmingham where they went on to have two daughters. But then he had an accident and damaged his leg so badly that he could only walk with crutches. His girls were still very little and his wife couldn't cope with looking after all of them. His own mother had died, so he applied for my mother to go to the UK for six months to help his family through this period. My mother didn't want to leave me behind, because she felt I was too young, so I went with her.

I found it very strange. Everybody was busy all the time. You could hardly find anybody at home. At the same time, there was hardly anyone on the streets. I missed my daddyji so much when I was at school here. I did learn a little English but I was bullied at school – there was a much older Indian boy who used to hit me and kick me. I complained to my uncle and he went and saw my teacher. In the end, the teacher would accompany me to the school gates and my uncle would fetch me from there. I used to be really scared to go to school because of this boy, but even though my uncle shouted at him a couple of times he didn't pay any attention. Towards the end of my stay I became very fond of an Indian teacher who used to speak to me in Hindi – the others were all white. When I went back to India I missed her a great deal. My brothers teased me about the bully, wondering how a girl who had been fattened on the ghee and milk of India couldn't fight back. But my stay in England gave me quite a lot of status back at our school.

When I returned from England, my teachers would tease me, saying that the Queen's daughter had returned. My older brother went to college briefly after school and then started working to support my father who was farming on his own. When I turned sixteen, I took on responsibility for keeping the house clean and doing all the laundry. My mother couldn't bend and wash the clothes because she used to have neck and backache. I think it was caused by the problems she had in childbirth. She couldn't even dispose of the buffalo dung, which has to be carried quite a distance; Daddyji had to do that. I also did most of the cooking. After that I would do all my school homework.

As soon as I turned eighteen, my mother started talking about my wedding plans and all the things that they would have to do. She would tell me how to behave with everyone in my husband's family; that I mustn't answer back even if somebody says something rude or hurtful, that I must respect my elders, but also the younger members. My friends and I were not even allowed to go out anywhere after school unless we were going to the gurdwara. I used to dream of falling in love like in the movies. I didn't fall for anyone in school although I used to get plenty of offers. I was worried that if I did anything wrong I would bring shame to my family. This sort of behaviour is not tolerated in the village. We wouldn't have been left alive. Once, when I was only ten, I got a love letter from a stupid boy. He must have been no more than twelve. Boys get up to all sorts of tricks even at a young age. Imagine giving a girl a love letter at such a young age! I showed the letter, without even reading it, to the headmaster and the boy was expelled from school.

It was a mixed school until the ninth standard when we turned thirteen. After that we studied separately. The boys were not allowed to play near the girls' section. Sikh schools are very strict. If the teacher discovers a relationship between a girl and a boy, they will be expelled. For example, there was a very modern girl in our class who had an affair with a boy and the head kicked them both out. As Sikhs, we are not allowed to cut our hair and this girl had her hair cut short. All of us used to tie our long plaits with ribbons. Another girl in my class fell in love with our teacher. They both came from the same village, which is a big no-no in our tradition. You must marry someone from another village because people from the same village are all supposed to be related. He was very highly educated although his parents were poor. When the teacher received a marriage proposal from America, the girl started saying that only she should marry him, no one else. They knew their parents wouldn't agree. They both took poison and committed suicide. You know how strict they are in India. When people fall in love, the parents usually react by quickly marrying them off to someone else. In India girls are dragged backwards, they are not allowed to go out, and their life is full of dos and don'ts.

When I finished school, my father was at first reluctant to allow me to go to college because I would be mixing with boys. My father let me go for a two-month sewing course in a village near us. Then I did a beauticians' course for a year which was quite expensive. I really wanted to do nursing, but my father wouldn't let me. One of his friends who was a doctor even offered to get me admitted on a course because my marks were so good – I got a first class when I matriculated – and suggested that I could stay with them while I was studying. It was really hard to get places on that course. That wish of mine was left unfulfilled. We have to obey our parents; there is no way out of that. Mummy would tell him that they would be able to find a nice boy for me if I was better educated. Even the teachers were putting pressure on him. All my friends were studying in a women's college. Finally, daddyji agreed. I enrolled on a BA. The college bus would pick us up and drop us off. My father would accompany me to the bus-stop. That college was also very strict. No men were allowed on the premises.

My father was strict. I was never allowed to go to the cinema, for example. If I wanted to see a film it would be a Hindi movie at home on the video. Although I was spoilt as the youngest child, there were many restrictions as I grew up. My father would go everywhere with me, whereas my brothers had freedom of movement. However, my brother was obliged to marry the girl my parents found for him although he didn't like the way she looked. But they're happy now. Sometimes I was allowed to play games on a stretch of empty land right opposite my house with my cousins who lived nearby. My brothers would tell my father that I was growing up and shouldn't be allowed to play. Daddyji would also tell me to concentrate on my studies. But my mother wouldn't say anything. On the contrary, she and my grandmother would sit on a *charpai* and watch us. We loved playing cricket and hopscotch and 'pittu'.

My parents were becoming anxious that I had reached a marriage-able age and that they needed to start looking. My mother had got married at eighteen. My cousins were all getting married, one by one. My friends' parents were also on the look-out for suitable boys. It made me think that perhaps I too had reached that age. In any case, we were not brought up to challenge our parents. I felt I was being pushed out of my own home. Why did they have to get rid of us so quickly? I had no choice. I couldn't object. My friends and I never even discussed sex. I remember when a baby was born in the extended family and we went to visit, I asked my parents where the baby had come from. I was told that God had thrown her from the rooftop and I believed it. I must have been about sixteen years old. Although I had watched Hindi films which were full of romantic love, I didn't realize that that led to babies.

I learned about sex just a couple of days before my wedding when my brother's wife, Dev, explained what the husband does to you, how you link up with the man when you sleep together on the first night. A woman did not have to do anything. She just waits for her husband to touch her. I was so shocked. I had never heard of such a thing. How, if the date was right, you could fall pregnant, how the body makes eggs. When I started my periods, I went to my mother to ask her how I could have hurt myself. She asked me where the blood was coming from. I said from down below. Apparently it was normal for girls to start periods at a certain age, but my mother didn't tell me why. My older cousin told me that we get periods in order to have children, but the connections still didn't fall into place.

My grandmother's friend said that she would look for a boy for me. My future husband was twenty-seven when he came to India in 2004 – his father's sister was the great-niece of my grandmother's friend. They were on their way to see another girl when the matchmaker, my grandmother's friend, told them about me. The whole family came to see me the following day. We bought cold drinks, and cooked a lot of food. My husband's family ate meat but we cooked only vegetarian food. We sat them in the new section of the house on the terrace. There were quite a lot of people. We had also invited my brother's matchmakers, who were related to my husband's family. I remember when my father was handing out Cokes, he tripped, and the glass of Coke smashed into pieces under my husband's feet. Maybe it was a bad omen.

I wore a Punjabi suit which is also known as a salwar kameez. It was a turquoise and dark-blue print which had been made especially for such an occasion. I didn't have any make-up on. Unmarried girls are not allowed to wear any. I had plaited my hair. This was my first experience of being 'shown off' to a suitor. I was petrified. I sat there looking down. My husband sat opposite me and was looking at me. I darted a quick glance at him. I thought, let me at least see what he looks like. He was no Shahrukh Khan,[5] he was quite fat and tall and wore glasses. My heart did sink, but you cannot say anything. At least he was clean-shaven. I didn't like beards. All my brothers and my father are clean-shaven. Only my grandfather wears a turban. He smiled at me. I smiled back. But he didn't say anything. Our families were talking among themselves.

The Sikh religion requires men to wear the five Ks – Kanga (comb), Kaccha (boxer shorts), Kara (steel bangle), Kirpan (small sword), and Kesh (hair). As they are not supposed to cut their hair, they wear a turban to keep it tidy. Turbaned Sikhs are usually considered to be more conservative than clean-shaven ones, although Amber thought there was no difference.

His mother, Satvant Kaur, asked me what I was studying. Then they sent me and him and his younger sister, Sukhvinder, into another room so that we could talk 'privately'. What would I say to him? Thank God his sister did most of the talking. She told me about their older sister, Narinder Kaur, and her son, Jasbir, who lived separately from them in London and had not come to India. The only question my husband, Amardeep, asked me was which singer I liked the most. I said I liked them all because I liked one song by one and another by another. He laughed and on my wedding day he explained that he found it funny because he just knew that I would give an answer like that. He was born and brought up in the UK. He spoke Punjabi halt-ingly, like a child. It sounded very sweet. His family called him Raj.

His mother came in and asked about my brothers. I don't know how old she was. She looked pretty healthy, although I have found out since then that she has false teeth. Narinder, her older daughter, was thirty-five years old. Maybe she was fifty-five years old. She took her son aside. He said that he liked me, but before he gave a final answer he wanted to show my picture to his uncle who had not been able to come with them and in whose house they were staying. His own father was dead and his uncle was like a father to him. I liked the sound of that. I thought, here is a young man who respects his elders. He must be a good man. They asked my father for a picture of me. Sukhvinder also took a picture with her phone-camera to send to her older sister. When his mother asked me what my surname was, she misheard and thought I had the same name as them because our names sounded fairly similar. By then she had already approved of me and thought for a moment that the wedding could not go ahead. We were both Sikh Jats but we do not marry people of the same surname because we consider ourselves to be related.

Jats are a tribe of people who are mostly Hindu although there are some Sikh and Muslim Jats too. They belong to the Kshatriya or warrior caste and were a prime target for recruitment into the British army because of their martial reputation.

One week later they phoned us to say that they wanted to go ahead. They wanted the engagement to take place immediately, before they returned to England. My parents thought he was suitable. I was not asked for my opinion. We organized the engagement in a hurry. We both had lots of relatives that we wanted to invite. There were at least fifty or so guests.

According to custom, we had to give them gold jewellery. Some of it my mother had collected in anticipation of just such a day. They booked a hall, or 'palace' as it is known, from 10 a.m. onwards. I wore an ordinary red, cotton suit because there was no time to get anything stitched. They bought me earrings and a necklace with red stones set in artificial gold. My husband and his family turned up late at about midday. It was all last minute for them too. On the way they picked up a moviewallah to film the ceremony. They also bought me a Punjabi suit and make-up because they are required to give something to the bride. First they filmed me in my clothes, then they made me change into their suit, then Sukhvinder did my make-up and they filmed me again. We served tea, sweetmeats and savoury snacks like *bhajia*. Then there was some more filming. We exchanged rings, my father put a gold chain around Raj's neck, he put a bracelet on me, and my mother gave his mother gold earrings. Everybody was very happy with the arrangements. But I was going to be leaving everything behind, and I began to feel like an outsider in my own family. What kind of family was I going to join? I didn't see them again until my wedding in February – his face would swim into my mind from time to time, but that was all. I comforted myself with the thought that if he showed so much respect to his uncle, perhaps he would love me too.

My mother-in-law (*saas*) would ring me regularly in the interval, but, after a while, she started saying some disturbing things, like they wanted a very big 'palace' for the wedding because a lot of people would be attending from their side. My father started to worry. He didn't have enough money. How would he be able to afford it? He was determined to do the best he could for the only daughter that he had. Then she demanded sets of gold jewellery (*a set usually consists of earrings, necklace and ring*) for each member of the family. I'm not sure how much money we're talking about, perhaps 4 or 5 Lakhs – 1 Lakh equals Rs 100,000, so about £4,500–£5,700. She also asked for a car! My father felt these demands were unreasonable. He began to suspect that they were just greedy and that I may not be happy with them, so he spoke to her saying that he couldn't afford to meet all their demands and would have to call the wedding off. Immediately my *saas* changed her tune, blaming the matchmakers for making all these promises. That reassured my father somewhat. He borrowed money from the money-lenders in the market-place – you pledge your entire harvest and borrow money against that. I spoke to Raj only a couple of times during this period. We had very little to say to each other beyond 'hello, how are you?' I was shy, and perhaps he was too. My *saas* did all the talking. She would ask me what I was doing, how I was keeping and advised me not to do too much work in my house now that I belonged to them.

The day of my wedding approached. My husband's family arrived two weeks ahead. My husband came about five days before the wedding because he could not get enough leave – he worked as an assistant bank manager. Narinder, Raj's older sister, came to see me too. We had to give material for suits and money to her young son. My cousin decorated my hands with henna. A lot of people had turned up from my maternal grandmother's village. Following tradition, they walked round the village singing bawdy songs, with silver pots decorated with sequinned red cloth on their heads. The pots were set on the ground and then weighed down with wheat grain, and a candle, or *diya*, was lit and placed on the lid. I walked at the head of the procession with a *diya* on a steel tray. The singing and dancing went on late into the night but I was not allowed to dance. This ceremony, called the *jago* ceremony, is carried out in the village of the bride and separately in the groom's village. I was surprised to find that they do this in Britain too. Then we had the *Choora* ceremony, in which my mother's brother put coloured glass, or nowadays plastic, bangles on me after dipping them in watered-down milk.

My parents gave me twenty-one Punjabi suits and two *lehengas*,[6] as well as the one I wore on my wedding day. All my things were laid out on display before the wedding at my parents' house and, afterwards, at my in-laws' house, where their gifts were added to the display. My parents had given me a gold set which consisted of a necklace, earrings and a *tikka* – a gold pendant with a long chain which is clipped to your hair with the pendant dangling on your forehead. On display also were the set that we had given to my *saas* and my sisters-in-law, the gold chain for Narinder's husband and her son, and a bracelet for my husband. There was also a ring and a chain for my father-in-law, despite the fact that he was actually dead. My *saas* had demanded it. She said that we can't leave him out just because he's dead. We have to keep his name alive. Everybody thought it strange asking for gold for a dead person, which would never be worn. They just wanted as much gold as they could get; I had never met such greedy people before. They had also given me a gold set, six gold bangles, one sari and about eleven suits – a mixture of plain, printed cotton suits to wear at home and heavily-embroidered ones for special occasions. They also gave me a simple *lehenga* made from pleated gold cloth but without any embroidery, which I didn't wear, even once. All these things are with my in-laws. I came away with very few things although I do have my wedding *lehenga*. They kept the wedding sari. It was gorgeous.

It is a tradition to give the bride 11, 21, 31 or 101 suits and perhaps more. Adding one to a number is considered auspicious. The clothes, along with the jewellery, are laid out on display so that friends and neighbours can troop in and examine them and be suitably impressed or disappointed. They signal the status and wealth of the family.

The following day I was driven to the beauty parlour in a car owned by my father's friend. My aunt came with me. I was weeping continuously while they were doing my make-up. They said, 'we can't do your make-up because it is running the moment we put it on you'. This was my last day in my childhood home. Everyone was saying, 'don't cry, all the girls have to leave home'. I wore a heavily-embroidered, maroon *lehenga* and a heavy gold jewellery set. When I got to the hall, the 'palace', my younger brother pretended not to recognize me. Everyone said that I was looking beautiful. But I was feeling very sad. I didn't eat anything that day, and the *barat* (*the groom, his friends and family*) was late, which didn't help. People were wondering what the groom would wear. In our village, people wore European suits on such an occasion but we had heard that it was fashionable for the men to wear churidar *kurta*[7] suits, which we found strange. My cousins reported to me that Raj was wearing just that and we all burst into laughter.

We then had the *milni* (*meeting*) ceremony, in which all the main members of the bride's family exchange garlands with their opposite numbers in the groom's family. The bride's family also give woollen shawls and gold chains to the groom's family on such an occasion, but as these are expensive my *saas* had told us that it was best to exchange them in advance, in private, so that we did not have to meet the demands of her extended family to be given these items. However, what she was really doing was putting on a show that we had given them nothing. The morning prior to the wedding, *shagan pani*, when we exchanged gifts at their house, they had taken all these things from daddyji. It had included a suit for the groom, a coconut, almonds, pistachios and some gold item which signifies that the boy is now ours. We didn't realize till later that she would use this to present the wedding in another light.

Then the *barat* entered the palace and my *saas* asked my family to bring the bride out so that she could be filmed. When I came out, my *saas* and other members of the family commented on how beautiful I looked. They were also impressed with my clothes and jewellery. They were exactly what they wanted. My husband and I were filmed. I glanced at him and saw that he was wearing those strange clothes with a red scarf and a turban, but he looked good. Everything had turned out well. I got quite bored by the filming. They make you pose in many different ways. They then took me off to a separate room and filmed me there. I had to feed sweets to my husband. He fed me in turn. He was trying to get me to eat, saying that I was thin enough.

First we served tea and snacks, then the *phere*, the wedding ceremony, began. To begin with, we had to circle our holy book, the Guru Granth Sahib, four times. Raj was walking really fast as if he had to catch a train. His sister tapped him on the shoulder and asked him to slow down. Then he slowed down so much that I kept bumping into him and tripping over my *lehenga*. The groom led with a scarf draped round his shoulders and I had to hold the other end and follow him.

My father handed me the other end of the scarf to signify that I now passed from his control to that of my husband. Then the Granthi (*priest*) sang hymns which described how a bride must behave with the man to whom she is now joined and at the home of her in-laws. I cried all the way through. The *phere* took place in a gurdwara which was in a different village. From there, we were taken by limousine back to the palace for the reception.

At the palace we were welcomed by a band. Everybody stood up as we entered the hall. People started dancing in front of us, including my younger brother. My sister-in-law told my husband to hold my hand. My husband's uncle held our hands over the knife and cut the cake. Everybody came up and stuffed a piece of cake in our mouths, as is the tradition. I couldn't eat so much sweet stuff, but they wouldn't listen to me when I asked them to stop. My brothers never got their turn because they were busy making sure that things were running smoothly. There must have been 400 guests in all, 200 from each side. About twenty people came down from Britain in the *barat*; the rest were local.

Then Raj and I sat on special chairs on the stage and exchanged garlands. The backdrop was heavily decorated with flowers. People queued up to throw money into our laps. Some of the money from my lap fell on the floor. One of Raj's relatives picked it up and put it in his lap. After that we sat down to our meal. While we were eating, a singer entertained us. Raj and I had to feed each other the first mouthful. That was all I could eat. Then Raj tried to give me a few more mouthfuls. Raj's mother had asked us to serve meat and alcohol, which made it all very expensive.

When the wedding was over, his mother wanted the *doli* (*the ceremony that marks the bride's departure to her husband's home*) to take place at our home. My family agreed reluctantly because there was quite a lot of work to do and it would have been quite a palaver for everyone to come back to ours. Not everyone could come back because of the size of my house. We had to serve everyone cold drinks. My brothers and my parents wept a lot. I didn't get that on camera because the video man didn't come back with us. The singer had come and he sang a few songs. It is a tradition for the bride to take a child with her. I took my uncle's son with me and also my younger brother in the limousine. As the weather was cold, the heating was on in the car and I was boiling. My brother was perspiring terribly. His collar got soaked. I hadn't eaten and with the heat I began to feel sick. The car was driving very slowly, perhaps because the roads are so small. Finally, my brother could bear the heat no longer and asked for the heat to be turned down. I still ended up being sick out of the window. There was a bar area in the car from which they gave me a glass of water and I felt much better.

When we got home there were other rituals. Raj and his family were staying at his uncle's bungalow. Their own home is quite old and the new home that they were building wasn't finished as yet. We were given two rooms, a large one for the whole family and one for me and my husband. My *saas* circled a container of clean water around me and Raj about five to seven times, symbolizing that she will share whatever troubles we face. She is supposed to drink the water while her son pleads with her not to. However, after the final round, he lets her drink it. My *saas* put bangles on me and we were filmed doing that. I sat alone with all the older women. My husband had disappeared somewhere. They were insisting that I eat, but I was still feeling sick. One lady gave me a drink of Coca-Cola with salt. That made me feel better. I ate a little after that. They took me upstairs. On the first night, husband and wife don't sleep together. I slept in the big room with his whole family. But nobody had thought to work out where my husband, *bechara*, would sleep. I had taken his place in the room. He stood outside the room and watched the proceedings. The door was open and we were all sitting and chatting. One of his aunts asked him what he was doing. He said no one was in the least bit interested in him. 'Should I go and sleep in the kitchen?' he asked. Everybody started laughing. 'Oh my God!' his mother said. 'I forgot about him completely.' Finally they gave him a bed in one corner of the room.

The following day I went home to visit my family with my husband and other relatives. They dressed me up in a sari. The matchmaker made a bun out of my hair. I was given a gold set and they put a *tikka*[8] on my forehead. Many of our neighbours and friends had turned up to satisfy their curiosity about how I looked on my first visit home. Again, my parents had to organize tea and snacks. On this visit the groom is supposed to give all my girl cousins inexpensive, silver rings along with a coconut.

I spoke to Dev, my sister-in-law, and said I was really nervous as we were going to sleep together for the first time that night. She advised me not to be scared; everything would be fine. It was also the last day of my period. That made it worse. We left quite late that day. On the way the family decided to eat at a restaurant as there was no time to go home and cook. It was a nice, glass-fronted restaurant. One aunty went to investigate it and walked straight into the glass. She hurt her forehead. We couldn't stop laughing. Then all the ladies wanted to go to the toilet. The same aunty slipped in the toilet and hurt herself some more. We became hysterical. Then they brought a bowl of hot water with a lemon in it for you to clean your hands. Someone told this aunty that it was for drinking and, because she was a village woman, that's exactly what she did. I had come first in domestic science in school. I knew exactly what to do with cutlery and how to lay a table. My *saas* was pleasantly surprised that I knew all this despite the fact that I lived in a village. One of the relatives suggested that they rent a room in this place and leave me and my husband there for a couple of nights, a kind of honeymoon. My *saas* thought that it was too dangerous, that there were thieves around and that they might kill us in order to steal from us.

When we got home we played some more games. For example, you add milk to a pot of water so it becomes murky. Somebody threw money into the pot and my husband and I were supposed to scramble around for the money to see who would come up with the most. My husband would win each time. His uncle said he was cheating. He would put his one hand on top of both mine to stop me from looking for the money while he used his free hand to feel around at the bottom of the pot. Then Narinder took me to our small room. Although there were no flowers on the bed, it had been nicely done up and was very clean. She sat me in the middle of the bed. She arranged the folds of my sari so that it looked like a flower like they do in the Bollywood movies. When she left, I started shaking. What will happen when my husband comes up? A hundred questions came to mind. He took ages – about twenty minutes. It was already very late. Maybe they were giving him training too. When the door opened, I became a bag of nerves. My God, he's here! He came in and shut the door. I kept remembering my sister-in-law's words. He changed into a *kurta pyjama*. Then he sat in front of me and started talking to me. He put his hands on my legs. I think he intended to do something, but when he felt them shaking he didn't proceed. There was a glass of warm milk by the bedside. They put this out for you on the first night. He told me to drink some milk. Perhaps he thought it would calm me. I had a little at his insistence. It had become cold. He said we should drink it so that tongues don't wag. I'm not sure what he meant.

He started telling me all about his family. Sukhvinder was hot-tempered. He said that I should tell him if she said anything hurtful, but not say anything directly to her. He did not want to upset her because she had become particularly sensitive after their father's death. His mother was also hot-tempered, but he told me not to worry. Slowly, slowly, everybody will change. Don't let any tension build up. I felt good that he was telling me all this. I thought, here is a man who will support me fully in life. Narinder did not mix with them very much. We kept talking until we both started yawning. He asked me to change my clothes. I asked him where I could change my clothes. He said, here, your nightclothes are on that chair. He promised to face away from me while I was changing. I quickly took my sari off and put on my nightie, darting quick glances at him to make sure that he wasn't looking. Finally he asked, laughing, if I had finished. Then we got into bed and fell asleep. Nothing happened between us that night.

In the morning, my *saas* walked in while we were still asleep and asked us to get up and get ready. When my husband left the room, my *saas* asked how the night had gone. I knew what she wanted to know. I said it was OK. She laughed. The family made plans to go out but they weren't supposed to take me – there is a *matha tekna* ceremony in which a new bride must visit the memorial built to the dead elders of the family before she can go out anywhere. This is often built in the fields or somewhere near your home. It is extremely small, made out of mud, and is often topped with a mini-dome like the kind you find on top of a gurdwara. She has to go and light a *diya* there and seek their blessings for her marriage. As I hadn't done this, I couldn't go out with them. My husband said that he wouldn't go either. His mother tried to explain that this is India, not England, this is the tradition. She took him to one side and got really angry with him. Finally she relented and we went to the elders' memorial. I think I fell in love with him that day. I felt he really cared for me.

On the second day, after the serious bit was over, husband and wife are supposed to play a game. Using light bamboo sticks, they pretend to hit each other with them. This is not a game that we played in our caste. Sukhvinder asked Raj, as a joke, to hit me really hard. He swung the stick from a very great distance and brought it towards me with such gusto that I got petrified. However, as it came within an inch of touching me, it stopped and brushed lightly against me. Then it was my turn. The sister said, 'this is your only chance to hit him hard'. But I just did it very gently. So the family said, 'she must love you a lot, Raj'. Then his uncle and aunt played the same game but they appeared to be really whacking each other. We had a lot of fun. Then we went to the gurdwara and went shopping before coming home. As my husband was due to leave shortly for England, they also had to visit various relatives. So we would be out from morning to night. The relatives gave us money and suits. If I was given any money, my *saas* would take it from me immediately. I didn't really care; I had no need for it anyway.

One morning, I heard Sukhvinder screaming outside our room.

When Raj and I came out to investigate, we found that she was beating up Jasbir, her nephew. The reason was trivial. His father had asked for toilet paper, and Sukhvinder refused. When Jasbir asked why, she started hitting him. Everybody tried to separate them. From that day on, I worried about how I would fit in with this family.

For the next few nights, Raj didn't touch me. Then one night it was raining. He said he loved the rain. At midnight he suggested that we go and take a shower in the rain on the terrace. It's pretty cold in February. We stayed in the rain for quite a long time. He said that his mother would get really angry if she found out what we were doing and if we fell ill. I didn't mind falling ill if he enjoyed the rain. We got completely drenched. My night suit was very silky and got stuck to my skin. He said, 'let's go, if you fall ill, my mother will wonder how that happened'. We came down the stairs as quietly as possible. I had no other clothes in the room. I couldn't go to the next room to get my clothes because that would make everybody suspicious. He said, 'take your clothes off and get into bed naked'. My God! He took his clothes off. I switched the lights off and got undressed. I wrapped myself with a towel and got into bed. Then he came near me. I was very shy as he clambered on top of me. He moved with confidence. It felt very strange especially when I bled. I let out a few shrieks. I was in a lot of pain. But what could I do? This was a necessary part of marriage. After that, I lost my shyness. I still never initiated anything or took an active part. It was he who did everything. I started falling in love with him.

One day we went to visit a family friend who was very wealthy and had a large mansion. We all got to sleep in our own rooms. Sukhvinder fell ill and started crying that she wanted to sleep with her brother. Everybody tried to dissuade her, reminding her that he was newly married. But she wouldn't listen. My husband and his mother let her have her way. She slept between me and Raj on a big double bed. They hugged each other and slept while I was at one end of the bed. If I was ill I might have wanted to sleep with my mother – but a newly-married brother?!!! When I told my family about it, they thought it was quite strange. Sukhvinder complained of a headache. I massaged her head almost the whole night through. In the morning my eyes were puffy from lack of sleep. Narinder remarked on it in the morning. When I explained, she said that was Sukhvinder's way. She made a big deal out of even the smallest of ailments. She said that I should look after myself and not give in to her demands. Strangely, Sukhvinder had told me that Narinder was not a nice woman. All of them had said unkind things about the older sister. I couldn't work out why. The way Sukhvinder behaved towards me makes me wonder now whether she was jealous of me.

My husband and I did not get much of a chance to talk. We were never alone. Then the time for his departure came. When he left for England, I wept. Everybody tried to reassure me that it would not be long before we were reunited. I had already got my visa. They had applied for my visa back in October. His uncle said that I had got a visa for two years but I would only get a full stamp after that.

An immigration rule, known as the two-year rule, applies to any marriage to a non-British spouse. Such marriages must last for two years before the overseas spouse can apply for leave to remain.

My *saas* and I left four weeks later. I was allowed to go home to my mother for one week. During that week, my *saas* phoned and asked for money to buy tickets to London for herself and me. My father got very upset. He said he didn't have the money. In that case, she would have to leave me behind. My father started crying. My brothers said that it's a question of Amber's whole life; that the money he had spent on the wedding would go to waste if he did not find the money for fares. I don't know where daddyji got the money from, but he did give her the Rs 21,000 (*£245 approximately*) that she had demanded. The day she came to fetch me from my mother's, Satvant Kaur fought with my family. Dev had applied henna to my hair because I had a headache and henna is considered to be cooling. My *saas* started shouting: she couldn't understand why I had to put henna in my hair; where I had come across this fashion; Raj would get really angry if he knew what I had done. She asked me to wash it straight away. I started crying, but I went and washed my hair. My father shouted at my mother for letting me put henna in my hair when I hadn't done it all my life. My mother was upset that she was yelling at me. It was a mistake and when I was told to wash it, I did. What was the problem? When I was leaving, my parents wondered how I would manage. I said, 'don't worry, I will win them over with love and patience'.

We then continued on a round of visits to various relatives. Before leaving the country, I asked if I could see my parents one final time. She couldn't see the point as I had only been with them recently. My grandmother is so old that she can't walk around and couldn't come to see me. She had fainted when I left, afraid that she wouldn't live to see me again. However, daddyji came to see me off in Delhi, from where we were going to catch the flight. On that occasion too I got a terrible headache. My *saas* showed no sympathy. She scolded me in front of everyone – 'why does your head get overheated?' she asked. We were staying with Narinder's in-laws in Delhi. My father was sitting upstairs with the men. I went up and told him that my head was hurting. He took me out to buy a Coke; perhaps I had a build-up of gas in my stomach and that was giving me a headache. When he took me out, she got very angry. 'What kind of a father thinks that young women suffer from gas?' In England she told my husband about it and added that my relationship with my father was suspect. What a terrible thing to say! I couldn't understand her hostility to me. Why did she torture me with these terrible allegations? It's very hard to tolerate an allegation like this. I never said that their relationships were suspect, despite the fact that Sukhvinder slept with her brother in front of my eyes. I cried so much that day. Did God give me life in order to hear such terrible things? I tried to tell myself, this is the family with whom I have to live; I must endure this without fuss. God knows the truth. She then asked me how much money I had been given. She knew that I had been given Rs 500 (£6) by each member of my family: my brothers; my mother; my grandparents; and various members in my maternal grandmother's house. She took it all from me, saying I had no use for it. I had never met anyone with such an attachment to money.

Raj came to the airport to fetch us. We went back to a simple house – there was a sitting-room on the ground floor, a toilet and kitchen and a little extension at the back. There were three bedrooms upstairs. Sukhvinder slept in the smallest bedroom, my *saas* in another and then there was one for us. At first, Raj was quite nice to me. We got on well. We were sleeping together and I felt he loved me, but after a week everybody started changing. I noticed that Raj would go out with Sukhvinder but never asked me to go with them. I was new to London, surely they would want to show me the sights? I would wake up at 7 a.m. and make breakfast for him and the others. He would usually eat cereal and go to work. Then Sukhvinder found a job at the airport in the Gucci shop and my *saas* and I were the only ones left at home. She started saying things like she didn't think I was the real child of my parents because they gave no dowry. I usually listened in silence. Sometimes I would ask why she was saying all these things when my father had done exactly as asked.

There are two positive things that can be said about the reprehensible practice of dowry. Some scholars argue that it was a way of passing on a girl's share of the inheritance prior to death at a time when inheritance was only passed onto sons. However, it was never an equal share. 'This disenfranchisement makes women even more dependent on marriage as a route to economic security, and makes it likely that women will toler-ate abuse within marriage', says Srimati Basu, an anthropologist.[9] The second argument is that dowry was given directly to women to afford them some financial independence if the marriage did not work out. However, in practice, given the lowly status of women, the dowry was passed onto the in-laws and was never in the control of women. In the case of marriage breakdown, the dowry is usually held onto by the in-laws. There is anecdotal evidence that some families contract marriages repeatedly as a way of accumulating wealth.

Occasionally my parents would ring me and I would tell them that I was fine. Raj's family would all be standing nearby, so I could hardly say anything else. I never rang them. I didn't even know how to call India at that time. My *saas* would say that their new bungalow was standing empty; surely my father could buy the furniture for it? She would ask about the car, hinting all the time that they should be sending more money. I couldn't ask my father for more when I knew the trouble he'd gone to, to raise money for my wedding. After all, he had given them a lot of gold. She said that if he couldn't afford it, why did he bother to get me married off?

They would leave me alone at home with Jasbir and go out – shopping or visiting relatives. I had to clean the whole house, wash, dry, iron everybody's clothes, put them away in their wardrobes and cook all the meals. When everybody came back from work in the evenings, I would have to make hot food for them. Although I did all the cooking, I wasn't allowed to make the things I liked. For example, when I first came I was not used to bread; it would make me sick. But that's all they would let me eat. My *saas* would scream that I was vomiting deliberately. But English-style bread didn't suit me. I would get the runs. She said that I was just acting. I wasn't allowed to drink juice or Coke. I had to cook meat for them. As I had never touched meat before, I would close my eyes while I was washing it, pretending that I was washing aubergines. It felt yeuchy to the touch. It made my skin crawl. My husband preferred meat to vegetables. For every meal I had to make chapattis, rice, one meat curry and a vegetable curry. Nobody ate stale food. That they gave to me. If I couldn't finish it, it would be thrown out. Even Narinder's husband would come to our house to eat his meals. He would have an early lunch and then take a packed meal for the evenings. Narinder worked at Homebase and visited us occasionally. Sukhvinder used to make digs at her. I took total care of all of them. I didn't mind; I was doing my duty. What saddens me is that they didn't do their duty by me. After all, it was a two-way relationship.

I also did the gardening. Nothing was growing in it except very tall grass when I first arrived. It wasn't a very big garden, but I grew coriander, spinach and fenugreek. I also planted flowers. One day my stomach started hurting. I had been so busy gardening that I hadn't stopped to eat all day. I had to do all the housework even when I was sick. They were very reluctant to take me to the doctor, but when I continued to have stomach problems they took me. I couldn't speak much English but my *saas* could say a few words. She spoke to the doctor on my behalf. The doctor looked Indian but he spoke only in English. He said I was not used to the water here and that they should give me bottled water rather than tap water. Instead, my *saas* made me drink a glass of water mixed with wheat flour, saying that the nurse had advised her that it was good for me. But it would make my stomach hurt even more. If I refused to take it, she would slap me. On another occasion she gave me some tablets that made me feel dizzy. In time, I stopped telling her that I was feeling sick.

We would go to the gurdwara every morning. I was quite popular with all the older women. I would touch their feet to show my respect. Slowly, slowly, my *saas* started resenting that. She stopped me talking to them, which made me feel bad because they must have wondered why I was being so unfriendly. She even put a stop to visits from a neighbour. Maybe they thought that if she came in their absence, she might put me up to something or I might tell her stuff. They told me never to open the door to her if I was alone in the house. Then I would come back and do all the work as instructed by my *saas* while she sat on the settee and watched TV. There was so much washing-up to do in that house, my God. She would then walk around the house, running her finger over ledges to check for dust. I had to clean the windows as well.

When it was time for lunch I would cook fresh chapattis for her. I wasn't allowed to make them all in one go. I had to make one at a time as she ate them. She would shout at me that I deliberately didn't give her a fluffed-up chapatti. A well-made chapatti swells with air and is a sign that it has been evenly rolled out. A good housewife's chapattis must be perfectly round and must always swell up. Sometimes chapattis don't swell up. It was not my fault. She just needed something to criticize me about. Her daughter was the same. She would shout at me if she found a stain on her clothes. She said I wasn't washing them well. She threw the remote control at me to emphasize her point. Or, if they were crumpled, she said I hadn't ironed them properly. On one occasion she kicked my hot cup of tea and it fell all over the carpet in the sitting-room. Then she would say, 'this is not your house, don't think of yourself as the mistress of this house'.

I don't know what she told my husband, but then he stopped behaving well with me. He would present her catalogue of complaints, asking for an explanation for what I'd done all day. He would accuse me of being idle. Then I would start crying. I had not sat on the settee for even one second. My back was hurting from scrubbing wooden floors – she wouldn't let me mop them with a long-handled mop, I had to get down on my knees and clean it with a damp soapy cloth, the way we do it in India. When Sukhvinder called me names like 'stupid' and 'mental', I told Raj, like he had told me to. He didn't believe that she would say such things to me. I said, 'why don't you ask her?' He called her down and asked if she had abused me. She said she had. I sat quietly. He then said to his sister, 'you should swear at her even more, that is all she is good for'. I couldn't understand what had happened to the husband I had in India. Why the transformation when I was not to blame? After all the care I took of them, is that what my husband thought of me? That day he broke my heart.

He still slept with me; even when I wasn't feeling well. He would slap me and shake me violently and want to know why I wouldn't have sex with him. Then he would rape me. In India we had normal sex. I used to get some pleasure from that. Here he began to rape me anally every night. My sister-in-law had never told me about sex from the back. When I told him to stop doing that because it hurt, he didn't believe that it could be painful. I used to bleed so much that I had difficulties going to the toilet. I would weep as I sat on the toilet, but I couldn't confide in anyone. I preferred death to this life. Was married life the same for everyone? If he loved me, he wouldn't do things like that. I started hating him little by little. Once he had his way, he would turn over on his side and make me scratch his back. I was so stupid that I wouldn't stop until he asked me to. I thought it was my duty to carry on until he fell asleep. My hands would be aching from the day's work. Every other night I would have to massage his hair with oil. I would also have to massage Sukhvinder's head. He never kissed me or showed me any affection. I could have tolerated abuse from the rest of the family if he had been on my side, but when your life partner behaves like that there is no hope. Then, like his mother, he started complaining that my family had given them nothing.

I never became pregnant. He would withdraw when he was about to finish and wipe it off with a towel. When I said I wanted a child, he said, 'you'll get one when you start thinking straight'. I thought that a child would be the best way to change them all. He would feel something for our child even if not for me. Blood is blood. He carried on having sex with me until two or three days before the end. On one occasion… I feel too embarrassed to talk about it… he laid a towel on the floor, made me lie down on it and then pissed inside me. I didn't realize what was happening until I felt something hot trickling out. The towel got all wet. I don't know why he did that. What a dirty thing!

One day when I was working in the kitchen, my *saas* started taunting me about my earlier visit to the UK. She said I had agreed to the marriage because I wanted to meet up with the other boy who I had met on that trip; that I wasn't really planning to live with Raj. I tried to explain that I was barely nine when I came. I said I could ask my uncle to send me the photos so they could see for themselves how young I was. My *saas* said that I would not be allowed to contact him. Then she dragged me by the hair to my bedroom upstairs and called out to the rest of the family to come upstairs. My *saas* grabbed me by the wrist and slammed my elbow against the wall; then she tried to strangle me. I said to her 'kill me, I don't want to live this kind of life'. Narinder asked her mother to let go, in case something happened and they were accused of murder. Then she got hold of my hair and whacked my face against the wall. I was crying loudly. Raj was cheering his mother on, saying 'go on, hit her some more'. He was watching the *tamasha* (*drama*) with great pleasure. Raj was also repeating his mother's taunts about my first visit to Britain. Even a servant is treated better than that. I felt like an animal in the jungle which has been ensnared and surrounded by hunters, all of whom are looking for different ways to torture it for their entertainment. That was the worst day. The only day worse than that was when they kicked me out.

Then my *saas* went to Narinder's house and rang my father from there and said all sorts of things about me. My father said he would swallow poison and kill himself. He asked to speak to me. When my *saas* wouldn't put me on the phone, he got worried that they might even have killed me. He rang Dev's cousin and asked her to visit me. I found out later that they lived nearby in Heston itself. Aunty came to visit me with her sons. I was crying. My *saas* hit me on my head with her hands to stop me crying. In front of them! She kept saying, 'tell them how happy you are with us. Have you lost your tongue?' Raj was staring at us. Aunty, of course, understood everything. She said to my *saas*, 'sister why are you treating her like this? You should have let her speak to her father on the phone. He is really worried about her.'

After she left, my *saas* said that they had no intention of keeping me and that her son could use me and abuse me as he wished. As if I was a prostitute. What *saas* talks like that? 'We just want to get our investment back on the money we spent on the wedding.' My passport was with them. She would threaten to have me deported to India. She would taunt me that my status here was dependent on Raj and he could send me back at any time; even two years later, if he didn't apply for me, I wouldn't be *pukka*. I used to pray to God that somehow I could settle down in their house; that the day would pass without fights and abuse. I would behave very carefully to avoid making any mistakes and giving her any reason to yell. But everyday she would start on me. I endured all that because I had nowhere to go.

After that day, they stopped talking to me altogether. When the family had gone out and left me with Jas, Narinder rang to talk to me. She was nicest to me. She advised me how to win them over. If I told my parents that I was happy and that they should not interfere in my life, then I would have a quiet life. She said I should fall at my *saas*'s feet and ask for forgiveness. I touched everybody's feet when they returned. I then spoke to my father in front of them and said that I was very happy and that he should not interfere. 'Please don't send people to visit me', I said. My father was crying. He knew that I was suffering, but what could he do? Although Narinder was usually nice to me, I remember on one occasion when she took me home to her place she slapped me, saying that my parents had not taken enough care of her. I knew that was rubbish because my parents were always telling me to take care of all of them equally.

Despite the fact that things were going badly, they held a big party in May, about two months after I came here, to celebrate our wedding. They had promised to invite all their friends to a party and they felt obliged to keep their word. Satvant thought the party was a waste of money, but Raj and Sukhwinder wanted to go ahead. It was a fairly good party held at a hall. That was the confusing thing. They made a public show as if it were a genuine marriage. They told me that I mustn't say anything to the guests at the party. They wanted me to look and act happy. They told me that when I danced with my husband I should talk to him. If anybody should ask why my parents hadn't come, I had to say that my father was not well enough to travel. Many people did ask. I followed their instructions to the letter. The party went off very well. They served alcohol. I wore the maroon wedding *lehenga*. He wore the same thing that he had worn on our wedding day. Narinder's husband, I think, had a drink that day and got quite merry. He picked his wife up and started kissing her. When we got home, my *saas* shouted at him for bringing the family into disrepute by his behaviour. They had always maintained that no one drank alcohol in their family. Apparently, Raj's father had died from alcoholism and that's why they all abstained. It was a lie. We wouldn't have minded if they had told us the truth. If they didn't drink, then why serve it? Even in India, they had demanded that my father serve alcohol and that, too, of the best quality. I think Narinder's husband had a drink problem. He said that was the first time he had a drink; he simply wanted to enjoy the party. That day my husband had a drink as well. You can always tell. If you had attended the party you would have thought that we were happily married. Aunty had been invited to the party reluctantly, to stop it becoming a big issue in India. She asked if I was happy. I said everything was fine.

Even though things had soured a week after I got here, there were moments when Raj was nice to me – twice in five months, to be precise. Once when I picked up a broken glass and started bleeding. He got a tissue and dabbed at it and ran out to buy some plasters from the shops. He scolded me for picking it up. But there was no pattern to his tenderness. One day in June, we were all watching a film on telly in the evening. It had been a good day. There had been no fights. Sukhvinder was sitting on the carpet watching telly. We were sitting on the settee and Raj put his arm around my shoulder. I thought he had had a change of heart. Maybe he had noticed how much I was doing for the family. That was the hope with which I lived there – that one day things would get better. Sukhvinder turned around and saw us. She went upstairs to her mother there and then and told her that Raj and I were hugging. She should have been pleased. I was his wife, not a prostitute. I went upstairs to my room. His mother went down and shouted at Raj, 'aren't you ashamed to behave like this in front of your sister?' He said, 'we weren't doing anything'. She said she didn't want to see us sitting together. Then she shouted at me for having no sense and allowing my husband to do that to me. I said nothing. We never sat together again. After that incident things got worse and the distance between us grew.

Raj started spending all his time on the phone. As soon as he came back from work, the phone would be stuck to his ear. I would watch him from the window – he would park the car and walk up and down the street talking on the phone. It was ages before he would come inside. He became so busy, I can't tell you. He became completely cut off. He would either be watching TV or playing games with Jas on his laptop. Then he started going out with his friends, and was coming home at 9 p.m., even though, as I discovered much later on, his office closed at 5 p.m. One day he was sitting at the computer in our bedroom. By chance I came up to put some clothes away and my eyes fell on the words 'I love you'. Whether it was a letter from him or to him, I never found out, but he immediately erased it. It was as if God had directed my eyes to those words.

There was a family wedding in August in India. His mother asked me to tell my parents that she was going to India and that she wanted Rs 50,000 (*£580 approximately*) spending money. If they don't agree, my life here would become even worse. Daddyji said, 'how can I arrange so much money? I have just got you married.' When she went to my parents' house, my father gave her Rs 6,000 (*£70*). As she was leaving, she said that the money was not even enough for a sari, what would be left over for her son and the rest of her family? She said 'if you can't afford more, wait and see what we will do to your daughter. We will send her back to India and get her killed off. Then you will see some sense.' Daddyji pleaded with her to spare me.

When my *saas* was in India, Sukhvinder told me that Raj had another woman. Sukhvinder said that it was their fault that they had made him marry me. Narinder's husband also confirmed it. When I asked my husband, he denied it. I asked how come he was on the phone so much when he didn't have any time for me. He hit me and told me to mind my own business. I asked him why he was so violent towards me when I hadn't done anything to him.

One day, he and Sukhvinder were getting ready to go out. As usual, they didn't ask if I wanted to join them. Then Sukhvinder said that he was going to meet that woman and asked if I wanted to see her. She offered to take me along. He said he had no room in his car for me. I said, 'I'll squeeze into any corner that you point out'. There was nothing in the car. Finally he pushed me to the back of the car and we went to Homebase. This was the only time I went out with them.

I was not introduced to her. She was a fairly old, divorced woman.

She had two children. One son had come with her. The way Raj was talking to her, with such joy and laughter – I had never seen him like that. He would go really close to talk to her. He was buying her some flooring and when she'd chosen the one she liked, he said he would find out the price. He whistled when he saw an assistant and swaggered towards him as if he was intoxicated. I was burning up with jealousy. Sukhvinder said, 'see? Now you know. Have you ever seen him so happy with you?' Raj spent entire days with that woman. He went to fit her floor. He didn't say anything to me. I was very upset. One weekend he left on a Saturday and didn't come back until Sunday evening. I couldn't understand why Sukhvinder was gloating. Surely every sister would want her brother's marriage to succeed. It was only when he was on the phone endlessly that I realized that he did not love me. But he never admitted to it. He used to say that she's a friend, that he respected her like a mother. Maybe he was on the phone to her to show his mother that he was not going to be too demonstrative with me.

On another occasion he didn't come back till 2 or 3 a.m. I sat up in the living-room waiting for him. I was starving. In our tradition you do not eat before your husband; this is the wife's duty. You have to serve them and then eat yourself. Generally, I would feed him first, then my *saas*, Sukhvinder and Jasbir, and then sit down myself. It would be 9 p.m. by the time I ate. At 10 p.m. I would warm up milk and give it to them before they went to bed. I rang him on his mobile but he didn't pick up, nor did he call back. When he came home, I said I was really worried that something had happened to him. He said he had been at a party and didn't hear the phone ringing. He went to bed without eating. So did I.

My *saas* had taken the gold set that was given to me by my parents to get it melted and redesigned as she thought it was rather old-fashioned. She rang Sukhvinder from India and said that a holy man had told her that Amber shouldn't wear jewellery because her stars were against it. Sukhvinder asked me to take off my jewellery. I didn't take it off at first. I went into the kitchen to work. So Sukhvinder repeated herself, screaming, 'didn't you hear me the first time? Take off the gold this minute.' So I did. She also made my husband remove his gold ring. I don't know why.

Next day was Tuesday 16 August. I made breakfast for Raj. He hadn't been talking to me for the last two or three days. He said he wasn't hungry and went to work. Sukhvinder had a day off from work. She was in a mood from the moment she got out of bed. I made her breakfast when she woke at 10 a.m. She said, 'this is not your house, bitch; I don't want you to live her any more, *chudhail*, you witch. I will take you to Narinder's place.' I said, 'I have come here as your brother's bride. Why are you saying these things when I take so much care of everyone?' She just kept repeating that I couldn't live there anymore. Now, when I think back on it, it was obviously all planned. I said, 'I am not going anywhere, I have work to do'. She caught hold of my hair and dragged me towards the front door. She pulled my hair so hard that it kept coming out in clumps. I got a splitting headache. She dug her long fingernails into my flesh and it started to bleed.

She then started hitting me. I picked up the cordless phone from the corner of the table. Perhaps I would have to phone the police to save myself. She pushed me and tried to grab the phone off me. She hit my head against the wall. I got a bump on my forehead. She kicked me and punched me and bit me on my right wrist and pushed me out of the door. Narinder turned up at that moment. I ran to her and cried '*didi*, sister, Sukhvinder's beating me up'. There was some stranger walking by on the pavement who stopped to watch us. Narinder said to him, 'oh it's you'. I don't know if she knew him or not. I'd never seen him before. I knew only one lady who lived on that road, who visited my mother-in-law from time to time. 'Can you take Amber with you? My sister is a little hot-tempered. I will try and calm her down. I will come for Amber in a little while.'

I was barefoot. I was feeling dizzy. I could hardly walk. The man held me up. My stomach was hurting where I had been punched. He lived three or four houses away. I found out later that his name was

Balbir Singh. I was crying buckets. He said, 'don't worry, I will look after you like a brother'. He was on his way to work when this happened. There was no one else in his house. I waited for Narinder, but she never came for me. Even though I was so unhappy, I was terrified at the prospect of having nowhere to go. The man wanted to phone the police and asked what I wanted to do. I wanted to talk to my parents first. They said they could do nothing for me. My mother gave me the telephone number of Dev's cousin. The man phoned them and they turned up at his house. He also phoned the police. They turned up with an ambulance. They took me to the hospital and gave me medicine for my severe headache.[10] I told the police, a woman and then a white man, the whole story. They asked me where I wanted to go. Aunty said, 'I will take her home with me'. They asked me if I wanted to have Sukhvinder arrested. I said, 'yes'. They did arrest her, but apparently she said that they had no proof as to who started the fight. As I had no witnesses, the police said that there was no case to pursue.

I have thought long and hard about this family to try to understand why they behaved like that towards me. I think that they arranged our marriage to get him away from that married woman. But that didn't happen. I don't know how long that relationship had been going on. A few days before she went to India, I even overheard his mother telling him to make sure that I didn't find out about the other woman. But she also told me, 'if I want, I can stop him from seeing her, but why should I when he is not happy with you?' Surely they should have done everything to bring us closer together instead of trying to make me jealous. They should have given us time together so that we could have understood each other. They could even have kept me on as a servant to do the work, if not as a wife. I didn't challenge anybody. If I shouted and was difficult to get on with, I could understand, but I swear to God that I obeyed every wish of theirs. I think that the only reason they broke us up was dowry. My family hadn't been able to satisfy their demands.

My things were still with them. We waited a couple of weeks for my *saas* to return from India before going to collect them. My aunty and a priest from the local gurdwara went to collect them. The police had said that if there was a problem, we should ring them. I sat in the car with aunty's son. At first they didn't answer the door. The priest then rang them on the mobile. My *saas* answered the phone. She opened the door to him. When she saw aunty, she got a shock. At first, aunty tried to persuade her to take me back. She said that they wanted nothing more to do with me. Aunty then asked for my things. She said that I had taken everything and shut the door. Just then a police car passed by. When the priest explained the situation to them, the police asked me to get out of the car and go with them to the house. My *saas* told the police that I had taken it all and shut the door in their face. Sukhvinder realized that you cannot behave like that with the police. She opened the door and asked the police to excuse her mother, who wasn't feeling very well. She told her mother that they will have to give my stuff to me otherwise they would get into trouble with the police. My *saas* wouldn't let anyone enter. They came back quickly. They had already packed all the things they were going to give me in a broken little suitcase. I opened it there on the doorstep and noticed that they had only given me some of my Indian clothes, including my wedding *lehenga* and one other *lehenga*. I asked for my blanket, my jewels and passport. They said they had sent my passport to the Home Office and that I had taken the other things. But I didn't really notice what else was missing. When you're grieving, your mind is not on material things. One police officer spoke Hindi. He said, 'don't cry, be grateful that you have escaped with your life; many women get killed in the process'.

Aunty was good to me. She looked after me. In those days my condition was very poor. I used to get continual headaches. I went to the gurdwara regularly, looking for peace. I used to help with the washing-up and making of chapattis for *langar*.

This is a wonderful Sikh tradition whereby a full vegetarian meal is provided to anyone who comes to the gurdwara. It was intended by Guru Nanak, the first Sikh guru, as a way of breaking down caste and religious barriers. Everybody sat down to eat as equals, and vegetarian food would not affect the dietary laws of Muslims, Jews or Hindus.

Aunty kept me for five months until the following January. Their son was getting married and the house was too small for all of us. They wanted me to make other arrangements. They rang my parents and told them. My parents told me that there was no way they would have me back. The shame would be too much. They had done their duty by me. They advised me to go back to my husband.

On Christmas day I went to see Raj. He was in the forecourt washing his car. I thought, it doesn't matter how badly they treat me, at least it is a roof over my head. I would rather die living with them than return to India. When he saw me, his eyes widened. He shouted, 'what are you doing here?' I said, 'please I want to talk to you, just once. Tell me what I did wrong. Why did you do this to me?' Then he started knocking on his front door, 'Mummy, open the door, open the door'. Maybe she was upstairs and didn't hear him. I fell at his feet and said, 'please, listen to me just once'. But he kept knocking on the door. As I stood up, he shoved me aside roughly and pointed to a spot ten feet away and said, 'go and stand there and talk to me from there'. He asked me who I had come with. I said, 'I have come on my own'. He said, 'go back to wherever you have come from'. I said, 'I have no one apart from you. Why did you kick me out of the house?' Just as I asked this question, the door opened. My *saas* saw me and asked, 'what is she doing here?' She started swearing at me – 'bitch, go away'. She caught hold of Raj and dragged him into the house. I heard her telling her daughter to phone the police.

I sat on the doorstep, weeping. A little while later, the police turned up. They asked me if I had been beaten and why I was on the doorstep. I explained that I wanted to live with my husband. They knocked on the door. I don't know what they said. They were talking in English and I was crying. Then they were inside and I was on the outside. I fainted. When I came to, the police came out and said 'they don't want you here'. The family told them to arrest me because I was harassing them. In the car, the police officer said the family were stupid to ask that I should be arrested when I had done nothing wrong. They said they would drop me wherever I wanted to go. I still kept saying that I wanted to live with my husband. They said, 'we don't have time, it's Christmas today'. I asked them to drop me off at a gurdwara. They dropped me off at a church in Hounslow. It was locked. I sat on the steps and kept crying. I then walked to the gurd-wara, which was close by.

I went again, a few days later. I thought I would go to the bank where he worked; maybe he couldn't talk to me in front of his family. So I went to Barclays bank in Hayes. A woman at my aunty's gurdwara had taken pity on me and given me some money so I used some of this to take the bus. In Hayes they said 'he doesn't work here' and gave me an address in Uxbridge. He didn't work there either, but then somebody looked up his name on the computer and sent me to the right place. They gave me the bus number and directions of how to get there. I saw him through the glass. He said, 'you can't come to my place of work, go away'. Again I pleaded with him to talk to me. He said he couldn't talk to me there. So I went outside because I didn't want to make any trouble for him at work. I waited outside in the hope that he might come out and talk to me. I waited and waited. I was hungry and cold. I had brought a *paratha* with me from the gur-dwara. I started eating it, but I was also feeling nauseous. So I put the *paratha* back in the bag. I wandered around. Then he came out and saw me and started screaming, 'are you still here? Go home.' His face was all angry and contorted, the way he used to look when he was about to beat me. 'This is not India, this is England. I can call the police and have you arrested.' I kept pleading with him to talk to me. He said, 'come back at 5 p.m. if you want to talk to me'. I went away happily. At least he was going to talk to me. When I came back at 5 p.m., I couldn't see him. I went and asked some women staff who were sitting in the bank. At first they said 'no one of that name works here' and started laughing. I said, 'no, he is the assistant manager and I am his wife and I want to talk to him'. They said that he had left a quarter of an hour ago. Then I realized that all was lost. The distance between us could not be bridged.

Aunty's brother had a friend who had a large house. They agreed to take me in. I have been living here since January 2005. Even here I used to do all the housework. I cooked and washed up for the entire family of six. They would not lift a finger to help. They would eat and not even clear their plates away. They had two young children, two and four years old, and I had to look after them as well, changing their nappies, everything. I even had to do painting and decorating. They have two houses. In the other house I stripped all the wallpaper. I couldn't object because I had nothing. I had to work for my board and lodging. Life was very hard with them. I used to cry a lot at the way my life had turned out. My husband applied for divorce in March. Aunty brought the divorce papers to me. It broke my heart. This really was the end. He alleged that I was having a relationship with somebody else, that I would refuse to go out with them, and that when they rang me at home, I was never there. I got so angry with him and his lies. I had to respond to his application. A friend of this family knew about SBS and took me to them. They found me a solicitor. I was completely broken. They put me together again. I was so depressed. I felt like dying. I thought I would go mad.

After four months I found a job at a beauty parlour. A cousin of the family I was living with was going to open a new salon and was looking for staff. She found out that I had done a beautician's course, came to interview me and offered me the job. SBS helped me apply for a National Insurance number. I am now earning £432 per month at £5.05 per hour. I work every day from 2–6 except Mondays and Sundays. I pay £35 rent per week. For a little while after I had started earning, I used to do the whole grocery shopping every other week. This would come to nearly £80. This went on for a couple of months. Meena, from SBS, pointed out how unfair that was when they were a family of six and I was just on my own. I told them that I would make my own arrangements for food as I found this arrangement too expensive. To my surprise, they agreed and suggested that I contribute

£10 per week for my food. Now I don't have to look after the kids. They go to their granny's. When I come back early from work, I cook dinner for everyone. Sometimes they make it. We all get together and clean the house.

I still have headaches and diarrhoea. But my counselling sessions at SBS with Shah have made me change my view that my life has come to an end. Shah makes me concentrate on the future, not the past, and to work to improve my future. When I get upset, I talk to her endlessly about my in-laws. Sometimes I talk about my parents. I have a lot of anger against them. Sometimes I cry so much when I am in my room. I complain to God for dealing me such a raw hand. This must be my karma.[11]

I will never know why they treated me like this. The thought goes through my head all the time. Tell me where I was to blame. Today I have more knowledge. I can go out and about on my own – not every-where, but I'm getting there. I am gaining in self-confidence. In November 2006, SBS organized a meeting on immigration rules that trap women like me in unhappy marriages and I spoke about my expe-riences. Meena helped me to write a short piece in English. I was quite nervous at having to talk publicly. I started crying in the middle. Meena came up and asked me if I wanted to stop, she understood how hard it was for me. I said 'no, I want to tell people what I have been through so that other girls do not have to go through the same experi-ence'. Afterwards, many people came up to me and said that they were sorry to hear what I had been through but very glad that I had found the courage to share my experiences with them. I felt good about that.

I think it is really wrong that parents do not ask their daughters whether the man they have chosen for her is to her liking. This is a question that will affect her whole life. They should give the young couple a chance to get to know each other. What can you tell from five or ten minutes? Of course, in my case, I may not have found out about my husband's true nature because he was nice to me in India. I want to tell other women in my situation that they should not just jump at the chance of a man who has come from abroad. If girls are to get anywhere, parents have to give them permission to develop and grow. So when girls face troubles, they don't just keep crying like me but confront them. The way I was brought up in India: I couldn't go anywhere apart from school or college, and even then I had to be accompanied by my father or brothers; I had to play in front of the house. Even here, I was not allowed out except when I went to the gurdwara with my *saas*. I knew nothing about life here.

I have cut off all contact with my parents because they thought it was my fault. I don't even speak to them on the phone. They should have supported me. I know what I had to endure. I wasn't planning to return to India anyway. I know what a big insult it is to your family if your marriage breaks down. If I returned to the village, I wouldn't be able to do a job and people would hate me. It would be hell. I earn my own money now; I pay rent. In that house, I didn't even have £1 in my possession. I think, yes, Amber you have got somewhere. Now you need to go further. I don't know what's written in my fate. I want to learn to speak English properly so that I can make progress and get a better job. Meena has told me about jobs at the airport. I would also like to do another beautician's course and open my own shop. As for men, I don't think I will ever trust one again.

In January 2007, with the help of SBS, Amber won her right to stay in the UK. The one-year immigration rule meant that many women faced violence or deportation if their marriages broke down before the year was up. As a result of the SBS campaign against this rule, the government introduced concessions in which women who could prove that they had faced domestic violence would be allowed to stay but extended the probationary period from one to two years. However, they would not be allowed to claim benefits or gain access to refuges. The choice that now faces non-British women is violence or destitution. In the case of Amber, we saw how her need for a roof over her head enslaved her again. Now that she has won her right to stay, SBS will apply to a housing association in order to get her a place of her own and she will take the first, nervous steps towards freedom.

PASSPORT TO FREEDOM

Of all the five people whose stories are featured in this book, there is only one who continues to feel trapped, and that is Farhia Nur. She does not have papers. She occupies a twilight zone between legality and illegality. The government knows that she has no obvious means of support and yet requires her to sign on, which means travelling to the reporting centre once every month and trying to survive in between. She is no longer enslaved because she has got married, in a *sharia* (Islamic) court, to a man who has a British passport but appears to be under some inexplicable pressure to remain married to his first wife although they have separated. In any case, under the current rules the government does not allow marriage between failed asylum seekers and British citizens. Farhia is no longer starving but is unable to work or study. In contrast to her situation, Natasha, Liu, Amber and Naomi who have won the right to stay – although Naomi will have to re-apply when she turns eighteen – now have the opportunity to follow their dreams.

There is no consensus on the numbers held in slavery today, and that is partly because there is no consensus on the definition of slavery. Kevin Bales, Director of Free the Slaves, defines slavery as 'the total control of one person by another for the purpose of economic exploitation'.[1] On this basis, neither Farhia Nur nor Liu Bao Ren nor Amber Lobepreet would be considered slaves because, technically, they were at liberty to walk away from their situations at any time, while staring destitution and homelessness in the face. With the campaigner's zeal, Bales seeks to convince us that, under his definition, it is possible for slavery to be truly abolished. I commend that impulse. The ILO defines slavery even more narrowly than Bales, adding that it is a permanent feature, often based on descent, where a person is under the total control of another, amounting to ownership. In this very narrow sense, slavery exists only in a part of west Africa and Sudan. In reality it is not possible to address the issues of modern-day slavery in such narrow terms. There is a significant grey area which is filled with notions of deserving and undeserving, and distinctions between choice and coercion, which can create huge distortions in how the enslaved are viewed and treated. For instance, people who are trafficked are seen as more deserving than those who have been smuggled in, because the first is seen as forced and the second is seen as voluntary. However, in practice both can end up in slavery.

Key features of modern slavery

It is delusional to believe that slavery ended at any given point in history. Slavery goes back 10,000 years to Mesopotamia, the area known today as Iraq,[2] and has continued in a variety of different guises since then. The transatlantic trade of the seventeenth and eighteenth centuries, which paved the streets of developed nations with gold, supposedly ended in 1807, followed by the Slavery Abolition Act of 1833 which made it not only illegal to engage in the trade throughout the British Empire but also gave freedom to all slaves. However, these laws did not bring an end to slavery. It is a shock to realize not only that slavery exists today but that it can be as brutal, and sometimes more brutal, than slavery in earlier times. In English society before the Norman Conquest, 10 per cent of the population were classified as slaves and could be killed by their owners without penalty. They did, however, have certain rights: to property, free time and entitlement to specified rations[3] – rights that, as we have seen, were not extended to Amber or Naomi.

Most of those who are enslaved in the UK today are 'foreign', they are not citizens of this country and therefore, their exploitation does not create much moral outrage. When people are packed into lorries and ships like goods then the equation of human beings with things becomes complete. Seventeenth-century British law recognized slaves as chattels and insured slave owners against loss. This led to the common practice of dumping sick slaves overboard in order to claim insurance payments. Dead slaves were worth more to the slave trader than sickly ones. Compare this with the fact that ship captains today throw their healthy human cargo overboard to avoid being caught for the criminal act of transporting people illegally. Are we not just as complacent and complicit as those who happily lived off the profits of slavery?

Across the world, we see that 'otherness' has been crucial to the justification of the most inhumane treatment. In the seventeenth and eighteenth centuries, English courts upheld the rights of owners to claim Negroes as property because they were not Christians. The Arab slave trade in Africa used African and European slaves at different points in its history although the middlemen, like the modern traffickers, often belonged to the same community as those who were being sold into slavery. Similarly, bonded labour in India comes from excluded groups like 'dalits' or ethnic or religious minorities – not just the poor. According to Krishna Uphadhyaya, 'Bonded labour is not exclusively an "economic" phenomenon. There are both sociological and political aspects.'[4] In Pakistan today over half of the 6m bonded labourers are Hindus and Christians while in the *bidi*-making industry (hand-rolled cigarettes) in India the bonded labourers are mainly Muslim. Bonded labour, which arises from a small debt borrowed by poor peasants at times of distress from a local landowner on terms that are completely open-ended, has survived for thousands of years despite the existence of rehabilitation funds and laws against it. The agricultural worker has only his life to offer as collateral and he must work for the landowner until the landowner decides that the debt has been repaid. Bonded labour can lead to a lifetime's indebtedness and may even be inherited by the children. Both Natasha and Farhia are examples of bonded labour today. Their board and lodging became a rolling debt which could never be paid off. A freed slave in Brazil said he was given paracetamol for malaria and told that he would have to work for two months to pay for it.[5]

What makes modern slavery worse, in some ways, is that the price of a slave has plummeted. Translated into modern prices, a slave in the eighteenth century would have cost the equivalent of £25,000 today. Slaveowners 'bred' their own slaves to avoid the expense of buying new ones. This meant that they incurred costs in housing, clothing and feeding entire families, even if the standards of care were poor. Old-style slavery had a maintenance cost which came naturally with 'ownership', but today's slave traders exercise control without ownership which leads to much higher profits. Today it is possible to buy and sell women for £3,000, as in the case of Natasha, or get them for nothing, as with Naomi. The 'cost' of maintenance is transferred to the slaves themselves as part of their debt bondage. Bales reports that one of his researchers recently bought two young men for £25 each in the Ivory Coast to prove the point.[6] Then there are those like Liu who *pay* smugglers handsomely to be brought to Britain only to end up in slavery.

Therefore, modern slave traders have little incentive to look after their investments with care. This has both positive and negative repercussions. They use more violence in order to control their slaves, not caring whether they can work or not if they are disabled by the violence, because the outlay can be recouped quite quickly. Even in the few months that Niki was in control of Natasha and knew that she would not be able to work with bruises, his anger overcame his need for profit and he would beat her into submission. 'Once the girl is worn out or she is infected by some sexual disease she is cast aside, just as you would a broken fridge', says Superintendent Chris Bradford, the Head of the Metropolitan Police's Vice and Clubs Unit.[7] They become 'disposable' in our one-use and throw-away consumer culture. As it is cheap to replace a runaway slave, not much money or energy is invested in chasing after them. Unfortunately, the vast majority of those who are enslaved are unaware of this, so they buy the lies and cower in fear, submitting to all kinds of humiliation to avoid being caught by what they are told are corrupt and brutal police or risk having their families visited by the network of criminal traders. The positive aspect is that modern slavery is 'temporary': it does not endure for a lifetime. Most people, as we saw from the individual stories, find themselves in this position from a few months to a few years. However, we cannot say this with any certainty. Perhaps there are people – women in forced marriages for example – who remain enslaved for a lifetime and therefore hidden from our gaze.

The most important feature of modern slavery is that, unlike the days of the transatlantic slave trade when slave ownership was socially respectable, it is generally viewed with abhorrence. Today, slavery and all the related activities of abduction, deceit, coercion, violence and abuse are criminalized to varying degrees across the world and certainly in Britain. It is, therefore, even more shocking that slavery is as rife as it is when we have all these tools to eliminate it at our disposal. The fact that we have not done more to eliminate it stems partly from our refusal to call a slave a slave.

Causes of modern slavery

Modern slavery is driven mainly by poverty in the developing world and immigration controls in developed nations which reduce migrants to poverty. While current economic systems are in place, while the profit motive drives development, world inequality will continue to grow and huge scabs of poverty will continue to disfigure the earth. Western aid and trade are supposed to stimulate the development of struggling economies and thus ameliorate poverty. Their primary value has been as vehicles of business opportunity to Western companies. Aid has been tied to various unpalatable conditions. In 2002, David Blunkett proposed that future aid to developing countries should be linked to their co-operation in curbing illegal immigration.[8] Trade policies are weighted against the developing world and, ironically, aid programmes which have a stated aim of poverty reduction can have the opposite effect in practice. Even the way in which aid is delivered by the West can decimate trade in beneficiary countries. For example, US food aid in the form of rice to Jamaica in the late 1990s undercut Jamaican rice imports from Guyana and dented the incomes of Guyanese rice growers.

Institutions like the International Monetary Fund (IMF), World Trade Organization (WTO) and the World Bank are more concerned with removing barriers on the activities of the multi-nationals and opening up the markets of the developing world to unrestricted trade, foreign investment and the free movement of financial capital than with the effects of their policies on indigenous peoples. Average income in sub-Saharan Africa, already so low, has fallen by 15 per cent per person over the past two decades, a fall in income exceeding that of the 1930s Depression in the industrialized world.[9] If Africa, east Asia, south Asia, and Latin America were each to increase their share of world exports by 1 per cent, the resulting gains in income could lift 128m people out of poverty. When developing countries export to rich countries, they face tariff barriers that are four times higher than those faced by rich countries in the opposite direction. Those trade barriers cost them $100bn a year – twice as much as they receive in aid.[10] The gap between the rich and poor is growing: a UN study published in December 2006 found that 1 per cent of the world owned 40 per cent of the wealth.

Much slavery, of course, happens within national borders, especially in the Third World. There are entrenched economic interests, such as landowners and factory owners, who benefit from its continuation. Despite the fact that there are laws against slavery on the statute book of almost every country in the world, there is a lack of political will to enforce those laws. People are trafficked within borders from poor, often rural, areas to urban areas for the purposes of forced labour or sexual services. They may not be aware of their rights or they may be prepared to surrender their rights when hunger is staring them in the face. Very few poor people have the resources, the skills, the knowledge and the spare cash to cross borders in the search for employment and an even smaller percentage make it to the developed West.

However, poverty is not the only reason that people migrate and not the only cause of slavery. The inhumane immigration laws of the West, the barbed wire on which migrants are impaled, also cause slavery. War, conflict, persecution, and environmental degradation are some of the reasons that force people to flee. Most of them end up in neighbouring countries. UNCHR figures for 2006 show that Kenya took in 150,000 refugees from neighbouring Somalia, where Farhia Nur comes from, the majority of whom probably ended up in greater poverty there. Only 36,000 came to the UK.[11] When these people end up in Europe, Canada and the US, the unwelcoming structures of their immigration systems decide who can and cannot enter legitimately, thus throwing those 'without papers' to the mercy of those who know how to capitalize on other people's misfortunes. These non-persons are infinitely exploitable because their lack of status in these countries puts them beyond the reach of state protection.

No other choice

The popular view that migrants come to the UK in search of 'a better life' implies greed and ambition on the part of foreigners who want to abuse British hospitality at worst and who are exercising individual choice at best. 'Migration for economic betterment, rather than being considered, as it should be and as it was when Europeans did it, a sign of enterprise and courage, is now regarded as criminal and somehow shameful.'[12] Even a refugee is arguably coming for a better life because the life left behind involves death and torture. What does choice mean when sheer survival is at stake? As John Berger says, 'To try to understand the experience of another it is necessary to dismantle the world as seen from one's place within it, and to reassemble it as seen from his... The well-fed are incapable of understanding the choices of the under-fed.'[13]

While the idea that choice as an inalienable right is fast taking hold of people in the West, it does not appear to be a contradiction for the same people to condemn those who migrate because they have no other choice. Or where 'choice' seems to be the primary driver of migration, it becomes a dividing line between deserving and undeserving. Those who are trafficked, i.e. brought here against their will or deceived in some way, are more deserving of our sympathy than those who were smuggled here, because they paid someone to break the law and bring them in illegally. If they end up in slavery then that is the fate they deserve. Similarly, the notion of choice in marriage becomes the dividing line between 'arranged' and 'forced'. Amber is bought and sold like any common slave. She was not dragged to the door of her future husband but she was brought up in such a way that she could not question her parents' wisdom when they arranged her marriage. She had no other choice but to marry. Was that forced or arranged?

There are many diverse, overlapping, incomplete and confusing ways of classifying migrants who end up in slavery. The government is keen to focus on mode of entry: were they trafficked or smuggled? Were they forced or did they choose to come? Legislation, especially the ECAT, clearly constructs victims of trafficking as deserving of sympathy and positive government action. It obliges non-governmental organizations (NGOs) to follow suit, to shape their concerns in the language and categories used by government. Those who are smuggled in are often asylum seekers, as they have no legal way of coming to Britain. As only a minority of asylum seekers succeed in their claim because of the government's ridiculously high hurdles, the rest are considered to be bogus and really economic migrants in disguise. The distinction between political refugees and economic migrants is a popular one with government. This argument does not rear its ugly head that often nowadays since economic migrants began to develop a halo after the government proclaimed that the British economy needs them. In fact, asylum seekers, bogus or otherwise, are getting a bit of a rest from tabloid attention, which is currently firmly focused on the hordes descending from the newly-expanded EU:

Poland, Romania and Bulgaria. Then there are those who entered legally but became over-stayers for a variety of reasons or women who are trapped in violent or forced marriages. However, all those who have no independent means of survival will end up in forced labour of one kind or another: agricultural, construction, domestic labour or sexual exploitation.

Real lives are too messy to fit neatly into any one of these boxes. Farhia's rapist pays a people-smuggler to deposit her in the UK, where she claims asylum, fails, is denied financial support and 'forced' into unpaid domestic servitude and sexual exploitation. As she loses her asylum claim, she is not a political refugee according to the government, but does that make her an economic migrant? Naomi, a fifteen-year-old child, is brought by her Lebanese employer from Sierra Leone and deposited with her employer's 'sister' for a life of domestic slavery. She runs away and is sheltered by a man who prostitutes her. She runs away again and finds herself on the street. Was she trafficked? Is she more deserving of our sympathy than Farhia? Liu is imprisoned for his religious views, pays thousands of pounds to be smuggled here and ends up in 'forced' labour. The difficulties with labelling are made explicit when Liu's claim to the Criminal Injuries Board, for the loss of his brother's life in the Dover 58 tragedy fails. The Board argued that the victims were party to the crime. The lawyers for the relatives argued that the victims were not willing partners, they did not choose their mode of travel and they were not told about the conditions of travel.

Is it useful for our purposes to differentiate between people-smuggling and trafficking? How does it matter whether the cockle-pickers chose to come to this country when they ended up doing work which they would not have chosen to do? The Director of Anti-Slavery International argues that no distinction should be made if the end result is forced labour.[14] Various governmental and UN documents are at pains to make the distinction. One of the distinctions they make is that there is no violence in smuggling while there is in trafficking, but we can see from Liu's story that it does not hold water. The only distinction that is indisputable is that trafficking can happen within and across borders but smuggling happens only across borders. From a governmental point of view, their keenness to make a distinction is understandable: they owe nothing to those who have been smuggled in because they are complicit in a crime. Until recently, government agencies were not that sympathetic to victims of trafficking either. When police raided a brothel for trafficked women, they were accompanied by immigration officers who seized upon any woman whose papers were not in order as an illegal immigrant and put her in a detention centre. Women were snatched from the pimp's prison and thrown into the state's prison. Many victims were deported without any assessment of what risk they might return to and without any prospects of their traffickers being held to account. This was especially true of those women who refused to assist with police investigations out of fear of retribution by traffickers, in spite of the fact that branches of the same criminal networks which brought them into Britain awaited them in their country of origin. Wherever possible, the government attempted to criminalize trafficked women so as to have no responsibility towards them. As international conventions on trafficking construct victims as victims of crime and not as criminals, it becomes important for NGOs to acquiesce in this distinction between trafficking and smuggling so that at least some 'illegal' migrants receive a sympathetic response.

Why people migrate

People come to Britain to marry, to study, to work, to run a business or a combination of any of these. These are people exercising choice in the more generally understood meaning of the term. This book, however, focuses on those driven to migrate. The flight from hunger, for example, is hardly a matter of choice. Grinding poverty is one of the reasons why people rupture the ties of family, friends, land, language, jobs, culture, religion, and familiarity with the place where they were born, and travel to another country. Some analysts believe that it is not the 'push' of poverty but the attraction of strong economies that 'pull' people like magnets in their direction: 'A boom in the destination area, not a slump in the sending area, stimulates movement.'[15] Some people will be targeted by traffickers who can see that they would make good sex slaves, domestic labour or agricultural workers. War and conflict lead to a breakdown in civil society, as has happened in Iraq, creating situations where young women in need of work are being lured across the border to work in Syria, in factories that do not exist, and end up as prey for sex traffickers.[16] Even a one-off natural disaster like the tsunami led to child-trafficking of orphans in places like Thailand. War creates poverty and takes away the means to a livelihood. Of course someone fleeing the consequences of war may be seen as an economic migrant, rather than a refugee. In reality the distinction is meaningless; these are categories that have been imposed for the convenience of governments and to justify the upside-down logic of draconian immigration measures. Even those who come to the West without invitation are usually people with skills and some level of education and wealth, like Liu. However, if they do not have adequate papers, they will be vulnerable to extreme exploitation and be engaged in unskilled jobs, which gives rise to the view that they are contributing nothing to this society and economy.

Only a small percentage of migrants are literally fleeing out of fear for their lives. According to the UNCHR, the number of refugees worldwide has been in decline since 1980, reaching its lowest level, 8.4m, at the end of 2005. Of this figure, there are a mere 307,064 in the UK, a little over 3.5 per cent of the world's refugees.[17] To put it another way, this number is less than the capacity of three and a half Wembley stadiums. It makes you wonder what the fuss is all about. Many of those places where there is war and conflict are run by regimes which have been armed by the British government: Sri Lanka, Turkey, Indonesia. Others, like Afghanistan and Iraq, have been invaded by Britain and the US. Although the invasion of Iraq was carried out by the USA with Britain in tow, it is Sweden, which was against the war, that is taking in Iraqi refugees. In 2006, Sweden accepted nearly 10,000 Iraqis, making them the country's second largest ethnic group after the Finns, whereas the US, which stands to gain most by its invasion, took in a measly 700 people.[18] To its shame, Britain received 600 applications, the majority of which were turned down, and it forcibly repatriated 38 Iraqis in February 2007. Meanwhile Syria and Jordan, bordering countries, took in 1m and 800,000 Iraqis respectively.[19] Part of the West's military strategy entails the setting up of military bases in remote parts of the world, evicting the inhabitants in order to use their homes as launching pads for future wars. There was a scandalous disregard for the people of the Diego Garcia and Chagos islands in the Indian Ocean, forced out of their homes in the 1960s and early 1970s when an airbase was built by the US, some of whom were allowed to settle in the UK. For years these people have been using every means at their disposal to be allowed the right to go home; they eventually won the right to do so after an appeal court ruling in May 2007.[20]

Centuries of industrialization and our current energy-consuming western lifestyle are having such an impact on climate change that scientists predict that there will be millions of refugees fleeing hunger and thirst and uninhabitable climates. The US is infamous for the fact that its population, which represents 5 per cent of the world's population, consumes more than 33 per cent of its resources. There are no international laws governing the plight of environmental refugees. People whose livelihood has been affected by the environment would be seen as economic migrants and therefore demonized and ignored. To date it appears that most such migrations have taken place within borders, usually from rural to urban areas. However, this will eventually drive people across borders. The Stern Report into climate change makes the unsurprising point that, 'The impacts of climate change are not evenly distributed... The poorest countries and people will suffer earliest and most'. A rise of 2°c in temperature combined with population growth could leave anywhere from one to four billion people facing water shortages. Disruption in agriculture could leave 30–200m people facing hunger, rise in deaths from malaria and dengue fever; and a rise in sea levels could permanently displace 200m people through floods and droughts.[21] Not many of these people will have the wherewithal to come to the West.

Refugees are also generated by the activities of multi-nationals. Millions of people in other countries have been forced to make way for large dams, oil pipelines and agricultural plantations in which UK companies are involved, often as a condition of UK aid money. Shell, for example, has a long and disreputable history in the Niger Delta (Nigeria). It has been extracting oil for over thirty years and its activities have resulted in land and water pollution which has led to the uprooting of the Ogoni people. Although their protests were largely peaceful, the corrupt Nigerian government under Abacha reacted with brutality and terror. Many of the Ogoni people left the region. Some no doubt ended up as refugees in the UK. The number of asylum applications from Nigeria shot up to 4,000 at the height of the troubles in 1994, the year when Ken Saro-Wiwa, a writer and political representative of the people, was executed. No Nigerian was given asylum in 1994 and only five were given exceptional leave to remain (ELR).[22] Even if all five had been totally supported by the state, it is likely to have been a pittance in comparison with the tax paid by Shell to the British treasury. As far as I am aware, no one has done such a cost comparison. Unfortunately the structure of multi-national companies is so complicated and the inter-relationship between the parent company and the subsidiaries so difficult to disentangle, that it would take huge resources to research that. Although much is written about the tax avoidance schemes of multi-national firms, I suspect that enough tax is paid to the treasury to make a strong financial argument against those who see migrants as a drain on this economy.

On every front, the industrialized West has been centrally implicated in the forces driving people from their homes. This point is succinctly made by Nicholas Hildyard:

> For every Kurd that comes to Britain, millions of pounds of UK
> taxpayers' money have been spent on supporting the Turkish
> regime that forced them to flee their homeland. For every

Congolese that comes here, millions of pounds of UK pensioners' money are invested in the companies that fuel the civil wars in the region through their extraction of minerals. For every Tamil, millions are spent on arms exports to Sri Lanka...[23]

Naturally, the West must face the consequences of its actions and that extends to its responsibility for migrants.

Who migrates?

Not everyone who migrates ends up in slavery. This book is not concerned with those who have easy access to this country because of their high level of skills, the size of their wallet or their financial contribution to British universities as foreign students. Nor is it concerned with those who come to join their British spouses in the normal course. Its main concern is with those for whom migration becomes an additional element in the web of forces that places them under the total control of someone else.

Given that government classifications of migrants are driven by administrative and political expediency, it is more useful from our point of view to explore the predicament of migrants according to where they ended up: prostitution, forced labour, forced marriage and failed asylum seekers although some of these categories are not mutually exclusive. The situation of children needs to be considered separately. Although they are found in each of the above categories, they deserve special attention because, by reason of age alone, they cannot be deemed to have given consent and consent, as we have seen, is very closely allied to culpability or at least collusion in immigration law. In the West, where children and animal charities pull most easily at the heartstrings, it is particularly damning that the government has double standards and 'foreign' children are not afforded the same degree of protection as 'British' children. It could be argued that women should be looked at as a separate category too. However, the reality is that women are disproportionately affected by poverty and are over-represented among those trafficked into the UK for sexual exploitation, for domestic work and for labour in the care sector. Of the 600,000–800,000 people trafficked across international borders each year, 70 per cent are women. The majority of these victims are forced into the commercial sex trade.[24] Non-sexual forced labour is made up of 44 per cent men and boys, and 56 per cent women and girls.[25] However, even exploited men do better than the women: Liu is the only one from our five stories who has been reunited with his family and whose life is coming together. The four women are struggling to settle down and, in some cases, still at a vulnerable point in their lives.

Prostitution

In no other area is the distinction between choice and coercion so starkly made and the response of state agencies towards those women who have been trafficked for sexual exploitation and those who may have come voluntarily so guided by concepts of deserving and undeserving. A whole raft of measures has been introduced for 'trafficked' women which is simply not available to those who have come here 'voluntarily'. And in no other area is the distinction more blurred by those with vested interests: the English Collective of Prostitutes (ECP) who argue that women go into prostitution out of choice; those who suggest that as it is the 'oldest profession in the world' it must somehow represent an acceptable career choice for women; and state agencies which emphasize choice in a bid to reduce their new obligations to trafficked women under the European Convention.

Although my focus is on the connection between sexual slavery and immigration controls, it is important to recognize that in the sex industry, rape, violence and the threat of it, and the fear of discovery of working 'dishonourably' are additional tools of enslavement even when women are here legally. Women do not feel able to use their legal status to seek protection from the state because the entrenched sexism of agencies like the police has meant that state protection has historically not been forthcoming to prostitutes. Women working with prostitutes report that even local prostitutes are 'enslaved by their pimps and their circumstances'[26] and that most are in it out of sheer desperation, often feeding a drug habit which may have been cultivated by a pimp in the first place, and are looking for exit strategies. Local women could have been internally trafficked from one part of the UK to another but this does not appear to be a particular concern of law enforcement agencies. Some overseas women in the industry are here legally and some illegally. Those who are here legally may have been trafficked and those who are here illegally may also have been trafficked or smuggled. In both categories, it may be possible to find women who are here 'voluntarily'. The complex nature of the industry highlights the inadequacy of an immigration focus in law enforcement.

By treating trafficked women as a separate and special case, the root of the problem, i.e. demand, is not being tackled. Feminist campaigners like Julie Bindel believe strongly that until the demand for sexual services is criminalized, a thriving sex industry will continue to act as a 'green light for traffickers'.[27] Trade is conducted so openly that slave auctions are reportedly taking place at coffee shops at Heathrow and Gatwick where brothel keepers are bidding for women.[28] Focusing on the human rights of trafficked women implicitly suggests that the human rights of local prostitutes who face violence and abuse are not of the same order. Of course, the situation of trafficked women is worse because they have no documentation, they are liable to be deported, they cannot look to the state for protection, and may feel isolated in a country far from home where they may not even speak the language. Piecemeal attempts to deal just with trafficked women, however, cannot work. The knotty issues of consent and choice which underlie discussions about the sex industry came to the fore with calls from various members of the government to convict men who had sex with trafficked women of rape, because a trafficked woman by definition has not given consent. Apart from the fact that rape convictions are at an historic low, just how would a man be convicted except by his own confession? Joan Smith, journalist and campaigner, calls for punters to show some responsibility when confronted by a woman who appears terrified and cannot speak the language, which seems a little naïve.[29] Natasha had learned not to show her fear; some women take drugs in order to numb the pain, while others who do not speak the language might be here 'voluntarily'. What is the morality underpinning all of this? Both categories of women are trying to escape poverty: those who go in with their eyes open are to be ignored while those whose eyes are closed are to receive state protection.

On 23 March 2007, the United Kingdom Human Trafficking Centre (UKHTC) published the UK Action Plan on Tackling Human Trafficking in a symbolic gesture to mark the bicentenary of the abolition of the slave trade. Despite the new emphasis on human rights violations, there appears to be establishment anxiety that more and more women will be given leave to remain here. This tension between the need to see them as victims without opening the flood gates to new immigration surfaces in police statements limiting the number of women to whom the term 'trafficked' can be applied. The police line is that 'trafficking' is an emotive term; that the word implies that women are snatched off a street, bundled into a car, brought to Britain and locked up in a brothel, but there is not much evidence of that. It is interesting that the police should push this line when the internationally accepted definition of trafficking includes deception and not just abduction. Superintendent Chris Bradford, Head of the Vice and Clubs Unit of the Metropolitan Police says, 'They are coming to the UK to be lap dancers, table dancers. That's only one step away from actually getting involved in prostitution.'[30] This is an eerie echo of those conservative judgments which threw out a rape case because a woman who was dressed provocatively was asking to be raped. The official line is that only a small percentage of prostitutes has been trafficked:

The vast majority of women in this environment are knowingly recruited as sex workers and may voluntarily engage in prostitution, others may have been duped by promises of legitimate employment, and so some of these people within our communities will be victims of human trafficking and will be the subject of unwilling exploitation.[31]

Where women enter prostitution for survival, a local economic boom leads to women leaving the sex industry in droves. With the growing prosperity of the Korean economy, for example, the sex industry was left depleted and special entertainment visas (E6) were issued to import women from Russia, Philippines and other places.[32] Similarly, on the basis of police estimates that ten years ago 85 per cent of women in brothels were UK citizens and now 85 per cent are from outside UK,[33] it could be argued that a booming British economy has led to local prostitutes leaving the industry and being replaced by 'foreign' women. However, the statistics are unreliable. The Chaste website (a Church initiative against sexual trafficking) says that 80,000 women work in prostitution and 70 per cent are recruited before their eighteenth birthday. This would mean that there are approximately 54,000 trafficked women here. Yet the most routinely quoted figure dates back to 2003 when a Home Office survey found that there are 4,000 trafficked women here at any one time.

The issue of trafficking for sexual exploitation first came to the attention of the authorities when the Metropolitan Police started documenting cases in 1991. The majority of women come from Eastern Europe, the Baltic States, and the Balkans, or from the Far East, especially China, Malaysia and Thailand. In 2006 the much publicized Operation Pentameter identified 84 victims of trafficking, following visits to 500 premises, 10 per cent of the estimated number of sex establishments in the country. All the victims were women, the majority aged between eighteen and twenty-five while twelve were aged between fourteen and seventeen. All entered overtly through airports, ports, railway and coach stations, but not necessarily with legal documentation. About 60 per cent arrived in the UK illegally, which means the remaining 40 per cent found themselves in these terrible situations despite having arrived in the country legally.[34] Human rights groups criticized Pentameter on the grounds that it was as much a campaign to find and deport illegal immigrants. The focus on illegal immigration is also apparent in the composition of the UKHTC, a multi-agency initiative, set up in 2006, which includes the Crown Prosecution Service (CPS), the Serious Organized Crime Agency (SOCA), and the IND.

There was no legislation dealing with trafficking until the UK Government criminalized all forms of trafficking under the Sexual Offences Act 2003 and the Asylum and Immigration Act 2004, under which there have been thirty convictions of trafficking as at June 2006.[35] The 2004 Act introduced new offences of trafficking for slavery or forced labour, human organ transplant or other forms of exploitation. Trafficking offences carry a maximum penalty of fourteen years imprisonment. In 2003, it was estimated that trafficking in human beings gave rise to a profit of $7–$10m.[36] The risks of getting caught are low because the relationship nurtured by traffickers with their 'cargo' is based on violence or threats of violence, making victims unwilling or unable to contact the authorities. As we saw in the story of Natasha, even when she was travelling alone by tube she had been so intimidated by her 'pimp' that she did not think of escaping. In the case of Naomi, although we cannot be sure if she was trafficked, her inability to read signs and direct police to the address where she was living means that no prosecutions are possible.

It is often only on arrival in another country that the danger becomes apparent to trafficked women, who will usually need protection from the traffickers in their country of destination. They will need time to come to terms with the reality of their situation and the levels of trauma they have experienced. Until 2001, when the POPPY Project was founded by Denise Marshall,[37] there was no agency to which rescued women could be sent for support and protection. The police often use accommodation provided by social services, as in the case of Natasha, which are not well enough resourced to match the range of services provided by POPPY. It is also true that young women disappear from social services care, as happened during Operation Paladin Child (discussed below, p. 269), a three-month project set up to assess the scale of trafficking in children.

Women at the POPPY Project have up to 30 days to consider whether they are prepared to give evidence to the police and whether they wish to claim asylum before there is any threat of removal. Initially the scheme criteria for admission specifically excluded women who intended to claim asylum, although this was dropped after lobbying by POPPY. Women then move on to Stage 2, which includes one year of 'acute' service and one year on 'resettlement'. During this time they must apply for asylum. These services are not available to those whose asylum applications have failed. In order to be eligible for temporary protection within the POPPY Project, victims of trafficking must be prepared to give evidence to the police. Women are also required to co-operate fully with the immigration authorities, including co-operating with arrangements for their own removal if and when police investigations are at an end and/or her asylum claim is unsuccessful. A study tracking the asylum applications of women at POPPY tentatively concluded that women's co-operation may have bearing upon the perceived credibility of their claims, 'If this is true, it is of concern. Whether or not a woman succeeds in her asylum claim should not depend on her willingness or otherwise to co-operate with the police and immigration authorities in relation to any prosecution they may wish to bring against her traffickers'.[38] The possibility of a period of reflection which includes time for making an asylum claim is an important mechanism to ensure victims' safety, and profoundly influences decisions about whether or not to co-operate with the authorities.

This period of reflection, originally granted by the government on a case-by-case basis, is now embedded in the ECAT, which the government finally signed up to in March 2007. The Convention allows for a reflection period of thirty days along the lines of the POPPY Project's Stage 1 support. Authorities are not allowed to deport anybody during this recovery and reflection period. In order to pursue compensation claims against the traffickers, victims have to be granted renewable residence permits because they need to stay in the country where the legal proceedings are being instituted. It had been recommended by the Joint Committee on Human Rights that residence permits should be issued for six months at a time. However there have been no compensation claims against traffickers to date.

The government had feared that these measures could become 'pull' factors which made no sense at all. Paul Goggins, then a junior minister at the Home Office, was anxious that the asylum and immigration system remained credible and robust.[39] If coercion and/or trickery are accepted as key elements in trafficking, then, by definition, there are no 'pull' factors. If anything, it is more likely to make traffickers 'downsize' their trade if legislation which encourages women to testify against them is supported. Some pressure groups are now calling on the government to agree to a 90-day reflection period and some are recommending the Italian model which provides for a six-month period regardless of whether victims of trafficking choose to testify against their trafficker. This has resulted in more survivors being willing to testify and a higher degree of success in prosecuting traffickers.

The right to remain here, and access all the services that will enable trafficked women to recover from the trauma of their experience is the best form of protection for them. Many women have said that a British passport breaks the grip that the traffickers have over them. It also eliminates the danger of being re-trafficked, the 'revolving door phenomenon' which is the fate that befalls many women who are deported. However, the government needs to prioritize human rights above that of immigration concerns. With every single category of slavery, the government's first response in tackling the problem is to restrict immigration rights, a strategy which does not work in any case, instead of liberalizing them.

Forced Labour

Current conditions in Britain – the demand for labour alongside more draconian immigration laws – encourage the growth of trafficking for forced labour at an almost uncontrollable rate. There are no reliable estimates for the scale of labour exploitation. The

Parliamentary Joint Committee on Human Rights Report on Human Trafficking concluded that information on trafficking for labour exploitation is even less adequate than that on trafficking for sexual purposes. The greater focus on trafficking for sexual exploitation may be driven by the greater numbers involved. 'Labour exploitation takes place across a range of sectors, specifically agriculture, construction, contract cleaning, domestic work and the care sector... in low-pay sectors, sectors where work can be described by the "three Ds" (difficult, dangerous and dirty)'.[40] There are two overriding fears that are exploited by unscrupulous employers which stop workers from complaining about conditions: fear of being sacked and easily replaced, and fear of being shopped to the authorities and deported.

There are many ways in which people end up doing forced labour. Those who have been smuggled here as political or economic refugees or whose migration status has become insecure over time may end up enslaved. As the borders are made more migrant-proof, smuggling becomes more expensive, which means that the people who are 'saved' are those with the most means and not necessarily those in the greatest danger. In true capitalist style, the quality of your journey depends on how much you pay. A 'no frills' journey can take ages, the conditions are dire and sickness and even death are distinct possibilities. Those who do not have the means then fall into a system of debt bondage like women and children in the sex industry or (Chinese) men in sweatshops. And families back home can be hit by debt bondage as they invest in one of their number going abroad to make their 'fortune'. The Chinese cockle-pickers who died at Morecambe Bay provide a vivid and tragic illustration of this phenomenon. The vast investment in their journeys had not been recouped because they had found one low-paid job after another, which barely covered the inflated rents and other expenses that the gangmasters dreamt up and drove them to take on riskier assignments like cockle-picking.

As a direct response to this tragedy, the government introduced the Gangmasters (Licensing) Act 2004, which only covers agriculture, not the cleaning, catering and hotel work where agencies for 'illegals' thrive. However, there has not yet been a single prosecution, despite high profile news reports like that broadcast by BBC TV in which an undercover reporter found Polish workers working for below minimum wage rates and being charged £50 rent per week for a bed in a room shared with twelve other people.[41] Gangmasters are supposed to be licensed, use of unlicensed gangmasters is a criminal offence, and gangmasters are supposed to recruit workers who are allowed to work legally in Britain. The BBC report did not tell us whether the gangmaster was licensed but the Polish workers were certainly here legally. However, a combination of lack of language and knowledge of their rights and desperation created this forced labour situation. These workers' conditions should be seen through the spectrum of employment rights. However, if you do not have a legal contract of employment, many of these rights are not available. Although the unions have demanded government action and recognize that exploitation of migrants affects all workers, they have been slow to organize this sector, many of whom are not and cannot afford to be unionized.

According to Anti-Slavery International's report on forced labour,[42] the majority of trafficked workers are here legally. Of course, it recognized the fact that those who came to their attention through channels like the Citizens Advice Bureau were more likely to be legal than not. This is the drawback of the government's approach to viewing trafficking as an immigration offence which leaves large sections of slavery untouched. Despite attention being drawn to the government's disproportionate interest in immigration, the trend looks set to continue, 'the new agency (UKHTC) would be devoting an increasing proportion of its effort to tackling organized immigration crime. SOCA has set itself the aim of devoting 25 per cent of its total effort to this crime area, representing broadly a tripling of activity.'[43]

The government has not made a commitment to eradicate forced labour but to tackle trafficking for forced labour. It is likely that the government will attempt to reduce its commitments, especially those of granting residence permits under the ECAT, by finding ways of tightening definitions, just as the official line on trafficking for sex suggested that most women knew what they were opting for, thus taking away one of the main planks of trafficking – deception. There is a hint of this with regard to forced labour in the Home Office's recently published Action Plan on Tackling Human Trafficking: 'One of the difficulties we will face in investigating trafficking for forced labour is distinguishing betw-een poor working conditions and situations involving forced labour. The element of coercion is an important indicator of the latter.'[44] Interestingly, deception has been left out of the equation again.

Another way of reducing its commitments under the Convention will be 'specific measures targeted at reducing demand. We are looking at ways to ensure that the realities of exploitation through prostitution are understood and also at ways in which employers understand their responsibilities when employing migrant workers as well as the penalties they face if they employ illegal migrant workers.'[45] Where sexual exploitation is concerned, the government is content to tackle demand by raising awareness, but where forced labour is concerned the government has proposed that employers be fined and even gaoled for not checking the immigration status of their workers.[46] The right response to trafficking for sex should be criminalizing buying of services. Apparently one in ten men now pays for sex, which represents a doubling of the figures since the 1990s.[47] Instead, the Action Plan talks of producing publicity material aimed at men who use prostitutes to be aware of the risk that the women may be trafficked. In fact Operation Pentameter 2, which is due to take place in 2007, is meant to develop further 'awareness-raising' strategies to reduce demand. Criminalization of demand in Sweden has made a significant impact on trafficking of women to that country. It seems irrational for the British government to criminalize use of illegal labour in a booming economy where, by all accounts, growth would be choked off without an adequate supply of labour. The rationale for penalizing employers is that they must stop the exploitation of illegal workers – a fine motive, but this move condemns them to further destitution in the absence of other means of support. As some of the forced labour is here legally, surely the government should criminalize those employers who ignore the employment legislation of this country and treat their employees like slaves.

The Joint Committee on Human Trafficking did not distinguish domestic workers as a separate category from those trafficked for forced labour. Around ten thousand people arrive legally in the UK to do domestic work.[48] As domestic workers are isolated, and dependent on their employers for both work and accommodation, many of them are deceived about the hours and conditions of work and could therefore be considered to have been trafficked. It is not unusual for them to work seven days per week without respite for eighteen hours per day, sleep on a kitchen or bedroom floor, and be paid about £200 per month. Perhaps the best known of such cases was that of Laxmi Peria Swamy, employed by Kuwaiti princesses who beat, whipped, imprisoned and starved her. She was supported by Brent Women's Refuge and Southall Black Sisters who helped her sue her former employers and, in a precedent-setting legal case, she won compensation of nearly £400,000 in 1989. This was nothing short of slavery, although Kalayaan, the main NGO supporting domestic workers in the UK, prefers to avoid the equation of domestic worker with slave, perhaps in a heroic attempt to elevate and dignify the domestic worker industry.

Proposed changes to British immigration law are likely to further weaken the position of domestic workers. Under the new points-based system (see below) of entry, migrant domestic workers will only be given six-month visas and they will be tied to one employer. This means they will not be able to leave their employer even if they are abusive. It reverses current practice, which had removed the link between the granting of a work permit and the requirement to stay with a specific employer in the UK, itself the result of a successful Kalayaan campaign in the 1990s. Kalayaan believes that the points-based system 'will establish legal channels to bring Migrant Domestic Workers (MDW) to the UK for the purpose of exploitation, removing even the most basic of their employment rights, leaving them powerless before abusive employers. It will effectively legalise trafficking.'[49]

Even where domestic workers have come to the UK with the right papers, unscrupulous employers control their workers by confiscating their passports (a characteristic of forced labour according to ILO Convention 29) and often not renewing their visas, thereby turning them into illegal immigrants, all the better to exploit them. Kalayaan has been running a campaign against this widespread practice. During August 2004 and August 2005, they 'registered 114 new migrant domestic workers at Kalayaan. Of these 114 individuals 65 of them – so well over half – had had their passports withheld by their employer'.[50] The first two demands in the Charter of Rights for Migrant Domestic Workers in Europe are connected to immigration status. The Charter asks for the right to an immigration status that recognizes that domestic work in the private house is proper work and asks for the right to an immigration status *independent* of any employer. This is a recognition of the direct links that exist between immigration status and slavery and exploitation.

Domestic workers fall between two stools. Although the overwhelming majority are women, they cannot access any of the services and/or refuges available to women facing domestic violence as domestic violence is defined as taking place between members of a family. As domestic workers are employees they should be able to use employment legislation to protect them from abusive employers and to access trade union support. However, trade unions have not historically paid much attention to those workers who cannot afford membership fees. It is a further disgrace that race and sex discrimination legislation does not extend to private homes so employers are free to discriminate on these grounds. SBS, in its current campaign to allow women of insecure immigration status to be eligible for public benefits when they have been forced out of the home through violence, has demanded that the definition of domestic violence be widened to include MDWs.

The status of domestic workers as workers is often muddied by the fact that poorer members of extended families are brought over on tourist visas of six months for a working 'holiday' for which they may or may not be paid. Naomi, the child domestic worker, was supposed to feel so grateful for the roof over her head that asking for wages on top would have been seen as ingratitude. Similarly, SBS has found that women who have been brought here as brides are often brought solely as domestic slaves. Although this is a component of many arranged marriages where the new bride is seen as additional domestic labour within an extended family set-up, there are situations where marriages may not have been consummated because the man is involved in other relationships and the sole purpose of getting him married apart from saving the family *izzat* (honour) is importing free domestic help. If the woman was forced into that marriage, she becomes a slave in all but name.

Forced marriage

The dividing line between forced and arranged marriages is a very fine one. As argued above, the notion of 'choice' becomes a guiding light in deciding who is deserving or non-deserving of state protection. This issue is further complicated by cultural relativism which historically meant that women and girls trying to escape the prospect of an 'arranged' marriage were met by a non-interventionist policy from social workers who saw it as racist to interfere with a minority culture. This notion of cultural relativism has also affected the trafficking of children for domestic work, particularly in African communities. As a result of demands made by feminists from minority groups most affected by the practice of forced marriage, the government has begun to make the right noises in damning the practice and, in fact, made opposition to it the litmus test of Britishness.

When the British government decided to tackle the issue, it did so with its customary zeal for tightening immigration law – the panacea for any social evil. Although there is some evidence of forced marriages taking place between cousins as a way of providing citizenship to extended family members, immigration law will not provide a way out of this practice. The government raised the age group from sixteen to eighteen for those getting married: not for everyone, only those who were marrying overseas spouses. Now there are proposals to increase the age limit to twenty-one. As SBS and other activists in the field have pointed out, women will simply be kept overseas until the appropriate age. The longer they are kept overseas, the more likely are they to have had children and to become further trapped in their situation. It would not have saved Amber, for example, who was twenty-one when she got married. Apart from the racism of a policy which introduces differential treatment of communities, this will not tackle the vast number of forced marriages that are taking place within national borders. Presumably, if enough white British men and women are affected by this change in age limits, the government will drop it, otherwise the differentials will remain.

Another piece of immigration law which adversely affects women in forced marriages is the two-year rule. It is a probationary period for trans-national marriages between British and non-British spouses. If the marriage ends before the two-year period, the non-British spouse could be deported. SBS started a campaign in 1993 against the rule, when the stipulated period was only one year, and won concessions in 1999 where a marriage had broken down on grounds of domestic violence. Women who could provide evidence of violence would be allowed leave to remain in the UK. Although violence may be a feature of forced marriages, women who cannot prove violence will not be able to leave a forced marriage within the two-year period. Indeed, the British spouse may not co-operate in applying for his wife's leave to remain within or even long after that period, which means that if she leaves the marriage without residence rights, she would become an over-stayer, and therefore an 'illegal' immigrant.

Measures to protect women from the prospect of forced marriage in the UK are likely to be more useful. To that end, a Forced Marriage (Civil Protection) Bill, which offers remedies and protection for women and children who might be at risk of forced marriage, was introduced in the House of Lords in January 2007 by Lord Anthony Lester, a Liberal peer, after consultation with SBS and family lawyers. At the time of writing, it looks set to become law after the government threw its weight behind it.

The Supplementary Convention on the Abolition of Slavery 1957 describes any practice whereby 'A woman, without the right to refuse, is promised or given in marriage on payment of a consideration in money or in kind' as a slavery-like practice. Anti-Slavery International lists forced marriage as a type of slavery. Despite the extensive use of dowry whereby women are bought and sold into marriage, there is no widespread acceptance of forced marriage as a form of slavery. When coercion and trickery are involved and/or the marriage turns unexpectedly into a state of sexual and domestic slavery, that should surely qualify victims of forced marriage to be considered within the framework of trafficking so that victims could have the same recourse to benefits under the trafficking convention whether or not they have suffered violence.

Failed asylum seekers

While the government has been slow to move on the issue of forced marriages taking place within UK borders, it has readily abrogated the right to marry for failed asylum seekers. Farhia Nur cannot marry the man who rescued her from slavery because she does not have a passport. Five British women who found themselves in this position, unable to marry the man of their choice because he was an asylum seeker, have set up Brides without Borders to campaign against the injustice of it. In May 2007, these restrictive marriage rules were successfully challenged in the courts as a breach of human rights but we do not know how the government will respond to this ruling at the time of writing. Other human rights of failed asylum seekers are trampled upon: there have been reports that those suffering from cancer or needing maternity care have been turned away from hospitals unless it is an emergency.[51] The right to liberty is taken away when asylum seekers are placed in detention centres without having committed a criminal act. Although the asylum system is vast and complicated, a quick look at the obstacles placed in the way of asylum seekers reveals how they are criminalized by the system and set up to fail even before they start the process.

With the huge rise in asylum seekers around the turn of the century, Tony Blair committed himself to halving the number of applications. It was a strange commitment to make. Refugees are supposedly generated by factors outside the control of any single government: war, persecution, conflict. When Blair commits himself to reducing the number of refugees, you would expect him to announce economic development initiatives in refugee-producing countries or, at the very least, a refusal to sell armaments to certain regimes. It has been argued that the NATO bombing of Kosovo in 1999 was partly carried out to prevent the mass exodus of Albanian refugees caused by Milosevic's Serbianization of the province because Europe was finding it hard to cope with previous waves of asylum seekers from the Balkans. Of course, the bombing campaign itself created refugees, some of whom landed up on the shores of Britain and many of whom were repatriated with unseemly haste when it appeared safe to return them. Jack Straw, when he was Home Secretary, was in favour of setting up schemes like the temporary protection scheme for Kosovan refugees in neighbouring Macedonia as a way of avoiding long-term responsibility for refugees. Mostly Blair has kept his commitment to reducing numbers not by going to war but by administrative stealth: introducing a number of measures designed to erode the provisions of the Geneva Convention and make it impossible for asylum seekers to reach our shores.

Britain is a signatory to the 1951 UN Convention on Refugees which was formulated in response to the humanitarian crisis caused by the reluctance of Western governments to take in, particularly, Jewish refugees from the Nazi holocaust. Under this convention, as noted previously, refugees must prove a 'well-founded fear of being persecuted for reasons of race, religion, nationality, membership of a particular social group or political opinion, is outside the country of origin of her nationality and is unable or, owing to such fear, is unwilling to avail her/himself of the protection of that country.'[52] During the Cold War, this convention gave the West a huge propaganda advantage by allowing them to offer asylum to those escaping Communism. Since the fall of the Soviet Union in 1989, the numbers have shot up from about 4,000 per year to 76,000 in 2000 in the UK. The rise in refugees appears partly to be connected to the end of the bi-polar world and the resulting implosion of eastern European economies, civil wars in the Balkans, Iraq, Iran and Afghanistan. Simply fleeing a war may allow someone to remain here on discretionary grounds but does not necessarily qualify them for refugee status. Even that is being further restricted by new legislation which makes that status temporary (five years) and returns people to their country of origin once the situation is deemed to be safe. There is a principle of non-return that applies to refugees where the situation in the countries they have fled remains dangerous. Fortunately the courts' interpretation of 'safe' has differed substantially from that of the Home Office, which has suffered a number of setbacks in trying to send asylum seekers back to places like Zimbabwe and Iraq.

The Convention requires States to consider any application for asylum made on their territory, however ill-founded. The Labour government has tried to circumvent this requirement on the basis of an absurd logic: 80 per cent of asylum applications are unsuccessful, therefore they are 'bogus', therefore people should be made to apply from 'over there', placing Britain's borders as far away from Britain as possible. Tony Blair mooted the idea of camps set up just outside the EU borders, in places like North Africa, which would be holding centres to which those who had claimed asylum within the EU would be sent.[53] The introduction of the safe third country rule in 1990 was another attempt at pushing the borders out. Asylum seekers were expected to claim asylum in the first safe country to which they travelled. If they did not, they were liable to be deported to that country. This is why Farhia and Liu lied about their travel route. If they had been caught out, their applications for asylum would have been turned down on that basis alone, even though it does not invalidate their claim that they were escaping persecution in the first place.

There is no lawful way for a refugee to enter the UK for the purposes of claiming asylum. There is no provision in the UK Immigration Rules for someone to be granted a visa in order to come to the UK to claim asylum. There are very few ways left to refugees wanting to enter Britain: to apply for a visitor, student or business visa; to buy an expensive forged visa; or to be smuggled in – all of which risk criminalizing refugees and weakening their case for asylum. One method used by the British government to prevent refugees coming here is to turn citizens of countries experiencing internal turmoil into 'visa nationals', i.e. people who have to get a visa from the British Embassy in their own country before travelling to Britain. The citizens of most former Yugoslavian states at the height of the Balkan conflict in 1992 were required to have visas. In 2002, when Zimbabwe was added to the list, there was a 61 per cent drop in asylum applications. The number of countries from which visas are required has shot up from 19 to 108 since 1991. The Refugee Council points out that the list of countries 'bears an uncanny resemblance to a list of refugee-producing countries; it includes Iran, Eritrea, China, Somalia, Afghanistan, Iraq, Pakistan, Zimbabwe and the Democratic Republic of Congo: the ten most common countries of origin for refugees reaching the UK this year' (2005).[54] In other words, the worse the human rights situation gets in a particular country, the more difficult it becomes to flee to the UK.

The Immigration (Carriers' Liability) Act 1987 makes it almost impossible for refugees to travel to the UK. Airlines are fined £2,000 for each passenger they bring to the UK without the right visa. The Immigration and Asylum Act 1999 extends these provisions to cover lorries and Eurostar. People who travel across the channel holding onto the underside of a train are forced to do so because the British government has clamped down on all humane entry routes for people fleeing persecution. Many asylum seekers are refused asylum because the standard of proof of persecution demanded of them is impossible to obtain in circumstances of flight. British officers are posted at those airports from where large numbers of undocumented travellers are expected to travel and their papers double-checked in an attempt to stop them coming to the UK. If refugees manage to negotiate this minefield to get to Britain, they must either claim asylum at the port of entry or within three days of arrival. Their applications may be fast-tracked or seen to be automatically unfounded if they have come from a 'white list' country, i.e. a country where there is no danger of persecution according to the Home Office – an idea which was introduced in 2002. This means that the applicant must return and appeal from the country of origin, which makes a mockery of the concept of escape and protection. Sri Lanka, for example, which has been ravaged by civil war since 1983, was put on the white list in 2003 and removed in 2006 only after a legal challenge. In making decisions on asylum cases, immigration caseworkers rely on country assessment reports (CIPU) which are published every six months on the thirty-five countries which produce the highest number of refugees. However, these reports are considered by experts and practitioners to be misleading, inaccurate, out of date and often falsely positive in their analysis. Among the reasons that Natasha was initially refused asylum was the officer's reliance on a CIPU report which stated that Russia had the infrastructure to protect her from the traffickers.

Interestingly, the judiciary has been more of a friend to asylum seekers than the government itself. Liberal interpretations of the UN Convention by the Lords have recently led to women from particular countries, facing particular issues, to be considered to have 'membership of a particular social group' by virtue of their gender. In October 2006, a test case involved a woman afraid to return to her country for fear of being forced into female genital mutilation and she was allowed to stay. Similarly, Natasha won leave on appeal to remain here under the Convention because of a precedent-setting case in 2003, when an immigration judge had argued that women who had been trafficked into the UK formed part of a particular social group and therefore the provisions of the Convention would apply to them. This case has influenced a number of asylum decisions for trafficked women. In Natasha's case, the adjudicator also ruled that if she were deported it would amount to a breach of Article 3 of the ECHR, which decrees that no one will be subjected to torture, degrading or inhuman treatment. The Government has also been ordered to pay compensation to those who were illegally detained and wrongfully deported. In one case the Government had to pay damages of £16,000 to a family of asylum seekers because it had ignored its own stringent legislation in the way that the family had been deported and left 'stranded abroad'.[55]

Failed asylum seekers are not illegal immigrants *per se* in that they are expected to sign on, not for benefits, but so that government can keep tabs on them, although those who have gone underground would be seen to be 'illegal'. Financial support and accommodation is cut off twenty-one days after the appeal process comes to an end. The Refugee Council has launched a campaign to end the destitution suffered by refused asylum seekers. The campaign argues that using poverty as a means of forcing people to leave the country is both ineffective and inhumane. The cards are stacked against asylum seekers. Is it any surprise that forty-one suicides were reported in the five years to 2005?[56]

In 2005, according to Home Office statistics, 15,685 asylum seekers and their dependants were removed from the UK. Efforts to deport people have been doubled but the targets set are impossible to reach. The National Audit Office (NAO) calculated that the cost of each enforced removal is on average £11,000. There is a backlog of hundreds of thousands of asylum seekers whose claims have been refused. In 2006 a committee of MPs concluded that it would take between ten and eighteen years to tackle the backlog at the current rate of removal. In 2004 the House of Commons Home Affairs Committee noted 'where the removal of a failed asylum seeker is delayed through no fault of their own, it is morally unacceptable for him to be rendered destitute'.[57] Some cannot return because their countries of origin will not issue them with travel documents, others have no functioning airports or they have a medical condition which makes them unfit for travel. There is limited help available for such 'hard case' failed asylum seekers but there is not much take-up of this. Many are not eligible because of the strict criteria. There are those like Farhia doomed to the hell of limbo, who have been through various appeals and failed but who come from countries deemed to be too unsafe to which to return people. They are known to the authorities because they sign on but they are being quietly destroyed by the absence of any government support and housing. It is the perfect recipe for slavery. Nor are they allowed to study, work or volunteer. Many of these individuals are highly skilled and frustrated at their inability to use their skills. An Institute for Public Policy Research (IPPR) study concluded that if they were regularized and allowed to work, they would boost the coffers through the tax they pay by £1bn. Taking into account the cost of deporting them at £4.7bn, giving them an amnesty would mean a net benefit to the UK of £6bn.[58] It is the same calculation that underlies President Bush's proposals to introduce a guest-worker programme which would require a visa to work in the US and to regularize the 12m undocumented workers currently in the US.

Current estimates suggest that between 155,000 and 283,500 rejected asylum seekers remained in the UK in May 2004[59] – less than half a per cent of the population. The absence of definite information provides ammunition to those scaremongers who believe that the government has lost control of its borders. However, it could also be argued that it is a project doomed to failure in the current situation: borders are porous, the forces driving the movement of people are irresistible and the advantages brought by migrants are too great to make it cost-effective for any government to try to keep people out.

Children

British commitment to human rights has to be questioned when it comes to the treatment of children. There has been a plethora of policy initiatives, in the wake of Victoria Climbié's death from gross abuse and neglect in 2000, starting with the White Paper, *Every Child Matters* – every child, that is, except asylum-seeking children. In the tension between border control and respect for human rights, border control emerges once again as the winner. Although Britain is a signatory to the UN Convention on the Rights of the Child, it has excluded immigration issues from the protections afforded by it. Internally too we see the same thing, 'Immigration legislation and duties under the Children Acts 1989 and 2004 are not easily reconciled, since immigration controls take precedence over welfare considerations.'[60]

The political imperative to keep numbers down plays itself out in various ways with regard to children. According to a report into the fate of unaccompanied minors, *Seeking Asylum Alone*, immigration officials tend to disbelieve a child's age on the basis of appearance and to assume that they are adults parading as children.[61] To uncover this presumed subterfuge, the government has announced proposals to carry out dental X-rays, a practice that was quite rightly banned in 1982 by the Conservatives. There may be a minority who will use age to evade controls. However, Debbie Ariyo, Executive Director of AFRUCA, an NGO which campaigns against cruelty to African children, says this is a genuine problem with many Africans who do not have papers and whose births are not registered as they are in the West. There are new proposals under active consideration, with specific reference to 500 Vietnamese children, for repatriating unaccompanied children to their countries of origin even if it is not in the best interests of the child.[62] This will be a reversal of a policy that has been in operation for at least a decade which allowed children Discretionary Leave to Remain until the age of eighteen. Before 1991 a majority of children had been allowed to settle. Naomi, as we have seen, would be ill-equipped to deal with returning to Sierra Leone even at the age of eighteen.

In 2005, 2,965 unaccompanied asylum-seeking children (UASC) applied for asylum. The main countries of origin were Afghanistan, Iran, Somalia, Eritrea, Iraq, China, Democratic Republic of Congo,

Vietnam, Nigeria and Guinea. No agency is able to estimate what percentage of these children had been trafficked, and many children who are trafficked are accompanied by adults as Naomi was. Once a child slips through passport control, they are lost to the system until they escape from their traffickers or are deemed by an immigration tribunal to have been trafficked. In the mid-nineties professionals believed that the vast majority of such children came from Africa. However, there is consensus now that children are being trafficked from India, Pakistan and Vietnam as well as Eastern Europe. Children from Africa are usually trafficked into domestic servitude, while those from Europe are trafficked for sexual exploitation. DCS Peter Spindler, Head of Child Abuse Investigations for the Metropolitan Police, gives an example of how vulnerable children are discovered:

> We know children are abused and sometimes it's sexual abuse – an eleven-year-old girl from Pakistan went to a hospital in Hillingdon a couple of weeks ago. She went in with stomach pains and gave birth to a baby boy. She is the youngest mum in Britain. Not some kid up north who is aged twelve who has had sex with a fifteen-year-old, been smoking, drinking, playing every trick that a teenager would pull. This one's different. We're supporting that investigation because the suspicion is that she's trafficked. When she arrived in the UK she was probably coming in for *a better life* [my emphasis] because both her parents were killed in the Pakistan earthquake. She's ended up with a number of adults in a house and one of those adults has had sex with her, has raped her. He's now charged and in custody. We'll convict, but with rape. But the trafficking won't get addressed because we won't be able to prove how she came in. There won't be any documentation, so we can't prove the route or anything like that.[63]

Operation Paladin Child, a multi-agency initiative was set up by the police, in conjunction with immigration and social services, to identify the number of children who were trafficked into the UK through Heathrow over a three-month period from August to November 2003. Of the 1,738 minors, 551 were considered to be at risk and referred to social services. Of these, the social services 'lost' 14 minors, a high proportion of whom were teenage African girls, which according to DCS Spindler, 'could confirm the NGO fears that this group fall victim to exploitation in domestic servitude or abuse through prostitution'. At the end of the survey period, the Paladin team could not identify any trafficked children because there were no systems and no resources for tracking the children once they had entered the UK.

Although the legislation exists, there have been no prosecutions for trafficking. According to Spindler,

> We've got all the offences but they are so complicated to prove…
> We have had a number of convictions for facilitation, where
> organized criminals have been paid to bring children in. The
> problem with trafficking is that you've got to prove exploitation.

Spindler goes on to add, 'I believe the greatest exploitation is of the UK PLC in the sense that the vast majority of the kids are coming in for a better life.' The culture of cynicism that pervades the immigration service has infected the police as well. 'A better life' is posited as criticism. Anyone escaping persecution is arguably coming for a better life but protecting such a person is surely part of the UK's international obligations. The concept of 'a better life' is common in cultural traditions in Africa where a child belonged not just to a family but to the whole community, which is a limited insurance against poverty. Richer relatives might be able to provide a better future but a system with positive values has become commercialized and paved the way for trafficking.[64] Spindler believes that the trafficking of children is on a different scale because there 'isn't enough money in children. You bring in adults and they will earn for you – they will go cockle-picking, working, grafting, women will be in prostitution. We would say it is more of a community issue, more disorganized; family members aren't traffickers, but they pay traffickers to bring kids and even those tend to be family-ish.'[65]

Just as in the case of forced marriage, it appears that cultural relativism has affected the response of social services to African children in situations of domestic slavery. As this is seen to be the norm in African culture, these children may have escaped the attention of the authorities. There may be different attitudes to child discipline and child labour within the home. However, social services should be guided by the human rights principles underlying the Children Acts. AFRUCA devotes a large part of its time to raising awareness among African communities to recognize child abuse. Debbie Ariyo says:

> It's going to be absolutely difficult to safeguard children from abuse if you don't know what abuse is... A lot of African people will tell you that child work is a must for every child. You have to work within the home, that's a cultural thing there. If you do something wrong, you have the right to be punished. If you put these things together and you visit a home where a child is doing abnormal work, it doesn't ring a bell because the child is just doing housework. And if that child is beaten, again you think there is nothing wrong, because the child has done something wrong and should be beaten.[66]

There is an ongoing debate about what constitutes childhood and whether international laws have been defined by Western perspectives on the incompatibility of childhood and work. 'This concept of childhood leaves little room for the realities of life in Less Developed Countries (LDCs).' It is not simply a question of First World versus Third World. Positing the debate in these terms hovers on the edge of cultural relativism. The children in well-off African families would not engage in domestic work. It is poverty that drives these standards. 'The second view holds that children have the right to work, while work is understood as a valued and meaningful activity which gives children "a status in society".'[67] An acceptable compromise between the two positions is when children's work becomes detrimental to their physical, mental and moral development and stops them from going to school. When that child has no form of escape, then the abuse is tantamount to slavery.

The view from over here

If we look at the immigration debate from the way it is conducted in the media and by the government itself, we can see how partial is the picture that emerges. Papers like the *Daily Mail* are full of stories about asylum seekers convicted of rape or found driving without insurance and, of course, engaging in benefit fraud. Generally, migrants are seen with suspicion: their presence deprives the British people of the benefits of living in Britain and British culture is about to be wiped out and replaced with something foreign and backward. Recently though, there has been some grudging recognition that immigration has helped the economy.

The whole picture is never placed before us. The factors that push people into migrating – from multi-national activity to climate change to war – for which the developed nations of the world bear a grave responsibility and from which they profit are rarely made explicit. While current links are invisible, historical links are dismissed as irrelevant by the passage of time. The role of the Empire in the making of modern Britain and in recruiting workers for the mother country has been well-documented and does not need to be rehearsed here. Black people came up with the slogan, 'We're here because you were there' to make that historical link explicit. It has, however, become fashionable to dismiss the Empire as something that happened so far in the past that harping on about it is not helpful. In fact, Gordon Brown went so far as to claim on his travels in Africa in 2005 that there was no need for Britain to apologize for the Empire, a theme picked up in Blair's refusal to apologize for slavery. Many of the countries where conflict and civil war continue to this day are ex-colonies of Britain or those of other imperial nations such as France. History also provides another interesting comparison: at least modern-day migration does not involve the death and destruction of the indigenous population the way it did when Europeans went to the Americas or Australia.

'Immigration is a luxury'

Immigration is a luxury we cannot afford, a view publicly enunciated by a former British National Party (BNP) candidate.[68] The economic arguments about the pressure on housing and public services, the impact on wages, overcrowding, rise in unemployment, appear eminently reasonable and are raised by people from the left and right ends of the political spectrum. However, if each of these arguments were to be stripped away and shown to be demonstrably false, we would be left with fears of cultural invasion and dilution of British values. Where once these arguments were made mostly on the right, we hear voices in support of 'progressive' values expressing fears that new migrants bring with them backward views on women and gays, to name but two examples. The immigration debate has from the start been balanced between national self-interest and the need to sell it to a public who may resist the influx of different cultures. However, if any government were prepared to sell it even on the basis of self-interest, let alone the moral and humanitarian arguments, we would see a shift in public opinion. Recently the government has been making a case for the need for 'economic migrants' with the right skills and qualifications and we have already seen public attitudes shift.

The argument that Britain is an overcrowded island is a familiar one, but what actually constitutes overcrowding? Bangladesh has 2,637 people per square mile while the UK has 640 people.[69] Those fearful of immigration have been saying that Britain is overcrowded since the introduction of the Aliens Act in 1905 when the population was approximately 39m. However, the fact of the matter is that the population size is not substantially different than it would have been if not a single person had come to settle in the UK and not a single person had been allowed to leave. The way in which the debate has been conducted over the last fifty years, who would have realized that *only* since 1993 has there been net immigration into the UK, i.e. more people entering the country than leaving it? More Britons live outside the country than there are migrants in the UK: 4.5m Britons live abroad, a far bigger diaspora in percentage terms than those of other rich countries like France, Germany, and the US,[70] as compared to 4m migrants living in the UK, which constitutes about 8 per cent of the population. Quoting figures, however, does not help when we are up against paranoia about immigration. It is comparable to the disconnect between the public perception that crime is rising and the reality that crime levels are actually dropping.

The most recent Home Office estimate suggested there are approximately half a million unauthorized migrants in Britain, with ministers admitting it is impossible to be more precise. They do the most dangerous and menial work. Bobby Chen, who works at the Central London Law Centre, believes that,

> To some extent, all governments know that illegal immigration happens and are happy that it carries on because it helps them economically. Whether you like it or not, toilets need to be cleaned and hospitals need to be staffed. If you clamp down too hard, it will destabilize the economy and the social structure.[71]

There is a view that it is only the dodgy employers, the ones who evade tax, that are the ones who employ illegal workers, as reflected in the Home Secretary, John Reid's 'shop a rogue' scheme launched in August 2006 to tackle those who employ illegal immigrants. However, it is legitimate businesses like Tesco, whose turnover is more than the GDP of Peru, that keep their profits up and their costs down by buying goods from suppliers who use illegal workers.[72] John Denham, Labour MP, writes, 'Most illegal work services the legitimate economy, from offices to building sites, hospitals to supermarkets. The companies that really benefit insulate themselves through complex webs of contractors and subcontractors.'[73]

There is talk of pressure on housing, health and other services, although the population is smaller than it would have been without movement in and out of the country: as indicated, there are half a million more Britons in the diaspora than there are migrants in this country. If the British population itself had expanded, government would have had to undertake measures to provide for their citizens so the real underlying argument is about us and them, of our inability despite globalization to see people as citizens of the world rather than individual nations. However, let us examine the argument of additional burdens of providing public services bearing in mind two facts: severe internal controls exist on who can have access to health and other public services; and, according to David Blunkett himself, migrants who make up 8 per cent of the UK population generate 10 per cent of the nation's wealth.[74] This means that migrants are more than self-financing.

While the benefits of immigration to receiving countries are clear, the costs are harder to assess. Most studies conclude that there is a small net gain. However, the studies are inconclusive and contradictory. A 1997 Organization for Economic Co-operation and Development (OECD) report on *Trends in International Migration* examined 17 studies of which 4 said the impact was zero or positive, 6 said it was zero or negative and 7 could not decide.[75] When immigrants first arrive, they are mostly young and single and do not make many demands on public services. Of course, when they settle and are joined by families, they will need housing, health and schooling, but they will have paid their taxes by then and will have no greater need of services than any other section of the workforce. Paradoxically, it is stringent immigration controls that encourage them to settle. If there had been free movement of labour as there is in the EU, they would, like the Poles, come and go in response to the needs of the British economy.

Furthermore, the British state will gain new workers without having to pay anything towards the costs of raising or training them. The average cost of raising a child to the age of twenty-one is £180,000 in the UK. No figures are available for the cost to the state. Every adult migrant is therefore a gift from a poorer country to a richer one, regardless of whether those workers were under-employed or unemployed in their country of origin. The issue of sub-Saharan Africa losing much-needed doctors and nurses to the West, for example, has been widely reported recently. Experts calculate that five years of medical training cost the British taxpayer £250,000. Every African doctor is therefore subsidizing the British economy by that sum. The cost of training, for example, a non-specialized doctor in a developing country is about £30,000. The Home Office estimated that 31 per cent of its doctors and 13 per cent of its nurses are born over-seas.[76] So immigration is a luxury, but not in the way that the BNP councillor meant.

One way of accruing all of the above benefits without having to shoulder any of the costs is to outsource the work. This strategy has been growing exponentially and countries like India with large, well-educated workforces who speak English have been the major beneficiaries of outsourcing. It also appeals to all the cultural purists. An American businessman describes the attractions of the scheme:

> Everything comes down to supply and demand. Obviously, it is labor demand, but it is also the fact that the supply of labor is cheaper. It's lower cost to import from other countries, which is what we're doing. I mean, this is similar to outsourcing, except it's outsourced labor that's delivered to our doorstep.[77]

By keeping labour in its original place, Western nations do not have to take on the cost of education, health and other benefits, while exploiting the full economic advantage of those workers.

However, there are some jobs that cannot be exported. We cannot ship our elderly to Mumbai to have their daily bath. As carers and cleaners, migrants help to improve the lives not just of the vulnerable sections of our society but also the professional elite at extremely affordable prices. The health, catering and hospitality sectors are turning to migrant workers to fill their skills gap. British workers are either unwilling or unable to do these jobs. It is the drive for profits that makes certain jobs unattractive. If the need to maintain purity of culture overrode all other considerations, including profit, then these sectors should pay extremely high wages and improve conditions to such an extent that the indigenous unemployed might be attracted to these jobs. The British economy is booming and needs labour. According to the TUC, the UK skills gap is costing the economy £10bn.[78] Is there any loss of jobs for local people? 'The thesis that immigrants cause unemployment seems to have little or no basis in reality. As is well known, unemployment was higher in the 1930s, when there was hardly any immigration, than it is now'.[79] Even the IOM, which favours managed migration, accepts that only a small percentage of the unskilled workforce in the receiving countries loses out. IOM argues that employers and migrants themselves gain. However, it is questionable how much migrants gain and at what cost. Liu, even though he worked in skilled jobs in the construction industry, only managed to get somewhere by living in conditions that would be abhorrent, and quite rightly so, to the indigenous population – working sixty- to eighty-hour weeks, sleeping six to eight in small rooms, going without food sometimes, and paying a pittance of a rent.

Not only do migrants help fill vacancies, their presence itself enables the economy to grow. Even an article in the *Daily Telegraph* in 2006 grudgingly conceded this point:

Three years ago, Britain had 600,000 job vacancies. Since then, there has been a net inflow of 700,000 legal workers and who knows how many illegal. Yet, the number of unfilled posts is still 600,000. The reason for this paradox is that, as well as providing services, immigrants also consume them. They add to demand as well as supply. Simply by going shopping, buying a coffee, catching a bus, they create jobs, thereby sucking in yet more immigrants.[80]

Of course, immigrants as consumers help to expand an economy that is healthy and can rise to the challenge. Malfunctioning economies such as those in the Third World faced by a large influx of poor refugees across the border can be overwhelmed rather than benefit.

Some analysts, notably Nigel Harris, argue that migrants are not so much pushed into leaving by conditions at home as attracted to going where there are jobs. There is no doubt that the presence of unskilled legal and illegal migrants creates a downward pull on wages hence they are much loved by businesses. Most economic surveys report that migrants have helped reduce inflationary pressures. The CBI welcomed the fact that their taxes helped to pay for public services and pensions, long after they had returned home, and that their presence had kept inflation low.[81] The downward pull on wages and the dilution of labour rights have long been a concern of the TUC, hence their initially hostile stance towards immigration. It was refreshing therefore to see the general secretary, Brendan Barber, argue, 'Stop blaming migrants – exploitation is the problem'. He points out that those parts of the country seeing job losses are not those where migrant workers are most prevalent because 'they will go where there are job vacancies, not dole queues'.[82] It is important from the point of view of falling membership numbers that unions call for the regularization of undocumented workers.

Just as importantly, workers are needed today to pay into the pension schemes of tomorrow. The truth of the matter is that the population of the UK is ageing and the fertility rate is declining. Not enough children are being born to replace the current population. In 1990 there was one pensioner for every four workers. It is estimated that in 2030 there will be two pensioners for every five workers. An academic, David Blake has worked out that the UK state pension system is unlikely to remain viable unless 500,000 immigrant workers come to Britain per annum.[83] If the next generation is smaller in number than the current generation, the current generation will have some stark choices: it will have to accept a cut in its pension, or save more while in work, or work longer and retire later, or accept more immigration. As we have seen from the recent debate about delaying the retirement age and reductions in pension payments, there will be huge resistance to the other options. A consumer society which has runaway credit problems is hardly likely to save more. There is a fifth unspoken option: that employers increase the amount of their contributions to compensate for reduced contributions from a smaller workforce. It appears that immigration is in the national interest: not a luxury but an economic necessity. These were the realities in 1946 when James Callaghan made the following speech in Parliament:

> In a few years time we in this country will be faced with a shortage of labour and not with a shortage of jobs. Our birth rate is not increasing in sufficient proportion to enable us to replace ourselves… it may be revolutionary to suggest that we ought now to become a country where immigrants are welcome, but that is really the logical development of our present position in the world… Who is going to pay for the old age pensions and social services we are rightly distributing now, unless we have an addition to our population which only immigrants will provide in the days to come?[84]

In 2005, as against 565,000 arrivals, 380,000 people – over half of them British citizens – left Britain, leaving a net increase of 185,000 to Britain's population,[85] well below the annual half a million figure needed to sustain the pension system. Almost a quarter of the new arrivals were students bringing much-needed finance and subsidies to the British education system. They contributed £5bn to British higher education. Most of the migrants came from India, China and Poland. Of this figure, asylum seekers contributed a net inflow of 11,000, the lowest figure since 1991, and yet they remain the bugbear of British public attitudes towards migration. Media commentators like Melanie Phillips tend to conflate the issue of asylum seekers with new immigrants, many of whom have been actively recruited by the government as workers or students.

British Aid

Western aid has been premised on the fact that without development there will be fewer markets for Western goods and increased poverty and instability will become a breeding ground for terrorism, an issue that is high on the agenda of Western governments at the moment. Whether aid achieves any of these goals is part of a bigger discussion and outside the scope of this book. However, migrants themselves are contributing to the aid effort by the amount of money they send home to their families. This benefits Britain in terms of creating markets and in taking the pressure off its aid budget. From the UK alone, remittances to developing countries are estimated to be around £2.7bn annually.[86] And this is likely to be an underestimate by as much as two to three times because many migrants send money through friends and private courier systems. Compare these figures with UK international aid which was £3.8bn in 2004/5, some of which is tied to conditions and can be detrimental to the recipients.

Instead of the British government trumpeting the amount of remittances that are sent back to migrants' countries of origin as part of the UK's overall effort to drive down poverty, we hear a deafening silence. Entire local economies are being kick-started as a result of these remittances, while these workers are keeping the British economy going by filling important, necessary and, to our shame, low-paid jobs. If the dishonesty underlying immigration controls was eliminated and the British government was prepared to recognize how immigration controls created slavery and unpaid or extremely poorly paid labour, it would take steps to end this situation as part of its effort on aid. Higher wages would lead to higher remittances. 'There is also, arguably, something morally incoherent about pursuing a generous policy on aid while adopting a very tough policy on refugees, especially of an economic status.'[87]

Human rights contraventions

The British attempt to fulfil its commitment to human rights is shot through with moral incoherence. Although the Government has signed up to a number of international human rights instruments, in many cases it has asked for special dispensation with regard to its immigration laws. The protection provided by the ECHR, for example, is available to everyone in the UK, regardless of whether they have the right to remain here. The way in which UK immigration law is applied can be seen to breach at least three separate articles. Article 3 of the Convention prohibits torture or inhuman or degrading treatment or punishment. Natasha was given leave to remain under this article as it was accepted that deporting her to Russia would amount to inhuman treatment. Similarly, this could be used against the detention system, as could Article 5 which protects the right to liberty and security of the person. Article 8 provides the right to respect for private and family life and can, under certain circumstances, be used to challenge immigration decisions where families may be split up because one member has Leave to Remain and the others do not.

The absence of any financial support or provision of accommodation for those at the end of the line like Farhia, a policy of enforced destitution, is in breach of the human rights of asylum seekers. It is what creates slavery. It is a means of forcing people to leave the UK or not to come to the UK in the first place. It has not had its desired effect. Successive legislation has conspired to deprive asylum seekers of housing and financial support. The fourth largest economy in the world reduces them to the level of beggars and they are then blamed by the public for bringing crime and degradation to the streets. Asylum seekers are not allowed to do paid or unpaid work. The cruel paradox of Britain's immigration policy is highlighted by Teresa Hayter: 'It recruits nurses in Zimbabwe, but imprisons Zimbabwean nurses.'[88] In the absence of support, many asylum seekers are driven to despair.

The Nationality, Immigration and Asylum Act 2002 excludes local education authorities (LEAs) from the obligation to educate the children of asylum seekers housed in accommodation centres in mainstream schools. These children may (not must) be educated in the centre itself, creating a system of educational apartheid which is in breach of various international conventions – for instance, the 1989 UN Convention on the Rights of the Child which provides for equality of opportunity within education and the right to participate in normal community life. David Blunkett justified it on the grounds that schools were being swamped by asylum-seeking children. Some of the most successful campaigns on behalf of asylum-seeker families against deportation have been fought by those who have become embedded in the lives of their community. In fact, Blunkett complained that 'the difficulty sometimes with families whose removal has been attempted is that their youngsters have become part of a school.'[89]

The whole repressive machinery of detention centres, which cost nearly £156m in 2003–4 to maintain, breaches the human rights of its detainees.[90] The conditions in detention centres are worse than those in British prisons. Halama, the mother of a newborn baby, who has experienced both regimes, says that in Holloway prison, breastfeeding mothers got an extra litre of milk every night, whereas at Yarls Wood detention centre they were asked to drink lots of water. Halama believes the only reason why their babies were treated better in prison is 'because in prison there are British nationals and at immigration removal centres we are all foreign nationals, that is why they don't care about our babies'.[91] Home Office figures record nearly 1,900 children under the age of eighteen as having left detention centres in 2005; more than 40 per cent were under the age of five.[92] Their only crime is to be born to illegal immigrants, which makes them illegal immigrants before they can ever be considered children.

Political refugees versus economic migrants

There is no clear water between the label 'refugee' and 'economic' migrant, as the stories in this book show – merely government expediency. Refugees are 'pushed' from danger and are by definition unwilling migrants,[93] whereas migrants are 'pulled' or attracted toward more viable destinations. The almost universal branding of asylum seekers as bogus continues despite the staggering consistency between asylum applications and those countries where situations of conflict are reported. It is amazing how a particular view can acquire the status of fact when all the statistics are against it. It is no coincidence that applications from Iraq, Afghanistan, Somalia and Iran are among the highest at the moment. There is a direct link: when the situation in Sri Lanka deteriorates, there is an immediate and corresponding rise in the number of asylum applications from that country. It has served the purpose of the Labour government deliberately to muddy the distinction in order to make the country inhospitable to asylum seekers by labelling the vast majority of those who fail the immense obstacles placed in their way as economic migrants.

The view of many practitioners and activists in the field is that it is a nonsense to try and separate the two categories. Bobby Chen says:

> Lots of the coastal provinces, like Guangdong and Fujian, have traditionally seen a large number of people leave since the nineteenth century. So they have a history and economic reasons too because they have difficulty finding a job. One can say that these are economic migrants. I don't make that distinction as such because losing your job and having to survive is not only an economic issue but also a political issue.[94]

Sometimes the two categories might be just different points on a timeline. In the case of the Ogoni people, for example, those who left early on in response to Shell might have been turned away as economic migrants by the UK, whereas those who stayed and fought the corrupt local government which was in collusion with a British company and fled only when their lives were in danger would have been considered political refugees.

Immigration law in Britain

The law and enforcement machinery of immigration legislation is based on the government distinction between political versus economic migrants. Immigration controls are not about keeping people out but about creating a climate of insecurity so as to maximize profit from illegals. 'In all other areas of the law it is the *act* that is illegal. In immigration law, the law of the slave, it is the *person*.'[95] In criminal law it is the act, the '*actus reus*', which results in punishment. Under immigration law it is status, or lack of status. It could be seen as recidivist under English law. It harks back not just to chattel slavery but to feudal law where the focus lay generally on status rather than activity.[96] 'Managing' migration is the buzzword and key strategy, but it hides all kinds of tough and heartless measures. No matter how tough the laws get, people continue to find their way here. Here is the paradox: the more restrictive the immigration laws, the more profitable it is for smuggling and trafficking rings and the more imaginative, dangerous and life-threatening are their attempts to circumvent the barriers. It is not just demand from migrants but the need for cheap immigrant labour in the West that drives people-smuggling by international criminal gangs like the snakeheads, a business which is almost as profitable as drugs and far less punitive for the perpetrators if caught by the authorities.

The government of Britain is inadvertently supporting slavery through its immigration legislation. Immigration law reflects a deeply embedded class bias. Anyone who has a spare £200,000 to invest can enter the UK on a business visa and in their fifth year can apply for permanent residence. Under the so-called 'Innovator Programme', you do not even have to have capital as long as you have a business plan that shows that you have the potential to bring economic benefit to the country. This is part of the five tier points-based system which will be phased in by 2008, in which applicants wanting to enter the UK will be awarded points on the basis of aptitude, experience, age and the needs of the British economy. Under the current immigration rules there are eighty different routes into the country and concessions outside the rules. The new system is meant to introduce transparency and simplicity; however, practitioners remain cynical of that. Three tiers will allow entry on the basis of skills and the other two will take into account students and temporary workers. It will allow the highly skilled to enter the country without having a definite offer of work, although all other categories of migrants will require sponsors. The focus on skilled migrants is likely to increase the risks of trafficking as the opportunities for regular migration, in particular for low-skilled migrants, will become limited. In fact, Britain is hoping to meet its demand for low-skilled labour with the accession of Bulgaria and Romania to the EU in January 2007 and the eight states, including Poland, which joined in 2004.

It is worth remembering that immigration controls are only a century old, starting with the Aliens Act 1905 which was brought in to keep out an expected influx of Jews after vigorous campaigning by extreme right and fascist groups. Before 1914 it was possible to travel between many countries without a passport. Apart from more refinements to the Aliens Act, the Coloured Aliens Seamen Order of 1925 and the British Nationality Act of 1948 which laid out a theoretical framework of who was British, there was nothing until the 1962 Commonwealth Immigrants Act followed by another one in 1968, specifically designed to keep out Ugandan Asians. In the last quarter of the twentieth century and since, however, we have a seen a plethora of laws dealing with the question of immigration and reflecting national paranoia: 1971, 1981, 1988, 1993, 1996, 1999, 2002, 2004, 2006, and we are currently on the brink of new legislation, the UK Borders Bill, 2007. In the last fourteen years alone, there have been seven pieces of legislation and fifty changes to the immigration rules. All of this points to the fact that immigration controls do not work despite government attempts to approach the issue every which way.

The UK Borders Bill will give legitimacy to the 'fishing raids' that police used to carry out in search of the immigration status of individuals if they were called to a home to investigate domestic violence or some other unrelated incident in the eighties. Many of the high profile 'terror' raids recently carried out netted nothing more sinister than immigration offences. Both police and immigration officials will now be empowered to check immigration status if they have arrested anyone in connection with another offence. Anyone subject to immigration control will have to have a biometric ID card. Any lawful migrant can be forced to live in a particular place and report to police or immigration officers as a condition of his/her stay. Worst of all for those who live on the margins, immigration officers can also seize cash alleged to be proceeds of immigration act offences which includes working in breach of conditions.

This, side by side with the New Asylum Model (NAM), will create a system of legitimized brutality that truly justifies the epithet 'barbed wire Britain'. Only one of the features of the NAM has been welcomed by NGOs working in the field – a dedicated caseworker will be allocated to every new applicant from March 2007 for the duration of the asylum process – in the hope that there will be some accountability in this new system. Financial support for asylum seekers will be dependent on voice-tagging (phone software which identifies a person by their voice) or electronic tagging as a way of keeping tabs on asylum seekers.[97] Speed is promised: decisions in most cases are to be made in twenty days, rising to 90 per cent of cases being resolved in six months by 2011. Although a speedy resolution would reduce the suffering of people like Liu and Farhia, the emphasis on fast tracking in the past has led only to injustices, while a large number of cases have remained in agonizing limbo. The suspicion among experts is that speed will lead to rapid removals but it will not necessarily mean that those with complex cases and in greatest need of protection can feel confident that the new system will be any more sympathetic to them.

Even from the point of view of the settled community of migrants, immigration law hangs like a sword of Damocles over their heads on something simple like the ease with which family and friends can visit them or something complex like forced marriage on which action is required from the government. As we have seen, the government's knee-jerk reaction is to tighten the law on entry as if that will somehow resolve any issue under consideration. The other tendency is to reduce government commitments under various international laws by narrowing the range of people to whom the term 'trafficked' could be applied or by eroding the principles of the UN Convention by administrative measures. Similarly, the row over the government's proposed cuts to English language classes for migrants has focused on the fact that it contradicts the government's own requirements that proficiency in English, a key part of the citizenship tests, will have to be demonstrated by potential settlers. However, this appears to be yet another back-door way of cutting down the number of people who will pass through the pearly gates.

The immigration and slavery nexus

The way the government understands the connection between the two issues is that when it carries out a raid and discovers slaves, it sends its immigration officials to swoop down and deport them, not worrying about any infringement of human rights that may have gone on before the raid or since. They are seen primarily as 'illegals' and criminalized rather than being treated as victims of criminals.

Of course, the root cause of slavery is poverty and the lack of political will in many countries to implement laws against slavery. As much slavery takes place within national borders, the ending of immigration controls will not eradicate all slavery. For example, the IOM found that the number of women being trafficked into the sex trade increased after Lithuania joined the EU. About two thousand women and girls were reported to have been taken out of Lithuania in the course of 2005. It became easier and cheaper to traffic them because they could come here with legal documentation. 'Immigration is a useful tool for traffickers but it's not the only tool' says Denise Marshall. They use sexual violence and the stigma of prostitution to keep women under their thumb by threatening to tell their families about what they do. The women's lack of knowledge of available help and poor language skills are also part of the traffickers' armoury. This example merely reinforces my point that poverty is the primary cause of slavery. However, the advantage that the Lithuanian women have over other slaves is that they are in no danger of deportation and have the right to full protection of the state once they are rescued or run away.

Similarly, in the case of the Polish workers featured in a BBC special report, legality was clearly not an issue because they had every right to be in this country for work.[98] That is when employment law must be brought to bear. Employment agencies are often in breach of the law and the government should do more to enforce the law.

Traffickers may use regular migration routes and work visas, but utilize debt bondage, the removal of documents and migrants' uncertainty about their rights and status to subject them to forced labour. The Anti-Slavery International report on forced labour found that,

> Many of the migrant workers believed they were dependent on
> their employer in order to stay in the country (e.g. for visa
> extensions). In other cases the employer retained the migrant's
> documents, sometimes claiming they had sent the documents to
> the Home Office for official purposes, until the workers became
> irregular and therefore much easier to exploit... This clearly shows
> that regular as well as irregular [or undocumented] migrants are
> subject to trafficking for forced labour and that strategies which
> look at trafficking only as part of organized immigration crime are
> not going to identify a significant number of people who are
> working in forced labour conditions.[99]

The government needs to de-link its anti-trafficking work from its hunt for immigration offenders.

We turn migrants into slaves or prisoners by placing them in detention centres. New government legislation will turn them into prisoners *and* slaves. The 2006 Immigration Asylum and Nationality Act stipulates that those held in removal centres and about to be deported, like convicted prisoners, will now be allowed to work but the national minimum wage will not apply.[100] The choices that are open to anyone who cannot squeeze through the eye of the needle are slavery, deportation or imprisonment, even though migration is a win-win situation viewed from any perspective except the xenophobic. There are strong humanitarian, moral and economic reasons for looking at the system of immigration controls from a completely different perspective than the one that has been popular with the government so far. There is only one solution. It is the 'programme that dare not speak its name'[101] and is discussed in the next chapter.

SQUARING THE CIRCLE

We are at a crossroads as far as the future of our civilization, indeed of our world, is concerned. Perhaps at the beginning of every century people have felt that the dilemmas facing them are unique and need fresh thinking and reassessment in order to assure the future of the human race. Certainly the questions facing us at the beginning of the twenty-first century feel earth-shattering, quite literally in terms of the environment but also in terms of an age-old problem which will not go away – the stomach-wrenching knot of poverty which gives rise to slavery and migration, two of the issues with which this book is concerned. We are prepared to think the unthinkable with regards to the environment: Stephen Hawking has floated the idea that the human race may need to migrate to another planet to assure its future, a possibility which certainly concentrates our mind on the task in hand. We know we must radically alter our levels of consumption, both at a personal and business level, so giving the earth a chance to recover. The way we use energy, the kinds of food we eat and how they are manufactured are issues that have begun to gnaw at our conscience. Consumer outrage at the use of child labour in the manufacture of carpets and footballs led to some changes. That anger needs to be harnessed against the enslavement of human beings in the production of our food or clothes, in the running of our homes, the care of our elderly and disabled and, scandalously, in keeping our sex industry alive.

Eradicating slavery means nothing less than the eradication of poverty – because war, persecution, and climate change disproportionately affect the poor – a goal that seems further away than ever given the growing distance between the wealthy and the poor. However, Kevin Bales, inspirational head of Free the Slaves, believes that the abolition of modern slavery is a small task compared to the eighteenth century when any call for the abolition of an institution on which rested the very foundation of that society would have been considered ridiculous.[1] His is a seductive argument, not least because he presents it as an achievable aim. He has had a stab at working out the economics of modern slavery, despite the uncertainty around numbers and definitions, and gives us this scenario: it would cost £19 to free a family of bonded labour in India from their historic debt and to rehabilitate them, and an average of £200 to free each slave around the world. This would amount to a total cost of £5.4bn, which is 1 per cent of the UK government's annual budget or one week's spend in Iraq for the US. If you take into account the fact that freed slaves would generate, even if they earned a pittance of $2 per day, $20bn per year, it would be a bargain. He proposes the setting up of a UN inspectorate to monitor the prevalence of slavery worldwide comparable to that of the weapons inspectorate – not backed up by the threat of invasion, of course! More debatably, he argues that there are no big economic vested interests to fight. What this analysis does not take into account is that poverty is the inevitable consequence of the economic systems in which we live, and while these systems remain unchanged they will continue to generate the conditions in which slavery flourishes.

There are large scale and effective programmes involving liberation and reintegration of slaves taking place in Brazil today. These were unemployed and desperate people who were internally trafficked in Brazil. In 2005, 4,000 slaves were freed when officials from the employment ministry raided 183 farms. £1.8m was invested in helping them to rebuild their lives. President Lula da Silva has prioritized this issue since he came to power in 2002 and in 2003 a blacklist of companies employing slave labour was drawn up. However, campaigners feel that until there is land distribution, this will not make substantial inroads into the issue – poverty remains the central challenge.[2]

My canvas is smaller both in terms of geography and the solutions proposed: eradicating slavery in Britain. Although it is a worldwide problem requiring worldwide solutions, why shouldn't Britain become a paradigm of what is achievable? Global warming, for instance, cannot be solved by one nation alone, but that did not stop Norway from announcing that it hopes to reach zero carbon status by 2050. There is a huge galvanizing momentum behind a courageous individual act. There are many ways in which slavery can be minimized, contained and ring-fenced, and much commendable work is being done by organizations like Amnesty International and the Refugee Council to lobby the government to make legislative changes or to enforce the laws that have already been enacted. Campaigns around trafficking have concentrated on getting the government to sign up to the ECAT, which it finally did in March 2007. Now the same NGOs are hoping to persuade the government to improve on the basic clauses in the convention: for example, to increase the reflection period for victims of trafficking from thirty days to ninety days and grant residence permits without the condition that victims should co-operate with the police. A year-long campaign launched in November 2006 for granting amnesty to the approximately half a million undocumented people who have been here for more than four years, Strangers into Citizens, has been successfully drawing attention to its cause and more and more MPs are signing up to it. Its success is partly attributable to the fact that in this bicentenary year, it is very hard not to be persuaded by the connection between immigration controls and slavery, especially when the economic benefits brought by migrants to this society are so clear. In the US, amnesties have been granted to approximately 5.5m illegal workers since 1986, a testimony to its need for workers and the disproportionate costs of finding and deporting people who have done nothing worse than carrying out the least popular jobs in the economy. Even the tax they pay on their low salaries brings a net benefit to the economy. There is no welfare state to attract immigrants to the USA. They come because there are jobs.

The idea that the British welfare state is a magnet for immigrants is based on disinformation. Welfare benefits and most medical services, apart from emergency assistance, can only be accessed with the production of a valid passport. A failed asylum seeker suffering from cancer, for example, will not get free treatment. Amnesty International published *Down and Out in London*, and Refugee Action brought out *The Destitution Trap* in 2006 as part of their campaign to draw attention to the destitution faced by asylum seekers and to demand that they be allowed to work. Others, like Liberty and the Joint Council for the Welfare of Immigrants (JCWI), fight a defensive battle against more immigration legislation like the proposed Borders Bill, while the Refugee Council also campaigns against cutting back classes in English; Save the Children has lobbied to prevent the detention of children through its Place for a Child campaign. Many NGOs produce facts and figures to counter the distorted media coverage of immigration and demand a fairer asylum policy. Even newspapers with a record of more balanced coverage shy away from focusing on the issues because immigration is not seen as 'sexy' enough, thus very little of the work undertaken by these organizations seeps into the consciousness of the general public. Groups like SBS, which have been stalwart in supporting women like Amber, find it impossible to get coverage for their campaign against the two-year rule, although the media flock to them for a comment on 'honour killings'.

There is a theme underlying all of these campaigns: the treatment of immigrants. Each of these demands is important, but piecemeal reform just moves injustice around the board. For example, the demand for turning Strangers into Citizens, although a worthy aim, introduces arbitrary criteria about who would be eligible and who would not, thus leaving large pockets of slavery untouched. Similarly, although the trafficking convention is one step further on than we were in 2006, what will happen to those who do not fit into their definition of trafficking, such as failed asylum seekers and those who have been smuggled here but have ended up as slaves? I wholly support the attempt of NGOs to draw as many people as possible under the trafficking banner so that they can become eligible for the rest and reflection period, psychological and material support, and residence permits while they help authorities to investigate the trafficking gangs; but from a human rights point of view it makes no sense at all that Natasha can be supported, but Farhia, who has as brutal a history as Natasha, cannot because of her label 'failed asylum seeker'.

The government is so nervous about making positive changes to its immigration legislation that sometimes it avoids drawing attention to them: witness its amnesty to domestic workers which ran from 1988 to 1999. Or it claws back positive changes like its domestic violence concessions for non-British spouses trapped in violent marriages, by extending the probationary period for such marriages from one year to two years. There is a philosophical problem with the whole issue of concessions. Concessions are made where grounds for 'compassion' exist, turning negative conditions into something desirable: ill health or domestic violence become 'desirable' factors because they enhance your eligibility for that all-important Leave to Remain. The government needs to lead from the front. By making a strong public case for the British economy's need for certain categories of migrants, we have seen some of the public hysteria around economic migrants fade away. The introduction of civil partnerships for the gay community shows how public opinion can be moulded in positive ways. Although a rump of homophobia will remain, we had papers like the *Daily Mail* giving positive coverage to Elton John's 'wedding' day.

What would give government more room for manoeuvre? We need the equivalent of the Stern report on climate change to look into the issue of immigration and slavery. The Stern report made a strong economic case for government action on global warming, producing figures which showed that – despite the huge investment needed today – it would be cheaper to act now rather than later. A well-investigated, independent report gave the government the justification for radical action and allowed it to carry public opinion with it. Whereas action on climate change requires sacrifices from all of us, it is hard to understand why there is a reluctance to open doors to new migrants when their presence brings financial benefits while, at the same time, there is no clear evidence of the pressure they put on services. To paraphrase Bob Sutcliffe's argument in *Nacido en otra parte*,[3] to weigh migrants in terms of their worth in gold is to dehumanize them. If that argument were to be applied to any other section of the population, like the disabled, the unemployed or pensioners, who may be seen as a net drain on the economy, we would end up arguing for mass euthanasia. Notwithstanding the dehumanizing aspects of a cost-benefit analysis of immigration, here are some of the issues that need to be considered to put the debate in perspective:[4]

Benefits to the UK
- Taxes paid by migrants as opposed to the services used by them. Migrants constitute 8 per cent of the population and produce 10 per cent of the wealth.
- Taxes paid by multi-nationals in the UK on profits made from business activities in Third World countries which lead to the displacement of people, like the Ogoni people, who may end up as refugees in the UK. This is one of the most hidden arguments about the benefits accruing to this country at a huge cost to overseas communities.
- Taxes paid by the UK defence industry from selling arms to countries in conflict, which generates refugees. Hidden benefits such as jobs created in the UK as a result of multi-national business abroad, i.e. a jobs gained versus jobs taken tally.
- Overseas students subsidize home students through their fees.
- Low inflation as a result of immigration.
- Migrants' contributions to the pensions of future generations.

- Savings for Britain, in terms of training and producing new workers while there is a net loss to sending countries.

Costs
- The skills gap is costing the British economy £10bn according to the TUC.
- Unpaid taxes by 'illegal' workers amount to £1bn according to the IPPR.
- The UK government spent a staggering £1.5bn on the IND in unsuccessfully keeping numbers down.[5]
- Detention centres cost £156m in 2003–4.

This cost-benefit analysis relies on a central assumption – capitalism's unquenchable thirst for profit – otherwise the need to maintain current pensions, for example, could be met simply by huge increases in company contributions to the pension fund and a corresponding decrease in profits.

While it is the economics that drive change, there are other balance sheets to consider in terms of British international and human rights commitments. In recognition of growing world poverty, Britain has led the way in abolishing the debt burden for some of the poorest countries. Migrants' remittances compare extremely well with the amount Britain spends in aid. The estimated amount of remittances sent by unofficial routes is two to three times the amount of British foreign aid. This is self-help by the world's poor and surely an effort that should be supported. If, against all the odds, we can believe that the trickle-down theory will eventually lift the poor from their misery, surely these remittances can be seen in the same positive light.

In terms of human rights, the British government has sought to reduce the number of refugees coming to Britain by the use of administrative measures that undermine the spirit of the UN Convention. Where its commitment to human rights has conflicted with its desire to maintain a robust immigration system, the latter has taken precedence and the government has made reservations to international law as highlighted in the previous chapter. This is what Liberty has to say about this issue:

> Many of the UK reservations, we believe, discriminate against particular sections of society and thus are anathema to the very universality of human rights…
>
> The main theme running through the majority of the UK's reservations to international human rights treaties is based on the UK's wish to protect itself from unwanted immigration. However, the protection of this immigration policy via reservations to human rights treaties, we believe, amounts to discrimination under international human rights law. We contend that the existence of reservations to human rights treaties are not necessary as human rights do not confer a right to immigration per se, they confer rights to have applications assessed fairly and to be treated properly in accordance with human rights principles.[6]

Immigration legislation runs contrary to our domestic legislation, for example, on children. Ensuring that a child's best interests remains paramount is the presumption behind all our family law and the various Children Acts and yet the government aims to return asylum-seeking children to a community or family that might have trafficked them in the first instance or to a war-torn and dangerous country. At the very least, we must call for Britain's immigration laws to be brought in line with its human rights obligations. For Britain to take that on board fully, it would have to dismantle its entire detention system because it breaches the principle of the right to liberty of those who have done nothing wrong.

Given that immigration brings so many benefits to Britain's economy and society, the question why such draconian controls remain in force, reducing to slavery the very people who benefit this society, has to be asked. If economic benefit can be proved beyond doubt, we are left with fears of racial and cultural dilution. Anyone who laments the passing of spotted dick for chicken tikka masala needs the kind of bereavement counselling that lies outside the remit of this book. It is a pointless debate, like debating the existence of God, which leads to a hardening rather than an exchange of views.

All my research into how to eliminate slavery in Britain points in one direction: open borders. Many of the people I interviewed for this book, who work in the field, support the idea of open borders but are not prepared to speak about it or campaign for it publicly because it is acknowledged that public opinion would not be on their side. No One Is Illegal is one of the few, perhaps the only, campaigning groups openly to oppose all immigration controls because, among other factors 'they are premised on the basest nationalism – the assertion that one group of people over all others have (sic) a franchise on any particular piece of territory'.[7] The public debate on immigration is so hysterical that to talk about open borders is to invite an intellectual lynching. This is no extreme programme being advocated by someone on the hard left. It is one that makes eminent sense and is even articulated by members of the establishment. No less than the Deputy Director of the CIA and the Chairman of the National Intelligence Council of the USA talked of the inevitability of free movement of people in a speech which explored the intelligence challenges for the CIA post the Cold War in the period up to 2015:

> US national interests will increasingly be tied to our dependence on global networks that ensure the *unrestricted flow* of economic, political, and technical information, as well as *people*, [my emphasis] goods, and capital – which, by the way, is my definition of 'globalization'.[8]

The case for open borders serves the interests of capitalism and is a free marketer's dream. An unclassified US intelligence report mapping the global future to 2020, predicts that an ageing workforce in Japan and Europe may inhibit their economic growth.[9] In January 2000, Alan Greenspan, head of the US Federal Reserve, said that if growth was to continue without inflation, immigration policies would have to be relaxed.[10] Another establishment view from the IOM also comes down in favour of relaxation of controls: 'Migration restrictions are especially surprising when the numbers favour openness – the benefits of migration tend to be immediate, measurable and concentrated, while the costs of migration, if any, tend to be diffuse, deferred and harder to measure.'[11] Even the venerable Parliamentary Joint Committee on Human Rights when examining the question of trafficking said, 'We broadly accept the argument that restrictions on legal entry will not reduce the incidence of trafficking. It has been argued that such restrictions divert migration into illegal channels and therefore increase opportunities for traffickers.' Of course it did not take this to its logical conclusion and argue for open borders. It said merely, 'we consider that the development of lawful and managed migration channels, which recognize the essential role that migrant labour plays in the British economy, is an essential part of a successful anti-trafficking strategy.'[12]

The whole spectrum of views from left to right supports a 'managed' migration policy, with those on the left emphasizing fairness and justice while the government's emphasis falls on the 'robustness' and 'integrity' of the system. However, the government's attempt to maintain its integrity sets up contradictions and divisions time and again. The rules on marriage to a non-British person are a classic example of this. Domestic violence concessions won by SBS will enable a woman facing violence within the marriage to escape the two-year probationary period. However a woman who has had a forced marriage and is arguably in as much need of support to escape her slavery cannot avail herself of this concession.

Apart from radical changes in the immigration system, much needs to be done in enforcing and introducing employment legislation so that employers who reduce their workers to slaves are penalized. The campaign for enhanced corporate social responsibility needs to find ways in which multi-nationals take on responsibility for the refugees they create (see Passport to Freedom chapter), perhaps paying for their rehabilitation in whichever country gives them refuge. With all this, the case for open borders remains overwhelming. Immigration controls are not working. 'Controls are like a dam; when one hole is blocked, another appears somewhere else.'[13] It is comparable to the campaign against drugs. Despite the millions being poured into prevention, detection and prosecution of drug traffickers, there has been no substantial change in the availability and use of drugs. Fresh thinking would lend support to those marginal voices in the debate who are calling for decriminalization. On the face of it, this sounds like surrender, but it is actually likely to reduce the number of deaths from impure drugs and turf wars between criminal gangs. The War on Drugs is failing and it is high time for the government to admit that the War on Immigrants is also failing.

While we have problems without borders – inequality, poverty and exploitation – people will not and cannot respect borders. No punitive measures, sanctions, walls or fortresses will keep desperate people at bay. The US situation demonstrates this problem perfectly. Its borders are long and porous, especially the one shared with Mexico which is nearly 2,000 miles long. It is impossible to police, no matter how much money is poured into creating 'Fortress America'. Approximately one million immigrants are caught trying to cross the southern border every year yet apparently three million make the attempt.[14] When sections of the border are tightened up, smugglers charge more to get people across but it does not stop the flow. The number of people who die in the attempt to cross the border grows in proportion to the rigour with which the border is policed. Estimates of the number of illegal immigrants in the US veer wildly between 7 and 20m.[15] 1m legal immigrants are accepted every year. These vast numbers have not made a dent in America's *per capita* wealth, which is second only to Japan despite the popular view that a country becomes impoverished by the presence of migrants.

The main fear with regard to open doors is that the country will be swamped and that services will not be able to cope. This is not a question that is easily answered because it is, by definition, speculative. We can look to the history of migration when borders were open but it is not possible to factor in current circumstances to calculate potential number of arrivals. What we can say with certainty is that we already have open borders – with the rest of Europe which contains half a billion people – and we have not been swamped. It is often argued that any country that opens its borders unilaterally is asking for trouble. Despite the fact that only three out of twenty-seven countries in the EU – UK, Sweden and Ireland – have opened up to those from Romania and Bulgaria, there has been no flooding. The number of people from Poland, Romania or Bulgaria may be larger than estimated but they have been mostly mopped up by a labour-hungry market. In any case, those who worry about the influx of people from the poorer countries of the EU take account of only one half of the equation. There is a reason why the EU expands its membership: the larger the internal market, the more the gains, especially for those economies, like the British, with services and goods to sell. The larger market creates more jobs and therefore benefits the individual countries in the EU.

Before Spain and Portugal joined the EU in 1986, a large number of their citizens worked in catering and cleaning in Britain; they came in the sixties and seventies and returned once their own economies were booming. In general, migration follows jobs. Poland, for example, has an unemployment rate of 18 per cent. When it joined the EU, it was not worried by the fact that open borders would mean more migration into Poland, which would exacerbate its own high unemployment, because it was unlikely that people would go there in search of work. However, the loss of Polish builders and plumbers to other European countries has created vacancies in the Polish construction industry which have been filled by Romanians prepared to work at lower wages than the Poles – an example of trickle-down theory in operation. If Britain's economy had a 'No vacancies' sign up, migrants would gravitate to other countries. As far as refugees are concerned, we have seen how British policies and economic activities generate them in the first instance. British multi-nationals and the government have a moral responsibility for them and should either plough back profits towards their care or suspend actions that create refugees.

When the British lease on Hong Kong ran out in 1997, in a grudging recognition of its responsibility for those 'subjects' who might have some claim to British residence, Britain offered 20,000 visas. Despite the media hype of being inundated by people from Hong Kong, only half that number came. Where there were no controls such as from the Commonwealth to Britain in the 1950s or from Puerto Rico and Cuba to the US or from French Overseas Departments to France, migration represented a tiny fraction of sending and receiving countries. Between 1950 and 1980, 0.6 per cent of the Caribbean population emigrated. It is estimated that if the same rate was applied across the world, it would mean an extra 24m migrants per year. If they were evenly distributed in industrialized countries, it would lead to a population growth of 2.4 per cent which could be seen as a useful way of counteracting ageing populations and the decline in birth rates.[16] Although international action, especially co-operation between industrialized nations in terms of open borders is the most rational way forward, it should not stop us from taking unilateral action.

Very rarely do economic self-interest and human rights considerations come together in a single demand. Any campaign that satisfies both these considerations can only result in success. It is a historic moment. Let us grab the moment and call for an end to immigration controls. Human progress must be measured by the extent to which we have ended slavery. We should be fighting for a future when the world truly belongs to all of us.

ABBREVIATIONS

AFRUCA	Africans Unite Against Child Abuse
ALG	Association of Local Government
ARC	Application Registration Card
BNP	British National Party
CBI	Confederation of British Industry
CIA	Central Intelligence Agency
CIPU	Country Information and Policy Unit
CPS	Crown Prosecution Service
DHSS	Department of Health and Social Security
ECAT	Council of Europe Convention on Action Against Trafficking in Human Beings
ECHR	European Convention on Human Rights (1950)
ECP	English Collective of Prostitutes
EEC	European Economic Community
ELR	Exceptional Leave to Remain
ESOL	English for Speakers of Other Languages
EU	European Union
FGM	Female Genital Mutilation
GDP	Gross Domestic Product
ICU	Islamic Court Union
ILO	International Labour Office

ILR	Indefinite Leave to Remain
IPPR	Institute for Public Policy Research
IMF	International Monetary Fund
IND	Immigation and Nationality Directorate
IOM	International Organization for Migration
JCWI	Joint Council for the Welfare of Immigrants
KMT	Kuomintang
LDCs	Less Developed Countries
LEAs	Local Education Authorities
MDWs	Migrant Domestic Workers
NAM	New Asylum Model
NAO	National Audit Office
NATO	North Atlantic Treaty Organization
NGO	Non-Governmental Organization
OECD	Organization for Economic Co-operation and Development
RUF	Revolutionary United Front
SEF	Statement of Evidence Form
SOCA	Serious Organized Crime Agency
SBS	Southall Black Sisters
TUC	Trades Union Congress
UASC	Unaccompanied Asylum-seeking Children
UK	United Kingdom
UKHTC	United Kingdom Human Trafficking Centre
UN	United Nations
UNHCR	United Nations High Commissioner for Refugees
US	United States
USC	United Somali Congress
WTO	World Trade Organisation

NOTES

Introduction

1. Kevin B. Bales, *Disposable People: New Slavery in the Global Economy*, University of California Press, Berkeley, CA, 1999, p. 4.
2. *Disposable People*, p. 198.
3. *Disposable People*, p. 9.
4. *Every Child Counts – New Global Estimates on Child Labour*, International Labour Office, Geneva, 2002, p. 6.
5. 'Map of World Slavery 2007', *Guardian*, 23 March 2007.
6. Steve Cohen, 'Migrants as Slaves', European Council, 2007.
7. International Organization for Migration, 24 April 2007, http://www.iom.int/jahia/jsp/index.jsp.
8. Milton Meltzer, *Slavery: A World History*, Da Capo Press, Cambridge, MA, 1993, p.5.

Farhia Nur: No Refuge

1. Abdi Abby, 'Field research Project on Minorities in Somalia', unpublished paper, October 2005, pp. 8–9.
2. http://lucy.ukc.ac.uk/EthnoAtlas/Hmar/Cult_dir/Culture.7870.
3. Xan Rice, 'The Wages of Chaos', the *Guardian*, 31 May 2006.
4. Abdi Abby, p. 17.
5. www.amnesty.org.
6. A Somali dress made from silk or other fine materials and worn when going out.
7. A negotiated sum of money given to the bride's family by the groom's family in a Muslim wedding.
8. Some of this procedure is likely to change if and when the new UK Borders Bill becomes law.
9. http://www.refugeecouncil.org.uk/infocentre/asylumlaw/seeking_asylum.htm.

Natasha Bulova: On the Run

1. Suzan Brazier, http://www.nelegal.net/

articles/propiska.html.

2. E. Koshkina, *Drug and alcohol abuse is soaring in post-Soviet Russian Federation*, Institute of Economic Forecasting in the Russian Federation, Moscow, 2003, from http://www.eldis.org/static/DOC9364.htm.

3. Marcus Warren, 'Lone crusader fights Russia's alcohol problem', *Daily Telegraph*, 3 February 2001.

4. 'Sex trafficking in Belgium', http://www.expatica.com/source/site_article.asp?subchannel_id=48&story_id=253, accessed 16 April 2007.

5. The Immigration and Nationality Directorate (IND) issues a registration card to all those who apply for asylum from outside the EU. See p. 39.

6. See Chapter 5, on Amber Lobepreet, for more on marriage and divorce because of domestic violence and its consequences for immigration status.

7. POPPY Project and Asylum Aid, *Hope Betrayed: An analysis of women victims of trafficking and their claims for asylum*, POPPY Project, London, 2006. See also p. 225.

8. ILR. See p. 40.

9. Email from Sonali Naik, immigration barrister, 25 July 2006.

Naomi Conté: I said OK

1. http://hypertextbook.com/eworld/kamakwie.shtml.

2. Lansana Gberie, 'War and Peace in Sierra Leone: Diamonds, Corruption and the Lebanese Connection', Partnership Africa Canada (PAC), Ottawa, 2002; http://action.web.ca/home/pac/attach/sierraleone2002_e.pdf, accessed 14 March 2007.

3. 'Tackling Human Trafficking – Consultation on Proposals for a UK Action Plan', AFRUCA, 2006, p. 9.

4. Paul Lewis, '500 Children face forcible repatriation', the *Guardian*, 18 August 2006.

Liu Bao Ren: Journey's End

1. Hsiao-Hung Pai, 'Another Morecambe Bay is waiting to happen', the *Guardian*, 28 March 2006.

2. Zai Liang and Wenzhen Ye, 'From Fujian to New York: Understanding the New Chinese Immigration', in David Kyle and Rey Koslowkski (eds.), *Global Human Smuggling: Comparative Perspectives*, Johns Hopkins University Press, Baltimore, 2001, pp. 187–215; from http://usinfo.state.gov/eap/Archive_Index/From_Fujian_to_New_York_Understanding_the_New_Chinese_Immigration.html.

3. Peter Kwong, *Forbidden Workers: Illegal Chinese Immigrants and American Labor*, New Press, New York, 1997, p. 61, quoted in *Global Human Smuggling*, pp. 235–44.

4. http://en.wikipedia.org/wiki/Triads_in_Great_Britain.

5. CIPU country reports are used

by immigration officers and the judiciary as the basis for assessing asylum claims. See p. 49.

6. http://www.cecc.gov/pages/roundtables/052305/Thornton.php.
7. http://www.fsmitha.com/h2/ch25prc.html.
8. http://www.interpol.int/Public/THB/PeopleSmuggling/Default.asp.
9. http://www.nationmaster.com/graph/peo_chi_pop-people-chinese-population.
10. Fifty-eight Chinese immigrants were found dead in a container lorry at Dover in 2000. See pp. 185.
11. Tony Thompson, 'Snakehead empress who made millions trafficking in misery', the *Observer*, 6 July 2003.
12. http://www.globalsecurity.org/security/library/news/2003/07/sec-030701-38e4efb5.htm.
13. http://www.amfoundation.org/tcm.htm.
14. http://www.wsws.org/articles/2000/jun2000/immi-j21.shtml.
15. http://english.peopledaily.com.cn/english/200105/12/eng20010512_69788.html.
16. http://www.realcities.com/mld/krwashington/news/columnists/tim_johnson/15606187.htm.
17. Email from Sonali Naik, immigration barrister, 13 October 2006.
18. Vikki Valentine, 'Health for the Masses: China's "Barefoot Doctors"', http://www.npr.org/templates/story/story.php?storyId=4990242.

Amber Lobepreet: I had Nowhere to Go

1. The 'ji' is added on as a mark of respect.
2. Beds made with light wooden frames and a rope weave.
3. Fried Indian bread.
4. A vegetable curry made from mustard leaves and cornbread which is a speciality in northern India.
5. The leading Bollywood actor.
6. A tunic top with a long skirt and embroidered stole.
7. Knee-length tunics with tight trousers that are so long that they are gathered up.
8. The red dot, which is a sign of marriage.
9. http://www.boloji.com/wfs/wfs159.htm.
10. The police report said that she had suffered ABH, actual bodily harm.
11. Amber's GP's notes make frequent reference to her state of depression when she went there for routine treatment like booster tetanus injections.

Passport to Freedom

1. *Disposable People*, p. 6.
2. *Slavery: A World History*, p. 9.
3. From D.B. Davis, *The Problem of Slavery In Western Culture*, Cornell University Press, Ithaca, New York, 1966, quoted in Anthony Lester and Geoffrey Bindman, *Race and Law*, Penguin, London, 1972, p. 27.
4. Krishna Upadhyaya, 'Bonded

Labour in South Asia: India, Nepal and Pakistan,' in Christien Van Den Anker (ed.), *The Political Economy of New Slavery*, Palgrave Macmillan, London, 2004, p. 119.

5. Tom Phillips, 'Raids across Brazil free 4,000 modern-day slaves', the *Guardian*, 16 January 2006.

6. Kevin Bales, 'Free the Slaves', keynote speech at *Twenty-first century slavery: issues and responses*, a conference organized by the Wilberforce Institute for the study of Slavery and Emancipation (WISE), Hull, November 2006.

7. Lucy Ash, *Trafficked and Trapped*, BBC Radio Five Live report, 7 December 2003.

8. C. Boswell, *European Migration Policies in Flux: Changing Patterns of Inclusion and Exclusion*, Blackwell Publishing, Oxford, 2003, p. 106.

9. Barry Coates, 'Calling Time on Corporate Globalisation: Putting people before profits', http://www.thecornerhouse.org.uk/item.shtml?x=52207#index-02-14-00-00, accessed on 6 March 2007.

10. Kevin Watkins and Penny Fowler, *Rigged Rules and Double Standards: Trade, Globalisation, and the Fight against Poverty*, Oxfam, Oxford, 2003, p. 5.

11. http://www.unhcr.org/publ/PUBL/4444afc42.pdf , accessed 17 March 2007.

12. Teresa Hayter, *Open Borders: The case against immigration controls*, second edition, Pluto Press, London, 2004, p. 64.

13. John Berger, *A Seventh Man*, Granta, London, 1989, pp. 93–4.

14. Aidan McQuade, conference on Twenty First Century Slavery, November 2006.

15. Nigel Harris, *The New Untouchables: Immigration and the New World Worker*, Penguin, London, 1996, p. 191.

16. Hugh Macleod, 'Despair of Baghdad turns into a life of shame in Damascus', the *Guardian*, 24 October 2006.

17. http://www.unhcr.org/statistics/STATISTICS/4486ceb12.pdf, accessed 17 March 2007.

18. 'Sweden Calls for EU Help With Iraqi Refugees', http://www.dw-world.de/dw/article/0,2144,2352881,00.html, accessed 21 March 2007.

19. 'UK: Failure to take share of Iraqi refugees is shameful', http://amnesty.org.uk/news_details.asp?NewsID=17276, accessed 21 March 2007.

20. http://www.guardian.co.uk/international/story/0,,2086261,00.html.

21. Executive summary, *Stern Review on the Economics of Climate Change*, HM Treasury, London, 2006.

22. http://www.homeoffice.gov.uk/rds/pdfs2/hosb1595.pdf.

23. Nicholas Hildyard, 'How UK foreign investment creates refugees and asylum seekers', accessed at http://www.thecornerhouse.org.uk/item.shtml?x=52207#

index-02-00-00-00,
28 February 2007.

24. US Department of State,
Trafficking in Persons Report,
Washington, D.C., 2004,
accessed at http://www.state.
gov/g/tip/rls/tiprpt/2004/34021.
html, 30 May 2007.

25. International Organisation of
Labour, *A Global Alliance
Against Forced Labour*, Geneva,
2005, p. 15.

26. Interview with Julie Bindel,
28 November 2006.

27. Ibid.

28. Jacqueline Maley, '"Slave
auctions" targeted in
crackdown on airport crime',
The Guardian, 5 June 2006.

29. *Woman's Hour*, BBC Radio 4,
30 September 2005.

30. Radio 4.

31. http://www.ukhtc.org/uk.htm,
accessed 27 April 2007.

32. Victor Malarek, *The Natashas:
The New Global Sex Trade*,
2004, p. 224.

33. Joint Committee on Human
Rights, *Human Trafficking*, 26th
Joint Committee Report,
2005–6, p. 29.

34. *Human Trafficking*, p. 32.

35. *Human Trafficking*, p. 45.

36. UNICEF, *End Child
Exploitation: Stop the traffic*,
London, 2003, p. 11.

37. See p. 100.

38. *Hope Betrayed*, p. 21.

39. *Woman's Hour*, BBC Radio 4,
30 September 2005.

40. Klára Skrivánková, *Trafficking
for Forced Labour: UK Country
report*, Anti-Slavery International, London, 2006, p. 9.

41. Allan Little, 'New Evidence of
Bonded Labour', BBC News, 25
and 26 April 2007.

42. See Note 40.

43. UK Human Trafficking Centre
(UKHTC), UK Action Plan on
Tackling Human Trafficking, 23
March 2007, p. 9.

44. Ibid., p. 5.

45. Ibid., p. 8.

46. http://news.bbc.co.uk/
1/hi/uk_politics/6657621.stm,
accessed 17 May 2007.

47. Alice Miles, 'Tis a pity for
the whores', accessed at
http://www.timesonline.co.uk/a
rticle/0,,1058-1991136,00.
html, 22 March 2006.

48. 'Britain's Streets of Slavery',
BBC 1, 27–30 March 2006,
http://news.bbc.co.uk/1/hi/
programmes/4810562.stm,
accessed 20 March 2006.

49. Kalayaan, *Legalised Trafficking:
the Cost of Making Migration
work for Britain*, 2006, London,
p. 1.

50. Oral evidence from Kate
Roberts of Kalayaan, *Human
Trafficking*, op. cit., p. 31.

51. Amnesty International UK,
*Down and Out in London: The
Road to Destitution for Rejected
Asylum Seekers*, London, 2006,
p. 6.

52. Art 1A(2), Convention Relating
to the Status of Refugees, 1951.

53. http://www.icar.org.uk/
?lid=18, accessed 24 May 2007.

54. Maeve Sherlock, Chief
Executive of the Refugee
Council, 'Closing the door: the
UK's Erosion of the Right to
Asylum', http://www.bihr.org/

lunchtime.html, lecture given at the British Institute on Human Rights, 8 December 2005.

55. Sam Jones, '£16,000 for illegally ousted asylum seekers', the *Guardian*, 21 December 2006.

56. Harmit Athwal, *Driven to Desperate Measures*, Institute of Race Relations, London, September 2005, p. 3.

57. http://www.amnesty. org.uk/content.asp?Category ID=10682, accessed 2 May 2007.

58. Nigel Morris, 'Amnesty on illegal immigrants is "worth £6bn to UK"', *The Independent*, 31 March 2006.

59. NAO, *Returning failed asylum applicants*, July 2005, p. 2.

60. http://www.safeguarding children.org.uk/docs/ asylum_imagefree.pdf, accessed 2 May 2007.

61. Jacqueline Bhabha and Nadine Finch, *Seeking asylum alone: UK Report*, President and Fellows of Harvard College, 2006, p. 55.

62. Paul Lewis, op. cit.

63. Interview with Detective Chief Superintendent Peter Spindler, 2006.

64. Marian Ouattara, 'Trafficking of Children in central and West Africa', speech at an AFRUCA seminar on the Trafficking of Children to the UK: Myth or Reality, 20 November 2002, p. 8.

65. Interview with Spindler, op. cit.

66. Interview with Debbie Ariyo, 2006.

67. Rachel Nizan, 'Child labour in Latin America: issues and policies in Honduras', in Christien Van Den Anker (ed.), op. cit., p. 139.

68. http://www.guardian.co.uk/ farright/story/0,,2016933,00. html, 20 February 2007.

69. World Population data sheet, Population Reference Bureau, 2006, pp. 8–9, accessed at http://www.prb.org/pdf06/ 06WorldDataSheet.pdf, 3 June 2007.

70. http://www.csmonitor.com/ cgi-bin/encryptmail.pl?ID= B2B0B0B4B0B7B2B0B0B9B4B 7B5B5&url=/2006/0831/ p01s03-woeu.html, Mark Rice-Oxley, 'Britain's border problem: The British are leaving' in *The Christian Science Monitor*, 31 August 2006.

71. Interview with Bobby Chen, February 2005.

72. http://commentisfree. guardian.co.uk/felicity_ lawrence/2006/04/tesco_ profits.html, accessed 11 May 2007.

73. John Denham, 'Immigration's real frontline', *The Guardian*, 26 July 2006.

74. Teresa Hayter, p. xiii.

75. Ibid., p. 161.

76. Home Office, *Migration: An Economic and Social analysis*, London, 2001, p. 50.

77. Victor Morales, *Voice of America* radio documentary, 19 July 2006.

78. http://www.tuc.org.uk/ skills/tuc-6213-f0.cfm, accessed 21 April 2007.

79. Teresa Hayter, p. 158.

80. Jeff Randall, 'Immigration – how New Labour got the

numbers completely wrong',
the *Daily Telegraph*, 27 July
2006.

81. Andy McSmith and Ben
Russell, 'Migrants are essential
for business growth, says CBI,'
the *Independent*, 3 January
2007.

82. Brendan Barber, 'Stop blaming
migrants – exploitation is the
problem', the *Guardian*,
12 September 2006.

83. David Blake, 'Is Immigration
the Answer to the UK's Pension
Crisis?', University of London,
2003, www.lse.ac.uk/
ubs/pdf/dp15.pdf, accessed
20 April 2007.

84. Steve Cohen, *No one is illegal:
Asylum and Immigration
Control Past and Present*,
Trentham Books, Stoke on
Trent, 2003, p. 74.

85. Alan Travis, 'Migrants swell the
population of Britain by
185,000', the *Guardian*, 20 April
2007.

86. Speech by the Economic
Secretary, Ivan Lewis at the UK
Money Transmitters
Association, 27 April 2006,
http://www.hm-treasury.
gov.uk./newsroom_and_
speeches/ accessed 17 March
2007.

87. Nigel Dower, 'The Global
Framework for Development:
Instrumentality or Contested
Ethical Space?' in Anker, ibid,
p. 193.

88. Teresa Hayter, p. xiii.

89. Steve Cohen, *No one is illegal*,
p. 32.

90. *Returning failed asylum
applicants*, op. cit., p. 44.

91. National Coalition of Anti-
Deportation Campaigns press
release, accessible at
http://www.ncadc.org.uk/
archives/filed newszines/
newszine72/nellie.html.

92. Asylum statistics 2005, accessed
at http://www.home
office.gov.uk/rds/pdfs06/
hosb1406.pdf, 25 April 2007.

93. Teresa Hayter, p. 155.

94. Interview with Bobby Chen,
February 2005.

95. Steve Cohen, 'From a Worker to
a Slave', unpublished paper,
2006.

96. Email from Steve Cohen,
21 May 2007.

97. Refugee Council Briefing, The
New Asylum Model, March
2007, p. 2.

98. Allan Little, 'New evidence of
Bonded labour', BBC News,
25 and 26 April, accessed at
http://news.bbc.co.uk/1/hi/uk/
6593827.stm, 28 April 2007.

99. Klára Skrivánková, op. cit.

100. Steve Cohen, 'From a Worker to
a Slave', op. cit.

101. Steve Cohen, *Deportation is
Freedom!: The Orwellian World
of Immigration Controls,* Jessica
Kingsley Publishers, London
and Philadelphia, 2006, p. 103.

Squaring the Circle

1. Kevin Bales, 'Free the Slaves',
op. cit.

2. Tom Phillips, 'Raids across
Brazil free 4,000 modern-day
slaves', the *Guardian*,
16 January 2006.

3. Quoted in Teresa Hayter, p. 161.

4. See Chapter 6 for a fuller discussion of the points below.
5. http://news.bbc.co.uk/ 1/hi/uk_politics/4695699.stm, accessed 25 April 2007.
6. Liberty, *Review of the UK's Reservations to International Human Rights Treaty Obligations*, accessed at http://www.liberty-human-rights.org.uk/pdfs/policy02/ interventions-dec-2002.pdf, 10 May 2007.
7. No One is Illegal, *Right to stay for all, not amnesty for some*, Bolton, 1997, p. 3.
8. Speech by John C. Gannon, 'The CIA in the New World Order: Intelligence Challenges Through 2015', 1 February 2000, accessed at http://www.odci. gov/cia/ public_affairs/speeches/2000/ dci_speech_020200smithson. html, 8 March 2007.
9. http://www.dni.gov/nic/ NIC_globaltrend2020_s1. html#exp, accessed 13 May 2007.
10. Teresa Hayter, p. 158.
11. IOM, *World Migration 2005: Costs and Benefits of International Migration*, London, 2005.
12. Human Trafficking, p. 39.
13. Teresa Hayter, p. 152.
14. Craig McGill, *Human Traffic: Sex, Slaves and Immigration*, Vision Paperbacks, London, 2003, pp. 171–85.
15. http://www.csmonitor.com/ cgi-bin/encryptmail.pl?ID= C2F2E1E4A0CBEEE9E3EBE5 F2E2EFE3EBE5F2&url=/2006/ 0516/p01s02-ussc.html, Brad Knickerbocker, 'Illegal immigrants in the US: How many are there?', *Christian Science Monitor*, 16 May 2006.
16. Teresa Hayter, p. 153.

ACKNOWLEDGEMENTS

First of all, I want to thank those at the centre of this book: Farhia Nur, Natasha Bulova, Naomi Conté, Liu Bao Ren and Amber Lobepreet (not their real names, of course) for giving up their time and dredging up past nightmares and sorrows in the hope that their stories will bring about change in the lives of others like them.

Secondly, thanks to all the following:

Xiao Xing Wang and Elena Addison, who translated from Chinese and Russian, for bringing whole new worlds to life.

My first stop, Beth Herzfeld, Press Officer for Anti-Slavery International, for giving me a number of leads.

A long chain of key individuals for putting in the effort to find the right people and their stories: Meena Patel, Joint Co-ordinator of Southall Black Sisters; Debbie Ariyo, Executive Director of AFRUCA; Mohammed Sesay, Practice Manager of the Unaccompanied Minors Team at the London Borough of Southwark; Julie Bindel, journalist and feminist campaigner; DC Carlo Narboni, of the Metropolitan Police Clubs and Vice Unit; and Bobby Chen of Central London Law Centre.

Denise Marshall, Chief Executive, Eaves Housing for Women, Julie Bindel, DCS Peter Spindler, Head of Child Abuse Investigations for the Metropolitan Police and his team, Debbie Ariyo, Fiona Luckhoo,

Co-ordinator of Kalayaan until March 2005, Beth Herzfeld and Bobby Chen, for talking to me at length and helping me think through the complex issues of trafficking and smuggling, of domestic and sexual slavery.

Sonali Naik, immigration barrister at Garden Court Chambers, and Steve Cohen, immigration lawyer and member of No One Is Illegal, who read large chunks of the manuscript and gave me generous access to their extensive knowledge of a complicated and fast-changing area of the law.

Shaila Shah, a friend and Director of Publications at the British Association for Adoption and Fostering, with a sharp eye for detail and flaccid arguments, for her valuable feedback.

Jabez Lam, Chinese civil rights activist, Frances Brodrick, Team Manager for the POPPY project, and Kate Roberts, Community Support Worker at Kalayaan, for setting me right on important aspects of their work.

My editors at Portobello books, Tasja Dorkofikis, for her ability to enforce deadlines with kind words, and Sarah Westcott, for her valiant attempts to cut back my verbiage.

Poonam Joshi and Kerry Smith, Gender Policy Advisors, and their colleagues at Amnesty International UK for incorporating the promotion of this book enthusiastically into their already tight schedules.

Southall Black Sisters for letting me use their interview room, and Jani and Alonco da Silva for lending me their home for the occasional interview.

The Royal Literary Fund for supporting the writing of this book by appointing me to a fellowship at Queen Mary College, London University.

Atiha, my daughter, for her faith in me and for transcribing the occasional interview, and Rohan, my partner, for tolerating his temporary widower status while I went underground to meet my deadlines.